Universal Service

AEI Studies in Telecommunications Deregulation
J. Gregory Sidak and Paul W. MacAvoy, series editors

TOWARD COMPETITION IN LOCAL TELEPHONY
William J. Baumol and J. Gregory Sidak

TOWARD COMPETITION IN CABLE TELEVISION
Leland L. Johnson

REGULATING BROADCAST PROGRAMMING
Thomas G. Krattenmaker and Lucas A. Powe, Jr.

DESIGNING INCENTIVE REGULATION FOR
THE TELECOMMUNICATIONS INDUSTRY
David E. M. Sappington and Dennis L. Weisman

THE FAILURE OF ANTITRUST AND REGULATION
TO ESTABLISH COMPETITION IN
LONG-DISTANCE TELEPHONE SERVICES
Paul W. MacAvoy

UNIVERSAL SERVICE:
COMPETITION, INTERCONNECTION, AND MONOPOLY IN THE
MAKING OF THE AMERICAN TELEPHONE SYSTEM
Milton L. Mueller, Jr.

Universal Service

Competition, Interconnection, and Monopoly in the Making of the American Telephone System

Milton L. Mueller, Jr.

The MIT Press
Cambridge, Massachusetts
London, England

and

The AEI Press
Washington, D.C.

1997

Published by

The MIT Press
Cambridge, Massachusetts
London, England

and

The AEI Press
Washington, D.C.

Illustrations on pages 58 and 102 are courtesy of AT&T Archives.

Library of Congress Cataloging-in-Publication Data

Mueller, Milton.
    Universal service : competition, interconnection, and monopoly in
the making of the American telephone system / Milton L. Mueller.
    p.   cm.—(AEI studies in telecommunications deregulation)
    Includes bibliographical references and index.
    ISBN 0-262-13327-X (cloth : alk. paper)
    1. Telephone—United States—Deregulation—Case studies.
    2. Telephone companies—United States—Case studies.
    3. Telecommunication policy—United States—Case studies.
    I. Title.   II. Series.
HE8819.M843   1996
384.6'3—dc20   96-35151
                                                              CIP

Printed in the United States of America

Contents

Foreword

DRAMATIC ADVANCES IN COMMUNICATIONS and information technologies have been imposing severe strains on a government regulatory apparatus devised in the pioneer days of radio and are raising policy questions with large implications for American economic performance and social welfare. Before the passage of the Telecommunications Act of 1996, one was compelled to ask, Is federal and state telecommunications regulation impeding competition and innovation, and has that indeed become its principal if unstated function? Is regulation inhibiting the dissemination of ideas and information through electronic media? Does the licensing regime for the electromagnetic spectrum allocate that resource to less than its most productive uses? Now that the 1996 act is in place, is it likely to correct any of those ill effects?

Milton Mueller provides a historical analysis of universal service that yields insights on the universal service provisions of the 1996 act. The study is one of a series of research volumes addressing those questions commissioned by the American Enterprise Institute's Telecommunications Deregulation Project. The AEI project is intended to produce new empirical research on the entire range of telecommunications policy issues, with particular emphasis on identifying reforms to federal and state regulatory policies that will advance rather than inhibit innovation and consumer welfare. We hope this research will be useful to legislators and public officials at all levels of government and to the business executives and, most of all, the consumers who must live with their policies. The volumes have been written and edited to be accessible to readers with no specialized knowledge of communication technologies or economics; we hope they will find a place in courses on regulated industries and communications policy in economics and communications departments and in business, law, and public policy schools.

Each volume in the Telecommunications Deregulation Project has been discussed and criticized in draft form at an AEI seminar involving federal and state regulators, jurists, business executives, professionals, and academic experts with a wide range of interests and viewpoints and has been reviewed and favorably reported by anonymous academic referees selected by the MIT Press. I wish to thank all of them for their contributions, noting, however, that the final exposition and conclusions are entirely the responsibility of the author of each volume.

I am particularly grateful to Paul W. MacAvoy, Williams Brothers Professor of Management Studies at the Yale School of Management, and J. Gregory Sidak, F. K. Weyerhaeuser Chair in Law and Economics at AEI, for conceiving and overseeing the project's research and seminars, and to Frank Urbanowski, Terry Vaughn, and Victoria Richardson of the MIT Press, for their support and steady counsel in seeing the research to publication.

CHRISTOPHER C. DEMUTH
President, American Enterprise Institute
for Public Policy Research

Acknowledgments

THIS BOOK TOOK SHAPE over a ten-year period. All throughout its gradual progress toward publication it seemed to provoke a bipolar response: either sharp criticism and opposition or intense interest and support. The author feels that both sides of that process deserve to be acknowledged, for the former strengthened the final product—despite the delays—and made the latter all the sweeter.

The book began as the author's doctoral dissertation at the University of Pennsylvania. His advisor, Dr. Carolyn Marvin, deserves thanks for making the Annenberg School of Communications a hospitable place for historical research in communication. The author gratefully acknowledges the receipt of the 1987 AT&T Fellowship in Telephone History, which provided both financial support for his research and unrestricted access to that company's priceless historical records. Robert Lewis, Alan Gardner, and Robert Garnet, who at that time worked at the AT&T archives at 195 Broadway in New York City, created a stimulating environment for research. Special thanks are also due to Linda Straub, archivist at the AT&T archives' new home in Warren, New Jersey, for the many hours of assistance she provided.

Over the course of the book's evolution, the author received helpful comments from Gerald Brock, David Gabel, Tim Brennan, Gerald Faulhaber, Claude Fischer, Almarin Phillips, and four anonymous reviewers from the MIT Press.

A special thanks is due to the series coeditor, J. Gregory Sidak, for adopting this work at precisely the right time and sticking with it despite everything.

Last, but not least, thanks are due to my wife Deborah for her infinite patience.

MILTON L. MUELLER, JR.

About the Author

MILTON L. MUELLER, an assistant professor of communication at Rutgers University, is the author of several books and numerous journal articles on telephony. He has served as a consultant to such organizations as the World Bank, the Port Authority of New York and New Jersey, the United States Agency for International Development, and Bell Atlantic in the areas of telecommunications regulation and reform. Mr. Mueller holds a B.A. in animation and film from Columbia College (Chicago) and a Ph.D. in communication from the University of Pennsylvania.

Universal Service

1

Introduction

THIS BOOK ATTEMPTS to change the way we think about competition, universal service, and interconnection in telecommunications by revisiting a critical period in the development of American telecommunications: the period of unbridled competition between the Bell System and independent telephone companies in the early 1900s.

Universal service as both term and concept originated during that period. Since then, it has been one of the touchstones of U.S. telecommunications policy. Although the meaning of the term has changed, its essential connotation is not hard to grasp. *Universal service* means a telephone network that covers all of a country, is technologically integrated, and connects as many citizens as possible. The importance of rapid, widespread telecommunications to government, business, and society can scarcely be overstated. Because communications infrastructure coordinates and unifies a country in countless ways, the universal service concept spans the realms of economic and social policy.

In recent decades policymakers have come to believe that universal telephone service was an achievement of regulated monopoly. Superficially, the fit between telephone monopolies and universal service objectives seemed a natural one. Monopoly simplified the process of standardization and so provided the basis for uniform nationwide connectivity. The absence of competition also made it easier for regulators to make telephone companies' rates conform to social policy goals. The use of long-distance revenues to subsidize local service, a practice common to telephone monopolies worldwide, found ready justification in the idea of making access to basic telephone service affordable to larger numbers of people.

The alleged historical link between the universality of the telephone and a monopolistic industry structure has set the stage for a momentous policy debate in contemporary telecommunications. The natural monopoly paradigm is eroding everywhere. Competition is spreading globally. If, as traditionalists claim, universal service was the raison d'être of regulated monopoly, what will become of it as competition revolutionizes the industry? Are competition and universal service compatible?

The importance and pervasiveness of that question has led to worldwide adoption of the peculiarly American phrase *universal service*, which is regularly invoked by telecommunications authorities all over the world. In the United States, the federal government is concerned not only with the financing of universal service in a competitive environment, but also with the extension of universal service ideals from simple voice telephony to the new technologies of a "national information infrastructure."[1] The Telecommunications Act of 1996 embodies that expanding notion of universal service.[2]

Reconciling universal service goals with the new market paradigms is one of the central problems of contemporary telecommunications policy. But the universal service issue is really a subset of a more fundamental problem posed by telecommunications competition—interconnecting competing networks. Few if any of the new, competing networks are stand-alone entities; they require access to users of the established telephone network via interconnection arrangements. Those relations of interconnection have the power to predetermine the winners and losers of competition. Overly restrictive interconnection arrangements may cripple new competitors. Overly liberal arrangements may undermine incumbents and destroy universal service by allowing newcomers to "skim" the most profitable markets while leaving costly services to the incumbent. Without exception, the countries that have introduced competition have been forced into long debates about conditions and prices of interconnection, all the while looking over

---

1. National Telecommunications and Information Administration, Inquiry on Universal Service and Open Access, Dkt. No. 940955-4255 (Sept. 19, 1994).

2. Pub. L. No. 104-104, 110 Stat. 56 (1996).

their shoulders at the universal service implications of their policies.

The essential issue in those debates is the impact of interconnection upon competition and universal service in telecommunications. This book attempts to illuminate that problem through a detailed historical examination of early telephone competition in the United States. From 1894 to about 1912, competition in the telephone industry in the United States was open. The Bell System was forced to compete with independent telephone companies in thousands of cities. The specific form that the competition took is important. Unlike today's telecommunications industry, the competing exchanges of the Bell and independent companies were not connected to each other. Their contests during the early 1890s were an extended experiment with an essentially unregulated market for interconnection.

A historical analysis of that experiment challenges some of the most cherished tenets of contemporary telecommunications policy. Contrary to the prevailing mythology, it was that period of systems competition, not the ensuing period of regulated monopoly, that gave birth to both universal service as a policy prescription and the physical reality of a geographically ubiquitous telephone infrastructure. Moreover, the refusal of Bell and the independents to interconnect with each other actually promoted the rapid geographical extension of the network. Our understanding of the concept "universal service" is greatly enriched by reexamining the historical background.

The policy emerged in the thick of the competitive battle between Bell and the independents. The universality of telephone service became an issue at that time because of the fragmentation of telephone users into competing local exchanges. At that time, universal service did not mean a telephone in every home or rate subsidies to residential users, but the unification of the telephone system so that all users could call all others. In other words, the original universal service debate was about interconnection. The policy choice faced at that time may seem eerily familiar to modern observers of the telecommunications and computer industries.

This book combines theory and history in a way that makes the historical data relevant to current policy problems and points out how policymakers should apply the lessons of telecommunications history to the challenges of the future.

2

Universal Service: A Concept in Search of a History

UNIVERSAL SERVICE ENTERED the vocabulary of American telecommunications in 1907. The slogan "one system, one policy, universal service" was coined by Theodore Vail, president of AT&T, and propagated in the company's annual reports from 1907 to 1914. Its appearance came at the peak of a fierce competitive struggle between the Bell System and thousands of independent telephone companies. The idea of universal service served as the linchpin of the Bell System's argument for transforming the telephone industry into a regulated monopoly. The emergence of the concept thus marked an important turning point in the history of American telecommunications.

Most historians and policy makers believe that when Vail invoked "universal service" he meant the same thing we mean by it today: regulatory policies to promote the affordability of telephone service through cross-subsidies.[1] That widely accepted view is incorrect. There is an important difference between Vail's concept of universal service in 1907 and the conception prevailing now. Understanding that difference is what this book is all about. At stake is not simply a question of historical semantics, but a reinterpretation of the history of telecommunications with significant implications for current and future telecommunications policies.

---

1. *See, e.g.,* Herbert S. Dordick, *Toward a Universal Definition of Universal Service*, in UNIVERSAL TELEPHONE SERVICE: READY FOR THE 21ST CENTURY? (Annual Review of the Institute for Information Studies 1991) [hereinafter READY FOR THE 21ST CENTURY?].

In contemporary discourse, universal service policy is synonymous with government policies to promote the affordability of
telephone service and access to the network. More commonly, it
refers to attempts to maintain affordable local rates by means of
rate averaging and cross-subsidies within the nation's telecommunications system. That might mean, for example, higher charges for
long-distance service than for local service, or charging the same
rates for all long-distance calls, even when economies of scale
make one call far less expensive than another. Whatever the
mechanism, pushing telephone penetration toward 100 percent is a
policy goal of sufficient importance to justify various forms of
public intervention in the industry.

Universal service in that respect is an expression of liberal
egalitarianism. More than just a telephone in every home, the
phrase implies that a ubiquitous communications infrastructure can
contribute to national unity and equality of opportunity. In debates
over the emergence of competition in the telephone industry in the
last three decades, the concept has become a pillar of the developed
world's postal, telephone, and telegraph monopolies.[2] Telephone
companies and regulators warned that universal service could not
have been achieved without the regulated monopoly structure, and
that competitive market forces had to be thwarted or tempered lest
those goals be undermined. More recently, advocates of a new
"information superhighway" have also drawn upon the concept to
promote broadened access to new technologies.[3]

That is the contemporary construction of universal service—
one that has prevailed from about 1975. Indeed, that modern idea
of universal service comes with a full-blown version of its own
historical origins. According to the conventional wisdom, universal
telephone service was a public policy mandated by the federal
Communications Act of 1934 and consciously brought into being
by regulators acting in conjunction with telephone monopolies.
"Telecommunications public policy crystallized in America with
the Communications Act of 1934. Its goal was clear: the provision

---

2. Nicholas Garnham, *Universal Service in Western European Telecommunications,* in European Telecommunications Policy Research (IOS
1989).

3. For a skeptical view of that trend, see Robert W. Crandall & J. Gregory
Sidak, *Competition and Regulatory Policies for Interactive Broadband Networks,* 68 S. Cal. L. Rev. 1203 (1995).

of universal service to every citizen in the country. . . . Telephones at the time were viewed as a 'social necessity' that should be provided to all.''[4] The crowning achievement of that system, so the story goes, was the fact that 92 percent of American homes had telephones just before the AT&T divestiture.

The authors of that claim offer no supporting evidence. Indeed, they merely repeat ideas that most business people, academics, and regulators involved in the telephone industry take as true. To that group, universal service is the offspring of a near-holy trinity comprising the Communications Act of 1934, regulated monopolies, and rate subsidies.

It is, however, surprisingly easy to cast doubt upon that belief. The words "universal service" do not appear in the Communications Act. Neither do they appear in any of the thousands of pages of the *Congressional Record* during the period that Congress was preparing the legislation. The bill's House sponsor, Speaker Sam Rayburn (D-Texas), explicitly stated that the act did not change existing law.[5] Indeed, no mechanism for subsidizing telephone service was created or authorized in the legislation. The Communications Act of 1934 was, in fact, little more than consolidation. Its stated purpose was to put federal authority over communications into one specialized agency. To do so, the drafters took those parts of the Interstate Commerce Act of 1910 that authorized the Interstate Commerce Commission to regulate interstate telephone service and combined them with the Radio Act of 1927, which regulated broadcasting. The result was a consolidated communications act and a single regulatory agency, the Federal Communications Commission.

Indeed, federal regulation could not have had much impact on the universality of telephone service in the 1930s or 1940s, or even the 1950s. The Communications Act gave the FCC jurisdiction over interstate telecommunications only, and in the years shortly before 1934 less than 2 percent of all telephone traffic crossed state lines.[6]

---

4. Barbara J. Farrah & Mike Maxwell, *Building the American Infostructure*, TELEPHONY 45 (Apr. 20, 1992).

5. "[T]he bill as a whole does not change existing law, not only with reference to radio but with reference to telegraph, telephone, and cable, except in the transfer of jurisdiction [from the ICC to the new FCC] and such minor amendments as to make that transfer effective." 78 CONG. REC. 10,313 (1934).

6. Smith *v.* Illinois Bell Tel. Co., 282 U.S. 133 (1930).

The 1934 act thus affected only a small portion of the overall telephone marketplace.

That brings us back to the point at which this chapter began. If the universal service concept originated not in the Communications Act of 1934 but in the Bell-independent competition of the early 1900s, why did a debate about universality emerge at that time? And if, as I have asserted, Theodore Vail and his contemporaries did not mean by universal service what we mean today, what did they mean? As usual, historical reality is more interesting than myth.

The universality of telephone communications became an issue in the early 1900s because the local telephone exchanges of the Bell System and the independents were not connected to one another. Competition took the form of two separate telephone systems in a city or town vying with each other for subscribers and for connections to other localities. Subscribers who joined one system could not call subscribers of the other—unless, as happened about 13 percent of the time, they subscribed to both systems. Duplicate subscribers (mostly businesses) had two separate telephone instruments, one Bell, one independent. Even when there was only one exchange in a community, that duplicate service divided subscribers. A Bell exchange could not make connections with subscribers of a competing independent exchange in another city, and vice versa. In effect, telephone users confronted the same kind of barriers to communication as IBM-compatible and Macintosh computer users of the 1980s and 1990s. The incompatibility, however, was usually due more to the companies' refusal to deal with each other than to technological incompatibility.[7]

"Dual service" was the contemporary name for competing, noninterconnected telephone exchanges in the same community. Dual service diverges so radically from our current universally interconnected telephone system that it is hard to appreciate just how widespread and long-lived the phenomenon was. It existed in some form for thirty years, from 1894 to 1924. From 1900 to 1915, at least 45 percent of the U.S. cities with populations over 5,000 had competing, noninterconnected telephone exchanges. During the peak of the independent movement's strength, between 1902 and 1910, that percentage was more than 55 percent.

---

7. Technological differences did play a role, however, as independents often used automatic switching during those years whereas the Bell System was still relying on manual switching.

Vail and other Bell spokesmen decried the fragmentation and duplicate subscriptions caused by competing telephone exchanges. Independents defended the fragmentation as a small price to pay for the price restraints, service improvement, and innovation promoted by competition.

"Universal service" was put forward in that environment by the Bell System as a policy alternative to dual service. To Bell, the term meant consolidating competing telephone exchanges into local monopolies so that all telephone users could be interconnected. It did not mean a telephone in every home, affordability, or government policies to subsidize telephone penetration.[8]

After 1907, the Bell-independent business rivalry was transformed into a political and ideological struggle between two opposing principles of industry organization: dual service and universal service. It was true that dual service competition restricted universality by fragmenting subscribers. But, paradoxically, such competition also rewarded the pursuit of universality by the telephone companies themselves in a way that regulation and monopoly have never been able to do. A telephone system with more people on it is, *ceteris paribus*, more valuable than one with fewer subscribers.[9] Competing systems that are not connected to each other gain a competitive advantage over their rivals as they extend service to more users and more locations. That dynamic was the driving force behind the Bell-independent rivalry of the early 1900s. Dual service propelled both systems into a race to wire all parts of the country and attract as many subscribers as rapidly as possible. Penetration and geographic coverage in the United States, particularly in rural areas, made the most rapid gains in that period.

Perhaps most important, recasting that period of telephone history leads to a fundamental reinterpretation of why the telephone system became a monopoly. Odd as it may seem, after three antitrust cases and scores of journal articles, the monopolistic character of telephone service is still a subject of intense historical and theoretical controversy. Traditionally, economists grounded

---

8. That interpretation, which is vehemently disputed by historians whose work has been supported by the Bell System, is documented in chapters 8, 9, and 11.

9. That phenomenon is known as the "network externality" in economics. Chapter 3 contains more formal analysis of its properties and its implications for early telephone competition.

their explanation in the theory of natural monopoly and believed that the structure of the telephone industry was the most efficient form of organization owing to the presumed existence of supply-side economies of scale and scope. Many historians and economists have rejected the natural monopoly explanation, however, and have insisted that the monopoly resulted from abusive and predatory actions of the Bell System. Until now, those two positions have defined the spectrum of opinion on the subject.

We should reject both views. A different explanation, which might be called the universal service theory of monopoly, is more persuasive. That theory portrays the telephone monopoly as a product of a conscious, publicly mediated policy decision to "unify the service"—that is, to eliminate the user fragmentation created by dual service. In chapter 3, I characterize that outcome in terms of economic theory as an attempt to realize what may be termed demand-side economies of scope. That characterization represents a new theoretical position, in that it shifts the explanation for the efficiency of monopoly from the supply side to the demand side, and from economies of scale to economies of scope. It is also a distinct historical position in that it stresses that the elimination of dual service was the product of a political consensus rather than a unilateral product of the Bell System.

Another historiographical issue that merits revisiting is the role of interconnection and its absence in the development of the American telephone infrastructure. That is a neglected and often misinterpreted topic in the historical literature. The most influential account of the competitive period, the *Telephone Investigation* of the Federal Communications Commission in 1939, devotes only a few dismissive sentences to dual service competition.[10] Its incomplete and inaccurate treatment of the subject has misled two generations of historians. Lipartito, Langdale, Fischer, and others with access to primary sources, barely mention dual service competition.[11]

---

10. Duplication of exchange service is dismissed as "wasteful from the viewpoint of investment and burdensome to the subscriber." FEDERAL COMMUNICATIONS COMMISSION, INVESTIGATION OF THE TELEPHONE INDUSTRY 133 (Government Printing Office 1939).

11. KENNETH LIPARTITO, THE BELL SYSTEM AND REGIONAL BUSINESS: THE TELEPHONE IN THE SOUTH (Johns Hopkins University Press 1989); John V. Langdale, *The Growth of Long Distance Telephony in the Bell System, 1875–1907*, 4 J. HIST. GEO. 145 (1978); Claude Fischer, *Revolution in Rural*

Since dual service has not been taken seriously by historians, data about its nature and extent have not been systematically collected or quantified. When the phenomenon of noninterconnection has not been simply overlooked, it has often been misrepresented. Policy analysts and economists who have written about the early competitive period generally treat the lack of interconnection as an anticompetitive abuse. From their work has arisen the general interpretation that Bell's refusal to interconnect with the independents ultimately defeated them. The truth, as subsequent chapters will show, is very different. Until 1910, the independents were as uninterested as Bell in interconnecting. Further, Bell's refusal to interconnect utterly failed to stop the independents from proliferating throughout the country. Conversely, Bell's decisions from 1901 to 1908 to aggressively interconnect its toll lines to noncompeting independent exchanges was a damaging blow to dual service and the most powerful method of promoting universal service. Furthermore, the Kingsbury Commitment of 1913, which is almost unanimously represented by historians as the "end" of the dual service era and the beginning of universal interconnection, has been completely misinterpreted.

If revisiting the dual service era leads to substantial revisions in the way we understand and categorize telephone history, it also has important implications for current and future telecommunications policies. Indeed, current conceptions about the competitive consequences of interconnection and the need for "equal access" are derived mainly from interpretations of telephone and telegraph history. The important issue is whether decision makers will be guided by history or myth.

This book reframes the debate about universal service. If the standard historical assumptions about regulated monopoly's role in the creation of universal service are true, then nations considering competition and liberalization must control and limit competitive forces to promote universal access. If, on the other hand, dual service competition played a critical role in the development of a ubiquitous telephone infrastructure, and that experience accounts for the tremendous U.S. lead in the extension of telecommunications service, government policies should be very different.

Telephony, 1900–1920, 21 J. Soc. Hist. 5 (1987); CLAUDE FISCHER, AMERICA CALLING: A SOCIAL HISTORY OF THE TELEPHONE TO 1940 (University of California Press 1993).

3

A Theory of Access Competition

ALTHOUGH THIS IS PRIMARILY a historical work, it must include a discussion of theory. I argue that the refusal of competing telephone companies to interconnect gave them a powerful incentive to expand the scope of their networks, which played a crucial role in bringing about universal service as we know it. More generally, my analysis of interconnection of competing telephone companies in the late 1800s and early 1900s illuminates the problem of interconnecting competing networks and shows how those interconnection relationships lead to competitive or monopolistic industry structures. To clarify the historical treatment of those issues, I outline a theoretical framework of network competition. This chapter is concerned primarily with the theory relating to competition between unconnected networks. It does not attempt to explain everything about the economics of telecommunication networks.

The chapter begins with a critique of the common assumption that telephone monopoly can be explained by means of supply-side efficiencies alone. It shows that from the standpoint of traditional natural monopoly theory, the telephone system has always been an exceptional and seemingly contradictory case. It sketches a theoretical alternative to the natural monopoly paradigm that avoids the contradictions and sheds new light on the interpretation of the historical events. In essence, a better understanding of the unique characteristics of telephone competition and monopoly must come from two sources: an improved definition of the output of networks and a focus on demand-side rather than supply-side economies.

Natural Monopoly Theory
and the Telephone

Economists typically attempt to explain monopoly organization by the theory of natural monopoly. Although that theory is the main conceptual tool available to account for the existence of a monopoly as pervasive and long-lasting as the telephone system, the uneasy fit between the two has been apparent for more than seventy years. I begin with an account of the theory and its development over the years and then cite six reasons why telephone monopoly posed a puzzle within that theoretical framework.

The Development of Natural Monopoly Theory

From the 1870s to the 1930s, business regulation by specialized commissions gained acceptance in nearly all states. That regulation was the product of a new school of political economy, born of the populist turmoil of the 1880s, which held that competition in certain industries was destructive and inefficient and ought to be superseded by government regulation. In their attempt to determine which industries should be regulated, scholars and regulators developed the concept of natural monopoly.

Natural monopoly theory concentrated on supply-side phenomena; it attempted to explain industrial organization by looking at a firm's costs. In 1887, Henry Carter Adams gave the simplest definition of the theory. He divided industries into three classes: those with constant returns to scale; those with diminishing returns to scale; and those with increasing returns to scale. Businesses in the first two categories, he believed, could be left to the regulatory pressures of the market. In industries characterized by economies of scale, however, competition was disruptive, inefficient, and temporary. A firm became more efficient as it controlled more of the market. "The control of the state over industries should be coextensive with the application of the law of increasing returns in industries," Adams wrote.[1]

Other theorists concluded that there was no single characteristic defining a natural monopoly, though the existence of economies of scale was always an important factor. Thomas Henry Farrer

---

1. Henry Carter Adams, *The Relation of the State to Industrial Action*, 1 Publications of Amer. Econ. Ass'n 465 (1887).

listed five separate factors defining inherent monopolies, four of them pertaining to the peculiarity of utility infrastructures.[2] The "natural monopoly" label was coined by Richard T. Ely. Like Farrer, he saw monopoly as the product of a conjunction of factors, including scale economies, a high proportion of fixed to variable costs, and physical obstacles to the multiplication of competing facilities.

Since the time of Ely and Adams, natural monopoly theory, like economic theory generally, has become more refined and formalized. Economists no longer equate natural monopoly with economies of scale, as such. In the 1960s, James Bonbright contended that a single firm could be the most efficient supplier even when the expansion of output results in increases in average cost.[3] A theoretical breakthrough came in 1975 with Gerald Faulhaber's work on the sustainability of cross-subsidies in markets that are naturally monopolistic.[4] The emergence of the "contestable markets" school of industrial organization theory—developed by William J. Baumol, John C. Panzar, and Robert D. Willig—verified Bonbright's observation.[5] In the new theory, cost subadditivity replaced scale economies as the recipe for natural monopoly. (Cost subadditivity means that the production costs of one supplier serving all of the market are less than those of any combination of multiple suppliers serving a portion of the market.) That improved formalization vindicated Bonbright's earlier observation that a monopoly could be the most efficient supplier in the absence of

---

2. Farrer's criteria of monopoly were: (1) that the product that the firm supplies is a necessity; (2) that the firm occupy peculiarly favored spots or lines of land; (3) that the product or service that the firm supplies is used at the place where and in connection with the plant or machinery by which it is supplied; (4) that the product or service can be increased in supply without a proportionate increase in plant and capital; and (5) that the business requires a "certain, and a well defined harmonious arrangement, which can only be attained by unity." Edward D. Lowry, *Justification for Regulation: The Case for Natural Monopoly*, Pub. Util. Fortnightly 18 (Nov. 8, 1973).

3. James Bonbright, Principles of Public Utility Regulation 14–16 (Columbia University Press 1961).

4. Gerald Faulhaber, *Cross-Subsidization: Pricing in Public Enterprise*, 65 Am. Econ. Rev. 966 (1975).

5. William J. Baumol, John C. Panzar & Robert D. Willig, Contestable Markets and the Theory of Industry Structure (Harcourt, Brace, Jovanovich 1982); *see also* William Sharkey, The Theory of Natural Monopoly (Cambridge University Press 1982).

decreasing costs. At a given output, scale economies are sufficient to make cost functions subadditive, but cost functions can be subadditive even when average costs are increasing.

That revamped industrial organization theory formalized the definition of natural monopoly. Gone were the clumsy lists of special features. But the refinement in the theory did not change its concentration on supply-side efficiencies. The key to industrial organization was still the way the production costs of a firm responded to changes in the quantity of its output. Despite the revolution in analytical technique, the basic conception of natural monopoly, as reflected in the oral definition, did not change. In 1973, before the contestability revolution in industrial organization, natural monopoly was commonly said to exist "when one firm can supply the entire market at less cost than two or more firms."[6] Nearly a decade later, the definition was essentially the same: "There is natural monopoly in a particular market if and only if a single firm can produce the desired output at lower cost than any combination of two or more firms."[7]

The Telephone as Natural Monopoly:
Six Anomalies

The theory of natural monopoly had developed primarily from observations of the railroad and natural gas industries in the 1880s. But the writings of the earliest observers of the telephone industry show a very different view of the rationale for a telephone monopoly. Instead of pointing to increasing returns or other supply-side efficiencies, the utility economists of the 1920s and 1930s asserted explicitly and repeatedly that the telephone industry had become a monopoly to "unify the service."

Published in 1925, Warren Stehman's *Financial History of AT&T* was the first comprehensive economic history of the American telephone industry.[8] Stehman asserted that "complete monopoly" was "the ideal condition for telephone service," and he added that the telephone industry, "perhaps to a greater degree than any

---

6. Lowry, *supra* note 2, at 22. *See also* Richard A. Posner, *Natural Monopoly and Its Regulation*, 21 STAN. L. REV. 548 (1969).

7. SHARKEY, *supra* note 5.

8. J. WARREN STEHMAN, THE FINANCIAL HISTORY OF THE AMERICAN TELEPHONE AND TELEGRAPH COMPANY (Houghton Mifflin 1925).

other public utility, [is] essentially monopolistic in character."[9] According to Stehman, however, "wasteful duplication of facilities" was not the primary reason for telephony's special status; it was instead the number of other persons with whom a subscriber could communicate.[10] Thus, the first anomaly concerning monopoly over telephony is that unification of the service, not increasing returns on the supply side, was cited by the most informed contemporaries as the reason why the telephone monopoly came about.

The second anomaly is even more striking: Those familiar with the telephone industry at the time it became a monopoly believed that it did not possess decreasing costs on the supply side. On the contrary, the average cost of providing local exchange service was thought to increase with the number of subscribers. The main source of the diseconomy was switching technology—specifically, the geometric increase in the number of possible connections as the number of subscribers grew. Within a city, growth in the density of stations could result in decreases in the expense per station, as additional subscribers led to more efficient utilization of outside plants. Growth in the size of an exchange, however, always increased the average costs associated with switching and maintenance.[11] That cost characteristic generally offset the other economies so that utility commissions usually granted rate increases as exchanges grew. During the 1930s, it was normal for textbooks about public utility regulation to contain explicit discussions of that peculiar aspect of the telephone system. For example, Jones and Bigham's *Principles of Public Utilities* (1931), recognized that subscriber growth produced diseconomies rather than economies. The ultimate justification for monopoly, they maintained, was not scale economies but "the necessity of a unified service."[12] Similar arguments were made in other utility manuals published before 1940.[13] Thus, the cost characteristics of the industry not only failed

---

9. *Id.* at 198.

10. *Id.* at 234.

11. For a quantitative discussion of those issues, see Cost of Exchange Telephone Service (memorandum from Joseph P. Davis to Frederick Fish) (Oct. 14, 1902), AT&T archives.

12. ELIOT JONES & T. C. BIGHAM, PRINCIPLES OF PUBLIC UTILITIES (Macmillan 1931).

13. G. LLOYD WILSON, JAMES M. HERRING & ROLAND B. EUTSCHER, PUBLIC UTILITY INDUSTRIES (McGraw-Hill 1936); JAMES M. HERRING & GERALD C. GROSS, TELECOMMUNICATIONS: ECONOMICS AND REGULATION 189 (McGraw-Hill 1936).

to conform to the expectations of natural monopoly theory, but actively violated them.

The Jones and Bigham treatise also dwelt on an even more central anomaly. In telephone service, the authors observed, the appropriate unit with which to measure increasing "scale" is not obvious. In early discussions of the diseconomies of "scale" associated with telephony, economists generally treated the number of subscribers as the measure of the scale of output. Jones and Bigham argued, however, that a telephone exchange that connected a user to a larger number of other users was offering a distinctly different service, not more of the same service.[14] The volume of traffic was also an important aspect of telephone system output. Perhaps, they speculated, some composite unit such as the "call-mile minute" could be developed to provide a more scientific measure of the telephone system's output.[15] Although neither the authors nor other utility economists of the period pursued the matter, the question they raised had profound implications. The concept of the scale of output is fundamental to economic analysis. Natural monopoly theory, in both its classical and modern incarnations, hinges on mathematical analysis of the relationship between scalar variables p and q. Yet here was an open confession that economists did not know how to define Q, the aggregate demand for a particular good. Thus, we are left with the third anomaly: In telephony, the unit of output is problematical.

Still, the most intuitively plausible definition of the "scale" of a network is the number of users. That is in fact the definition used most often by classical and contemporary economists. Yet that definition produces a fourth anomaly: Equating the number of users with the Q scale has the paradoxical effect of creating an upward-sloping demand curve. In their 1985 article on network externalities, for example, Katz and Shapiro treat the number of users as the output scale of a network, and they explicitly state that firms will raise their prices as subscribers join.[16] Although that assump-

---

14. "To one who uses electricity, gas, water and street railways it matters not whether he be served by the same company as his friends, but to the user of the telephone it is highly important that he be on the same system with them and with all those with whom he might wish to get in touch." JONES & BIGHAM, *supra* note 12, at 89–90.

15. *Id.*

16. Michael Katz & Carl Shapiro, *Technology Adoption in the Presence of Network Externalities*, 94 J. POL. ECON. 822 (1985).

tion accurately describes how consumers value a growing network, it contradicts everything economics tells us about marginal utility and the slope of demand curves. That problem was noted in 1988 by David Allen, who went to extraordinary lengths in an attempt to square that anomaly with orthodox economic theory.[17]

By the time of the debate over the AT&T divestiture in the late 1970s and early 1980s, the issue of monopoly organization in telephony had been fully absorbed by the supply-side paradigm. The historical basis of telephone monopoly in universal interconnection, and the early doubts about the paradox of diseconomies and the definition of output, had been largely forgotten. Instead, during *United States* v. *AT&T,* econometric studies of Bell System cost functions were brandished by both sides. The odd result of those studies yields the fifth anomaly: Empirical studies of the supply side failed to uncover conclusive evidence of scale and scope economies. They made clear that there were significant economies of density—that is, urban areas were cheaper to serve than rural areas—but some of the most comprehensive studies failed to support the hypothesis that there were economies of scale and scope across all telecommunications services.[18] Other studies, using different statistical techniques and different measures of output, concluded that there were significant economies of scale and scope.[19] Once again, defining output was problematic. In his 1979 review of empirical studies of returns to scale in telecommunications, Stephen Littlechild observed that the only obvious scale economies were in long-distance transmission, whereas the least clear pattern of scale economies was in the local exchange.[20]

---

17. David Allen, *New Telecommunications Services: Network Externalities and Critical Mass*, 13 TELECOMM. POLICY 257 (1988).

18. MELVYN FUSS & LEONARD WAVERMAN, THE REGULATION OF TELECOMMUNICATIONS IN CANADA (Economic Council of Canada Technical Report No. 7, Mar. 1981); David S. Evans & James J. Heckman, *A Test for Subadditivity of the Cost Function with an Application to the Bell System*, 74 AM. ECON. REV. 615 (1984).

19. Baldev Raj & H. D. Vinod, *Bell System Scale Economies from a Randomly Varying Parameter Model*, J. ECON. BUS. 247 (1982); J. B. Smith & V. Corbo, Economies of Scale and Economies of Scope in Bell Canada (Mar. 1979) (working paper, Department of Economics, Concordia University).

20. STEPHEN C. LITTLECHILD, ELEMENTS OF TELECOMMUNICATIONS ECONOMICS (Institute of Electrical Engineers 1979). Ironically, long-distance transmission is precisely where new competition took root, and local exchange service to this day is still largely monopolistic.

Subsequent empirical studies by Shin and Ying also failed to find economies of scale or scope in local exchange services.[21] Thus, the results of studies of supply-side costs have been equivocal, despite the industry's long-term status as a monopoly.

Occasionally, a modern economist resurrects the old puzzles. The most notable example is in Alfred Kahn's classic two-volume treatise, *The Economics of Regulation*. In the course of arguing for a definition of natural monopoly as a product of long-run decreasing average costs, Kahn said of the telephone system:

> There are cases of natural monopoly that would seem at first blush not explicable in terms of long-run decreasing costs. [A]s the number of telephone subscribers goes up, the number of possible connections among them grows more rapidly: local exchange service is therefore believed to be subject to increasing, not decreasing unit costs, when the output is the number of subscribers. And yet, it seems clear that this service is a natural monopoly. . . because one company can serve any number of subscribers (for example, all in a community) at lower cost than two.[22]

That passage bears close analysis. Kahn recognized that the requirements of connecting telephone users force a competitive system to completely duplicate the network of its rival, and that subscribers in such a competitive market would be forced to pay twice for essentially the same service. But for him, the simple observation that one company can interconnect "any number of subscribers . . . at lower cost than two" is sufficient for it to qualify as a traditional natural monopoly. The argument appears persuasive and has often been cited by others. In reality, it highlights the sixth theoretical anomaly: The efficiencies that allegedly make telephone service a natural monopoly occur on the demand side and not the supply side. Contrary to natural monopoly theory, Kahn's rationale

---

21. Richard T. Shin & John S. Ying, *Unnatural Monopolies in Local Telephone*, 23 RAND J. ECON. 171 (1992); affidavit of John S. Ying (Mar. 24, 1994), Motion of Bell Atlantic Corp., BellSouth Corp., NYNEX Corp., and Southwestern Bell Corp. to Vacate the Decree, United States *v.* Western Elec. Co., No. 82-0192 (D.D.C. filed July 6, 1994).

22. 2 ALFRED E. KAHN, THE ECONOMICS OF REGULATION: PRINCIPLES AND INSTITUTIONS 123 (John Wiley & Sons, Inc. 1971; MIT Press rev. ed. 1988).

for monopoly is entirely independent of the scale of output (if users are taken as the unit of scale); the elimination of the need for duplicate subscriptions occurs whether a telephone system has 100 subscribers or 100 million subscribers. Moreover, the argument proves that a single firm is more efficient not because it makes telephone service cheaper to produce, but because it makes telephone service cheaper to consume by eliminating the need for duplicate subscriptions.

In sum, the application of industrial organization theory to the telephone system has generated a series of puzzling inconsistencies: contemporary observers of the monopolization process insisted that its object was to "unify the service" and not to realize supply-side efficiencies; a firm's unit costs appeared to increase rather than decrease as the size of its network grew; there was considerable doubt about the proper definition of a network's output; the most reasonable definition of the scale of a network, the number of subscribers, resulted in a paradoxical, upward-sloping demand curve; empirical studies failed to verify the existence of the theoretical cost characteristics of a natural monopoly; and the most convincing argument for the efficiency of a single system was based on demand-side rather than supply-side phenomena. Despite the number and the long-term persistence of those issues, few economists have been willing to make an explicit break with the natural monopoly paradigm.

There is an alternative conceptual framework for the analysis of network competition, one that resolves those problems. It has two elements: a redefinition of the output of networks, and a focus on demand-side rather than supply-side economies as the critical determinant of market structure. The latter draws on a new branch of economic theory, the "network externality" literature, which began in the mid-1970s, independent of the natural monopoly tradition. It uses game theory as well as standard economic techniques to model the way one consumer's demand for a product is affected by the behavior of other consumers. Originally applied to understanding telephone demand, the theory found fruitful application in economic analysis of standardization and new technology adoption as well. The pioneers of the literature on network externalities are Jeffrey Rohlfs, Paul David, Brian Arthur, and Joseph Farrell and Garth Saloner. They did not, however, apply the theory to the early period of telephone competition.

COMMUNICATIONS ACCESS NETWORKS
AS RADICALLY HETEROGENEOUS

A key assumption underlying natural monopoly theory, and indeed most economic analysis, is that a firm's output comprises homogeneous units. Each unit of q must be the same as any other unit. That assumption seems plausible enough when the product in question is an easily distinct one, for example, potato chips, soft drinks, or wheat. It is easy to imagine identical units of such items increasing or decreasing in quantity along a scale q. When the product is communications access, however, the assumption of homogeneity is both false and misleading.

The most important output dimension of an access network is the people and places it connects. From an economic point of view, neither users nor the locations connected are interchangeable; each one is *sui generis*, as is demonstrated forcefully by a wrongly dialed number. If a user does not reach her desired party, the system has failed as surely as a server who brings sake and tofu to a customer who ordered beer and pizza.

If each unit of access is a different good, the growth of a network involves an enlargement of a product's scope rather than an increase in scale. Economists have made similar arguments before.[23] With one recent exception,[24] however, even economists who explicitly recognize that point tend to ignore or back away from its implications. For the sake of simplicity, they assume that access is homogeneous and proceed with the business of normal economic analysis.[25] To do so, however, assumes away the central

---

23. GERALD W. BROCK, TELEPHONE PRICING TO PROMOTE UNIVERSAL SERVICE AND ECONOMIC FREEDOM (Federal Communications Commission, Office of Plans and Policies Working Paper No. 18, 1985). A telephone network is described as $N*(N-1)/2$ different products, where N is the number of persons and $N*(N-1)/2$ is the number of potential conversations.

24. NICHOLAS ECONOMIDES & LAWRENCE J. WHITE, ONE-WAY NETWORKS, TWO-WAY NETWORKS, COMPATIBILITY AND ANTITRUST (New York University Working Paper EC-93-14, July 1993). That paper characterizes networks as complementary components. Customers tend to be identified with a particular component (for example, an access line in telephone service). Service is a composite good. The addition of users to a network creates economies of scope in consumption.

25. A typical example is the testimony of Nina Cornell, former economist for the Federal Communications Commission, in a 1992 court case regarding telephone interconnection in New Zealand. Cornell testified that ''it could be

problem in the economics of network interconnection and competition. Ignoring the heterogeneity of access is understandable (if not entirely justifiable) in an environment of widespread telephone penetration and interconnected competitors. It is particularly troublesome, however, when analyzing early telephone competition, in which differences in the access units supplied by the networks played a crucial role in the contest.

Figure 3-1 is a simple but useful representation of network output. It is a matrix in which each member of the population (*A* through *n*) is assigned a row and column. Each cell in the matrix represents an access link or connection between a specific pair of users. Each cell is a separate output (*Q*) and thus has distinct supply characteristics and its own (downward-sloping) demand curve. Any combination of cells represents a distinct output scope. From the supply side, the efficiency of a network depends on how successfully its engineering can realize economies of scope by sharing facilities across cells. Economies of scale are meaningful

Figure 3-1
Matrix Representation of Network Output

	A				
B	Q_{ab}	**B**			
C	Q_{ac}	Q_{bc}	**C**		
D	Q_{ad}	Q_{bd}	Q_{cd}	**D**	
n	Q_{an}	Q_{bn}	Q_{cn}	Q_{dn}	**n**

argued that each potential connection from customer *A* to customer *B* is in a separate market from a customer's perspective'' but later added:

> looking at each potential as a separate market . . . is commercially unrealistic. Most customers, when offered a choice among several carriers, select a single carrier to supply a group of such potential connections, rather than selecting a separate carrier for each.

Brief of Evidence of Nina W. Cornell at 9 (High Ct. N.Z., filed Mar. 1992), Telecom Corp. of New Zealand *v.* Clear Communications, Ltd. (1995) 1 N.Z.L.R. 385 (Judgment of the Lords of the Judicial Committee of the Privy Council, Oct. 19, 1994). The testimony goes on to state that ''as long as all local exchange providers are interconnected, duplicate access facilities only raise the cost to consumers with no added benefits.'' Thus, the heterogeneity problem is passed over by assuming that local carriers will be interconnected and hence that competition involves no choice among imperfect substitutes.

only within one of the cells. From the demand side, the addition of new users to the network creates an economy of scope for existing users. Users obtain additional service capabilities without a proportional increase in their payments for access.[26]

The preceding discussion of network output involves some deviation from standard usage of the term "economies of scope." Traditionally, economists have considered the joint provision of local and long-distance service, and ancillary services such as security alarms or telegraph service, as an example of scope economies in a telephone network.[27] My framework, however, views every pairwise connection between telephone stations as a separate and distinct output. That is what I mean by the "radical heterogeneity" of network access.

ACCESS COMPETITION

I stress the heterogeneity of communications access because the concept neatly explains many unique features of competition in the supply of communications access. When competing networks are interconnected, it is easy to ignore the heterogeneity of access because the bundle of connections offered by each network appears to be the same. Heterogeneity becomes particularly important and noticeable, however, when competing networks are not interconnected or compatible, which was the case in the early era of telephone competition.

Access competition occurs when two or more networks supply access services that could be used as substitutes for one another, but do not provide access to each other. In that type of competition, the scope of the networks becomes one of the most important dimensions of rivalry. Each network offers consumers a different bundle of access units. Networks increase their value to consumers by attracting more users or by supplying more access than their rivals. The competitive process is complex, however, because users face inherently imperfect substitution choices, and the choices one user makes are affected by the choices other users make. That process differs greatly from the type of competition economists

---

26. We shall examine the concept of demand-side economies of scope further in the discussion of access competition and appropriability that appears later in this chapter.

27. More technically, economies of scope tends to mean supply-side cost subadditivity for the special case of orthogonal outputs.

normally consider; thus, it is worthwhile to make the distinction in more formal terms.

In the competition models of neoclassical theory, the quantity of a good demanded by society (Q) is divided up among numerous competing firms ($q_1, q_2, \ldots, q_n$). The output of each firm is assumed to be homogeneous. Once that assumption is made, two corollaries follow. First, each unit produced by the competing firms is a perfect substitute for every other unit. Second, each supplier's output comprises an additive share of the total output Q that would be produced by a single firm supplying the entire market; thus, $Q = (q_1 + q_2 + \ldots + q_n)$. An economist interested in industrial organization can then ask whether the amount Q is produced more efficiently under competitive or monopolistic conditions, or whether firm A or firm B has lower costs in producing amount Q.

Those assumptions and corollaries do not hold when the output represents communications access. Networks are combinations of many different Qs (communications access units). When competition exists, the market is not divided into additive "shares" of an aggregate, homogeneous quantity Q; instead, different users join different networks. Assuming that the networks are not interconnected, a user who joins one network is not accessible to the users of another—unless she also purchases access from the second network. A form of rivalry exists, in that users can choose the combination and price they prefer, but the combinations offered are not identical and therefore are imperfect substitutes. Moreover, the "shares" of communications access-units offered by competing networks do not sum to constant quantities in different conditions.

Imperfect substitution choices give the competitive process a special dynamic. On the demand side, they set in motion a coordination game in which users try to assure themselves of access to all desired parties through joint consumption of the same network. The theoretical literature of network externalities has greatly expanded our understanding of that process, generating a colorful set of terms to describe the unique properties of access competition. Formal models have shown that at any given price for access there can be multiple equilibria. The equilibrium achieved is "path dependent." That is, it can be influenced both by the sequence in which users join and by other small, random events. There is the problem of achieving the "critical mass" of users required to make joining a network worthwhile. "Bandwagon effects" arise when users who have been "fence sitting" flock to a particular standard or network once critical mass is achieved. There is the danger that users who have committed themselves to a losing standard or network can become technological "orphans." The demand for access and compatibility can also exhibit what Farrell and Saloner call "inertia," or what Arthur and David call "lock-in" effects: Users who have converged on a particular network become unwilling to risk sacrificing the benefits of joint consumption by moving to a new network, even when the new alternative is technically more efficient.[28] By making themselves accessible to users of both systems, duplicate subscribers play an important role in stabilizing that process.

On the supply side, access competition puts a premium on universality. Networks with a larger scope are more likely to attract users. More specifically, noninterconnection of competing networks creates three incentives to enlarge the scope of a network.

The incentive to be the first to serve unserved areas or markets. The inertia associated with joint consumption makes it difficult to attract existing users away from an established network. New competitors are most likely to gain ground by identifying and attracting new user groups. Thus, access competition is more likely

---

28. Theoretical work began with Rohlfs's game-theoretic model of interdependent demand for communications access. Jeffrey Rohlfs, *A Theory of Interdependent Demand for Telecommunications Services*, 5 BELL J. ECON. & MGMT. SCI. 16 (1974). *See also* GERALD W. BROCK, THE TELECOMMUNICATIONS INDUSTRY: THE DYNAMICS OF MARKET STRUCTURE (Harvard University Press 1981); W. Brian Arthur, *Competing Technologies, Increasing Returns, and Lock-In by Historical Events*, 99 ECON. J. 116 (1989); Paul A. David, *Clio and the Economics of QWERTY*, 75 AM. ECON. REV. 332 (1985); Joseph Farrell & Garth Saloner, *Installed Base and Compatibility: Innovation, Product Preannouncements, and Predation*, 76 AM. ECON. REV. 940 (1986); Joseph Farrell & Garth Saloner, *Standardization, Compatibility, and Innovation*, 16 RAND J. ECON. 70 (1985); Michael L. Katz & Carl Shapiro, *Technology Adoption in the Presence of Network Externalities*, 94 J. POL. ECON. 822 (1986); Michael L. Katz & Carl Shapiro, *Network Externalities, Competition, and Compatibility*, 75 AM. ECON. REV. 424 (1985); and Shane Greenstein, Invisible Hands vs. Invisible Advisors: Coordination Mechanisms in Economic Networks (Jan. 1993) (unpublished manuscript). One problem with that literature is its failure to identify the expansion of networks and compatibility as an increase in scope rather than scale. Katz and Shapiro, Besen, David, and others erroneously refer to standardization as a product of "demand-side economies of scale." With the exception of Rohlfs's, the models tend to treat users as homogeneous and communication patterns as uniform and thus to overstate the tendencies to converge.

to take place when a market is relatively undeveloped. As a corollary, it is difficult if not impossible to initiate access competition when an incumbent network is nearly universal in scope.

The incentive to lower the price of access. The demand for telecommunications consists of two parts, access and usage. A regime of access competition encourages producers to reduce the cost of, and perhaps even temporarily cross-subsidize, access relative to usage. Access competition also encourages the development of technologies that reduce the cost of access.

The incentive to interconnect users in noncompeting networks. The quickest way to expand an access universe is to establish connections with an existing network that has already attracted a critical mass of users (assuming, of course, that the existing network is not one's competitor). Competing networks will thus bid for interconnection rights to unaffiliated and noncompeting systems.

All three of those incentives are clearly visible in the historical data developed in subsequent chapters. Together, those three incentives form the basis of my argument that access competition promoted universal service.

Of course, there are corresponding disadvantages to access competition. It is often a transitory process—someone wins the competition and secures a monopoly, posing problems of inertia and regulation. Once a certain level of development has been achieved, the existence of separate networks can restrict rather than expand the scope of the system. Duplicate users may be saddled with significant demand-side diseconomies; fragmentation can be irritating and inconvenient to users. I do not argue that access competition represents the ideal state of affairs: Rather, that access competition played an indispensable part in providing telephone companies the impetus to expand their respective scopes, and that it bears the major responsibility for the achievement of universal service in the United States.

ACCESS COMPETITION AND APPROPRIABILITY

Economists typically frown upon exploitation of exclusive control of access for competitive advantage. They view the leverage derived from control of access as an exercise of monopoly power.[29]

---

29. *See* JOHN T. WENDERS, THE ECONOMICS OF TELECOMMUNICATIONS 171–90 (Ballinger Books 1987) (describing as an abuse of monopoly power a

Assuming that there are no insurmountable barriers to the duplication of access facilities, however, it is more accurate to say that access competition represents a qualitatively different kind of competition rather than a perversion or suppression of competition. In access competition, rivalry takes place over the scope of the product, not over just its price. Competition on that dimension is not necessarily socially undesirable because widespread scope is one of the most important determinants of a network's social utility.

In the absence of interconnection or compatibility, a network with a superior scope is able to fully appropriate the economic value of its bundle of access units. Connecting rival networks can eliminate or undermine their ability to appropriate the value of their particular combination of access units. Once again the root of the problem is network externality, or the interdependence of demand. If the value of a network increases as new users are added, it may be socially efficient to charge some users a price below access costs and make up the difference by charging higher access rates for users who value the addition of the new users more than the increase in their rates. As Gerald Brock has demonstrated, an access pricing scheme that discriminates among users will be more efficient than one that is uniform or is based entirely upon cost.[30] A discriminatory pricing scheme that optimizes the scope of a network can be sustained, however, only when free interconnection with a competitor is not required. If interconnection is required, a competitor can undercut the higher access prices and rely on an incumbent to supply access to the users who could only be induced to join his network at a lower price (perhaps even below cost).[31]

telephone company's use of its control of local exchange subscribers to exert leverage over the long-distance market); *see also* David Evans and James J. Heckman, *A Test for Subadditivity of the Cost Function with an Application to the Bell System*, 74 AM. ECON. REV. (1984).

30. GERALD W. BROCK, TELECOMMUNICATIONS POLICY FOR THE INFORMATION AGE: FROM MONOPOLY TO COMPETITION 72–73 (Harvard University Press 1994).

31. *Id.* A two-person network connecting *A* and *B* charges each $1 for access. Assume that one unit of access costs $1 to supply. A third person, *C*, is added. Assume that *A* and *B* both value access to *C* at $0.4, and that *C* values access to *A* and *B* at $0.4 each also. *C* would therefore be willing to pay only $0.8 to join the network. *A* and *B*, on the other hand, would be willing to pay up to $1.4. Brock shows that a price vector of $1.3, $1.3, $0.4 will induce all three to subscribe, exactly cover total costs, and make each person better off. If a unit of access costs $1 to supply, however, a competitor could undercut an incumbent's price of $1.3 and offer service to *C* via interconnection.

Thus, an incumbent network's ability to appropriate the value of its access bundle deteriorates.

The issue of appropriability played a major role in the historical drama of telephone competition. Both the Bell and independent telephone interests argued against compulsory interconnection of their networks on that ground.

DEMAND-SIDE ECONOMIES OF SCOPE

Understanding the heterogeneity of network output does more than clarify the unique nature of competition among networks; it also improves our understanding of the economic basis for monopoly. The framework above can be applied to show that imperfect substitution choices can result in user convergence on a single network. The economic gains driving that process come from the demand side rather than the supply side. The framework can also be used to analyze which users have an interest in a monopoly network and who the winners and losers from convergence might be.

As long ago as the 1880s, the promoters of the telephone business remarked that the value of a telephone exchange increased as more people joined it and that the demand for telephone service by one person depended on who else subscribed.[32] The observation, in fact, formed an important part of Theodore Vail's argument for universal service.[33] Modern economists call that phenomenon "network externalities." I give it a slightly different construction.

The increasing value of networks with a broader scope can be explained as a product of demand-side economies of scope. A user acquires access to a network by buying or leasing facilities, such as a telephone set and a local line. Those investments supply a gateway into a network, allowing a user to consume a specific set of access services. As additional users join the same network, the number of access services available through those gateway facilities expands. That expansion of service may take place without any increase in the user's investment. Even if the rate paid for access rises, the increase is likely to be less than what the user would have paid if access to the additional users were purchased separately.

---

32. GEORGE BARTLETT PRESCOTT, THE ELECTRIC TELEPHONE 236 (Appleton 1890).

33. AMERICAN TELEPHONE & TELEGRAPH CO., ANNUAL REPORT 17 (1907). Vail's views on that subject are discussed in more detail in chapter 8.

Thus, a demand-side economy of scope is realized: Additional access units are acquired for a less than proportional increase in user payment.

Conversely, dividing a market into fragmented, competing networks can create demand-side diseconomies of scope. Users whose desired calling partners are divided among two or more networks must invest in two or more gateway facilities and subscriptions if they want to maintain access to all of them. Those duplicate investments in access facilities may not be utilized as efficiently as they would be in an integrated system. Using the matrix model (figure 3-1), imagine the costs that a user would incur if each pairwise connection—each cell in the matrix—required a separate transaction between the two users involved, a separate pair of instruments, and a separate line. Even with comparatively small networks, the multiplicity would quickly become monstrously inefficient. Users achieve economies when access units are bundled together.

Integrated networks almost certainly create some supply-side economies of scope as well. But demand-side economies of scope can produce efficient user convergence on a single network even when the supply-side costs increase as users are added. That can be illustrated with a simple model (figure 3-2). In a population of N people, assume the cost per subscriber of supplying telephone service increases as the number of users approaches N. The population is evenly divided between two competing, incompatible networks, each of which charges $5.00 per month for telephone service. Under those conditions, a user who wants access to every other user must purchase access to both systems. Thus, universal access costs $10 per month. Now suppose that the two systems consolidate their exchanges. The additional costs created by enlarging the integrated system's scope increase the monthly rate by 20 percent, to $6 per month. Although the rate goes up, the duplicate users have still realized a significant demand-side economy of scope; they now pay $4 less for universal access. Moreover, all users who wanted universal access but were unwilling to pay more than $6 for it have also benefited from the consolidation.

What was a paradox in natural monopoly theory is now easily explained: One telephone system can be more efficient than two even when the per-user supply-side cost of one large system exceeds that of two or more smaller, competing systems.

The model may make it appear as if a monopoly or a fully

Figure 3-2
Supply-Side vs. Demand-Side Scope Economies

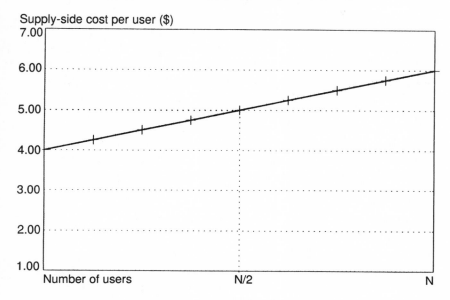

Supply-side cost per user ($)

interconnected system is prima facie more efficient than the alternative. Not so. The realization of demand-side economies of scope in that simple example depended on two assumptions. First, subscribers had to value access to all other subscribers more than the additional cost created by expanding the scope of the network. Second, consolidation had to allow duplicate users to reduce the number of access lines for which they paid.

Empirically, either one of those assumptions may be false. With respect to the first assumption, not everyone wants or needs a system that is universal in scope. Each individual order from the "menu" offered by a universal telecommunications network is different: some are highly extended and others are localized and restricted. Under those conditions the elimination of dual service may save money for some groups while raising the costs for many others. The model makes clear that the distribution of the demand for access among users and the politics of the transition are important empirical issues. (Those questions are explored in chapter 11.) As for the second assumption, large businesses almost always require multiple access lines from a telephone company. Buying

access from two competing networks would not necessarily consti-
tute a waste under such circumstances, although it might be an
inconvenience. A company that ordered six access lines under dual
service (say, two from one network and four from another) will
likely need six access lines from a consolidated system. Unless
monopoly reduces the number of access lines needed, there is
no demand-side economy of scope. (Empirical evidence about
subscriber fragmentation and duplication patterns is explored in
chapter 7.)

It should also be noted that the existence of a monopoly can
restrict the scope of communication as much as, if not more than,
the fragmentation caused by competition. A monopoly can charge
higher prices for access than it would if faced with competition. In
addition, a system exempt from competitive pressures can be
indifferent about increasing the scope of its service.

INTERCONNECTION OF COMPETING NETWORKS

Thus far the analysis has assumed that competing networks are not
interconnected, which may seem strange, if not downright per-
verse. Contemporary regulations routinely require open interconnection and equal access. But that "obvious" solution to the
problems of access competition did not exist until recently. Why
did public officials not initially mandate interconnection rather than
permit access competition? And why did they not choose to achieve
universal service by interconnecting the independents and Bell,
instead of by consolidating the system into a monopoly?

Those questions will be answered later, but the issue of how
interconnection affects the competitive process is relevant to the
theoretical issues raised by this chapter, and is taken up now.

Interconnection homogenizes access. It makes the scope of
rival networks appear to users as identical, even though they are
not. Thus, a firm can offer a substitute for one unit of access
without offering a substitute for the entire network. To the customer, the access universe offered is the same, regardless. Users
can choose, for example, the local access service of one company
and the long-distance service of another. By the same token, a
competing network can benefit from the customer access created
by a larger network's facilities while invading only those markets
that look profitable. Interconnected networks thus have a dual
status: They are both complements and competitors. Part of their

value is derived from their links to the other network, yet they present themselves to users as substitutes for each other. The long-term effects of that process are still unknown, but theory suggests that it encourages unbundling of the combination of access units making up the network, and discourages rate averaging and cross-subsidization among the units. Most important, the process seriously undermines a network's ability to appropriate the value of its scope. A network no longer gains a competitive advantage by maximizing its scope, neither can it maintain price discrimination that will optimize its scope.

Far from being ignorant of that issue, the telephone companies, users, and municipal and state officials of the early competitive era showed an appreciation of the economic consequences of interconnection that was in many respects more sophisticated than today's reflexive support for it. The main reason that access competition persisted was that both competing telephone interests supported it. Chapters 5 and 8 describe their reasons in detail, but essentially, both wanted to appropriate the value of their networks, and both thought they had a chance to win the competition. Is their attitude any different from the current promoters of incompatible wireless telephone technologies, computer operating systems, or software applications? Clearly, in the developmental stages of a technology, different approaches to compatibility and interconnection seem appropriate. Also, at that period in history, the courts were more willing to accept appropriability based arguments regarding the property rights of the telephone interests.

Aside from the legal barriers to compulsory interconnection, access competition was often supported or tolerated by users and public officials because, at that time, access competition was synonymous with competition. Eliminating it via interconnection, they feared, would lead to a state of complementarity between the networks rather than true competition.[34] Access competition was not an accident or a blunder. City councils deliberated carefully before authorizing dual service competition, and they were cer-

---

34. Stehman, for example, knew that competing companies could be required to interconnect and exchange traffic. But he rejected that as an adequate solution to the problem of service unification. While it eliminated the barriers to communication created by competition, interconnection required the competing companies to make joint financial arrangements and to work so closely together that the result was tantamount to monopoly anyway. STEHMAN, *supra* note 8, at 234.

tainly aware of the alternative of a single system. In the later stages of the competitive period, there were also experiments with interconnection of competing exchanges. As chapter 10 explains, the experiments tended to confirm the suspicion that competition would cease if rivalry over the scope of the network was eliminated.

Another important factor was the supply-side cost of interconnection. The network of the early 1900s was not electronic and digital but a mixture of manual and electromechanical analog devices. Interconnecting exchanges involved intricate coordination of armies of operators. That cooperation would have had to have taken place among entities with a twenty-year history of hostility and cutthroat competition. Both Bell and the independent companies were skeptical of the feasibility of such cooperation. Then, too, cities balked at the huge expenses necessary. Unknown benefits were outweighed by known "costs."

CONCLUSION

The output of a communication network is radically heterogeneous. Each connection between users is a separate output, a distinct service. Increases in the number of users attached to a network increase its scope and generally its value to users. Competition over the scope of a network leads to an entirely different kind of business rivalry from competition among firms with outputs that are homogeneous and substitutable.

In this chapter we have explored some of the properties of that peculiar form of rivalry and have given it the label "access competition." The Bell-independent rivalry is a history of that access competition. Many aspects of its outcome, including the achievement of a ubiquitous telephone infrastructure in the United States, can be attributed to the peculiar incentives generated by competition over the scope of a network. Likewise, the convergence of users on a single network or standard can be seen as a product of demand-side economies of scope.

4

Prologue: Telephone Development before Competition

COMMERCIAL DEVELOPMENT of the telephone business began in 1877. From 1878 to 1880, there was a brief bout of competition when Western Union Telegraph Company attempted to enter the business using instruments invented by Thomas Edison and Elisha Gray. Bell sued Western Union for patent infringement, however, and won. The victory cemented Bell's control of the business from 1880 until 1894, when the last patent protecting Bell's original invention expired.[1]

Those fourteen years of monopoly set the stage in three distinct ways for the heated rivalry that followed. First, the Bell organization fought an unrelenting legal battle to preserve its patent monopoly, despite numerous indications that it was not meeting the demand for telephones. Second, growth of the system led to rate increases, leading to continual conflict with the public. Finally, the Bell interests took a nationwide systems approach to telephone development, an approach modeled after its historical predecessor, the telegraph. That particular vision of universal service left huge pockets of demand unmet.

---

1. In the out-of-court settlement of November 1879, Western Union agreed to withdraw from the telephone business for seventeen years, to sell its exchanges to the Bell Co., to transfer all telephone-related patents to Bell, and to pay 20 percent of the cost of any new Bell telephone patents for seventeen years. Bell agreed to stay out of the telegraph business, to forward to Western Union all requests for telegraph service that came through its exchanges, and to pay Western Union 20 percent of its rental on telephones. FEDERAL COMMUNICATIONS COMMISSION, TELEPHONE INVESTIGATION 124 (1939).

A LEGACY OF SUPPRESSION

The Bell System's patents did not automatically give it a monopoly. Indeed, throughout the 1880s any number of people who understood voice transmission by electrical analogue made telephone instruments, patented them, and entered the fray. Bell attempted to mow down all those competitors through patent-infringement litigation. At stake was not who invented the telephone, but who would profit from its commercial development. Patent claims, no matter how spurious, gave promoters the pretext they needed to organize companies, sell stock, and begin to install lines and phones.[2] There were huge profits to be made and there was always a chance that their claims might be sustained by the courts. Not until 1887, when the U.S. Supreme Court upheld the controlling nature of Alexander Graham Bell's patents in a case combining many challenges to his rights, was the issue clearly settled. In the interim, the electrical journals of the 1880s routinely published notices of non-Bell telephone companies being formed—and of their closings after a few months for infringing the Bell patents.[3]

A specific case from the mid-1880s illustrates the nature and consequences of Bell's strategy of suppression. In May 1884 two promoters formed the Baxter Overland Telephone and Telegraph Company in Utica, New York. By October of that year, the exchange had 300 subscribers, and the physical capacity to serve 800. Clearly, that was a serious effort to provide telephone exchange service.[4] When the Bell exchange began to lose subscribers, it shut down the Baxter exchange with an infringement suit.

---

2. The importance of making and defending patent claims is clarified by George Smith's observation: "Typical of the organization of all the major firms in the electrical industries, telegraph and telephone company organization 'crystallized around patent rights,' and so whoever desired to enter or sustain business in either field had to come to terms with the holders of significant patents. . . . Survival (in that as well as in most emerging high-technology businesses of the era) required almost obsessive attention to patent claims wherever they arose." GEORGE SMITH, THE ANATOMY OF A BUSINESS STRATEGY 9 (Johns Hopkins/AT&T Series in Telephone History 1985).

3. HARRY B. MACMEAL, THE STORY OF INDEPENDENT TELEPHONY 27–29 (Independent Pioneer Telephone Association 1934).

4. The construction and service quality of the new company were reputed to be exceptional, and its rates were less than half those charged by Bell. *Id.* at 43.

There were many other like instances. Throughout the 1880s, scores of local and national business interests were willing and able to compete with Bell in supplying telephone equipment and service. For fourteen years those forces of spontaneous development were held in check by injunctions, fines, and confiscations. The expiration of the Bell patents was not the beginning of the competitive movement; it was more like the disintegration of a dike that for many years had protected the company from a raging flood.

The suppression of independent activity before patent expiration also helps to explain the ideologically charged character of the later rivalry. Here was a distant, impersonal corporation growing rich by maintaining a legal stranglehold on a popular, useful device. Bell could not have been a better archetype of the corporate evil promoted by populism. The publicity organs of the independent movement ceaselessly reminded their readers of what it was like in the bad old days of monopoly. Even the names of the early legal independents often mirrored those of the suppressed companies of the 1880s, for example, the Peoples Telephone Company, the Citizens Company.

The experiences also deeply impressed the national Bell company. As one independent propagandist put it, after fifteen years of skirmishes with patent violators, Bell management "had come to believe, and believe honestly, that anyone who attempted to enter the telephone field, no matter through what gate, was an interloper and a lawbreaker."[5] Bell's refusal to interconnect with the independents in the 1890s, and the independents' response in kind, was in part a reflection of that hostility.

RATE WARS

Bell's successful defense of its patents gave it the power to make monopoly profits on its telephones and the company was not bashful about exploiting that power. It required its licensees to *lease* rather than buy the telephones manufactured by its Western Electric subsidiary at an annual charge of $14 for each set. Since the machinery itself cost about $4 to make, Bell guaranteed itself large profits on every telephone in service. As protected monopolies, the operating companies were able to recover those costs in their subscription rates. The instrument lease price paid to Bell

---

5. PAUL A. LATZKE, A FIGHT WITH AN OCTOPUS (Telephony Press 1906).

accounted for one-fourth to one-half of the subscription price in small and medium-sized exchanges.

But the price of the telephones themselves was only one source of discontent over rates. Far more important in the long run was that the licensee companies' operating costs steadily increased throughout the 1880s. The resulting rate increases were not abuses of monopoly power but were legitimately rooted in the economic and technical characteristics of the telephone exchange.

In 1877, Bell managers had assumed that the local companies were basically in the business of leasing telephones. The telephone did not catch on, however, until the development of exchange service. As switching became more important, the licensees' functions changed. They became operating companies with large labor forces and huge investments in switchboards and outside wires and cables. As the business underwent that transition, Bell managers made a disturbing discovery: The average costs of telephone exchanges increased as they grew. Like their subscribers, Bell managers had expected their operations to realize economies of scope as more subscribers joined the exchange. In fact, the reverse was true.[6]

By 1881, Bell managers had come to a rather grim conclusion: Expansion had to be accompanied by rate increases. Only three or four of the more than 300 exchanges in operation in 1881 were able to pay for themselves at then-existing rates.[7] In noting that it would probably be necessary to raise rates $5 a year for every 100 new subscribers, one Bell exchange manager warned: "Any system which does not provide for that expansion is going to be involved in continual conflict with the public."

That warning was a prophecy. The need for growth-induced rate increases did involve the Bell companies in continual conflict with the public throughout the 1880s. Users responded to higher prices with outrage and frustration. They expected a bigger exchange to offer lower rates, as in any other normal business endeavor. With no alternative to the Bell company, they felt helpless and exploited as rates went up.

The public responded first with boycotts, then with attempts

---

6. 3 National Telephone Exchange Association Convention Minutes (1881), at 46, AT&T-Bell Laboratories Archives, Warren, N.J. [hereinafter AT&T-BLA].

7. 2 National Telephone Exchange Association Convention Minutes (1880), at 137, AT&T-BLA.

to control rates by legislation. Neither technique gave the tele-phone-using public the kind of redress it desired. Boycotts were a costly and ultimately ineffective weapon. Legislation was too clumsy, arbitrary, and drastic. In that context, the idea of starting alternative telephone companies backed by local capital and man-aged by local businessmen looked very attractive. As noted earlier, hundreds of localities chose that option during the 1880s in flagrant disregard of its illegality. Most, however, were forced to acknowl-edge that any form of competition would infringe the Bell patents, so local telephone users swallowed their frustration, paid their bills, and looked ahead to a time when challenges to the monopoly would be legal.

The link between exchange growth and rising costs would return to haunt Bell's competitors. Independent exchanges found it easy to undercut Bell rates when they first entered the field. They soon attracted so many customers, however, that their unit costs increased. Because many localities conceived of competition as a method of rate regulation, they wrote provisions fixing rates into any new company's franchise. As an independent grew, however, it was forced either to lose money or to ask for a rate increase, thus reneging on its promises and calling into question what many citizens saw as the justification for its existence.

ONE SYSTEM, ONE POLICY

Conflicts over rates, service, and patent infringement all contrib-uted to a simmering public resentment on which the independent movement capitalized. But two other factors, pertaining to the organization and goals of the Bell System itself, were equally important in setting the stage for the competitive struggle. Those were, first, Bell's contractual relations with its local operating companies, which were consciously designed to protect its control of the business by weaving its members into an integrated system; and second, Bell's vision of the telephone system as a substitute for the telegraph system—a network of voice communication to serve business users in principal towns and cities. The development plan that flowed from that vision left most of America without telephones or exchanges.

Theodore Vail, who later became president of AT&T, was the general manager of Bell Telephone from 1878 to 1887. Looking back after Bell had weathered fifteen years of competition, Vail claimed that the Bell System had been organized to achieve universal service all along. "The Bell System was founded on the broad lines of 'one system,' 'one policy,' 'universal service,'" he wrote in AT&T's *1909 Annual Report*. In 1918, he made the same claim even more emphatically. "From the commencement of the business," he wrote, "one system, one policy, universal service is branded on the business in the most distinctive terms."[8] By that claim, Vail meant that Bell intended to establish a centrally coordinated monopoly, a nationally integrated system whose subscribers could all talk to one another.[9]

As general manager, Vail consciously pursued that vision of a nationwide, fully interconnected system. Vail's intentions were clearly revealed in the patent settlement negotiation with Western Union about which company would control toll lines. Western Union wanted Bell to confine itself to the local exchange business and allow the telegraph company to control all interexchange connections. Vail, however, adamantly insisted on Bell's right to construct and operate long-distance lines.[10] The contracts defining the relationship between the national Bell organization and its licensed operating companies provide even stronger evidence of the nature of Vail's vision. Because Bell had neither the will nor the ability to construct and operate exchanges directly, it licensed local operating companies to develop the business. Those operating companies had franchise-like agreements to lease telephones, raise capital, and build and operate exchanges in an exclusive territory.

In return for the right to lease telephones, an exclusive Bell licensee in a territory agreed to certain conditions, which bound it to the national Bell organization far beyond the life of the patents. One of those provisions was Bell's reservation of long-distance interconnection rights. As Vail said in 1918, "it gave us control of the connection of every exchange under license with the outside. . . . [W]e believed that no exchange could exist without being more or less tied up with the others."[11] Any licensee com-

---

8. Gerald Brock, The Telecommunications Industry 102 (Harvard University Press 1981).

9. Chapter 8 contains a more extensive discussion of Vail's usage of those terms and their meaning.

10. Albert Bigelow Paine, In One Man's Life (Prentice Hall 1920).

11. Testimony of Theodore N. Vail, Read *v.* Central Union Telephone Co., Superior Court of Cook County, Illinois, Chancery General No. 299,689, at 1086.

pany that attempted to break away from the Bell System could be isolated by its inability to connect with any of the surrounding Bell exchanges.

In short, Bell wished to create a unified system, impervious to fragmentation and competition and capable of providing an end-to-end communications pathway to all its customers. Monopoly control and universal interconnection were mutually reinforcing categories in Vail's mind: The conditions that led to one necessarily led to the other. The supply of systemic interconnection required centralized control. Systemic interconnection, however, was not merely a product to be offered to customers—it was itself a powerful lever by which Bell's control of the telephone business could be maintained against centrifugal or competitive forces.

Universal service, in the sense of service everywhere, to everyone, is not the same as universal interconnection within a system. A system can be universal in the latter sense while being very restricted in scope. In fact, the phrase "universal service" never appeared in any Bell documents until 1907, the peak of the independents' strength, and by that time the scope and usage of the telephone had been transformed so profoundly that the concept of a universal system had taken on a meaning far different from what Vail had meant when he spoke of a "grand telephonic system" in 1878.

What Vail had in mind during those early years was not the "universal service" of 1907, much less the ubiquitous network of 1990. The closest model was the telegraph system of the 1870s—a nationwide, business-oriented message communications network linking terminals in all the principal commercial centers.[12] The telephone would reach largely the same people and places, but improve the efficiency and speed of communication by relying on direct conversation instead of written messages and the mediation of telegraph operators. As Lipartito has noted, Bell's idea of what telephone users wanted was based on an "image of a world of businessmen, engineers, and professionals communicating with

---

12. The telephone operated in a communications environment dominated by telegraphy for its first twenty years, fulfilling the role of adjunct to, complement of, or substitute for its predecessor. 1 HISTORY OF ENGINEERING AND SCIENCE IN THE BELL SYSTEM 489 (M. D. Fagen ed., AT&T 1975). *See also* Joel Tarr, Thomas Finholt & David Goodman, *The City and the Telegraph: Urban Telecommunications in the Pretelephone Era*, 14 J. URB. HIST. 38 (Nov. 1987).

one another. Such a world demanded a high-quality long-distance system because its residents had many and distant correspondents and contacts."[13]

That this was the model on which his vision was based is, to borrow Vail's words, "branded on the business in the most distinctive terms" if one looks at the system's pattern of development in the first two decades. In 1894, after seventeen years of commercial development, the Bell company had installed only 240,000 telephones, one for every 225 people in the United States. Nearly 90 percent of those phones were in businesses.[14] The remaining were generally in the homes of businessmen who wanted to be able to communicate with their offices from their residences. A noted Bell agent often assessed the demand for exchanges in smaller towns by examining its commercial register.[15]

Of course, many new technologies "trickle down" from business to the home as their costs decrease. But in the case of the Bell System, the overwhelming predominance of business users reflected a deliberate policy, a specific vision of what the telephone was for and who would be interested in using it. From the beginning, Vail was committed to matching the telegraph network in geographic scope. The telegraph made most of its money in intercity communication. If the telephone could supersede telegraphy in local communications, would it not be even more profitable to replace telegraphy's hold over long-distance business communications?

Until 1889, local and long-distance telephone service were literally two separate, stand-alone systems. A subscription to long-

13. KENNETH LIPARTITO, THE BELL SYSTEM AND REGIONAL BUSINESS 92 (Johns Hopkins/AT&T Series in Telephone History 1989).

14. A detailed breakdown of subscriber categories in the Buffalo, New York, exchange in 1892 is contained in the transcript of the third AT&T Switchboard Committee meeting, New York, March 15–18, 1892, at 276–77. Residential telephones made up 289 of the total 1,850 stations in the city; the rest were in business offices of various types. By 1907, in contrast, residential telephones comprised 50 to 60 percent of the total in the cities, and a larger portion in the rural areas.

15. In describing his methods for assessing the most promising places for small exchanges, Thomas Doolittle of AT&T wrote, "Reference was had to Bradstreet or Dun's Commercial Registers, which disclosed the invested capital or what might be called the commercial standing of each place." AT&T, 1906 ANNUAL REPORT (1907), Box 2020, AT&T-BLA.

distance service, which was always purchased separately, cost about 35 percent more than local service. AT&T soon discovered, however, that the development of the toll business was being retarded by its separation from the local exchange business. Most customers did not subscribe to the more expensive long-distance service and therefore were largely inaccessible to the users of the toll network in other cities. To increase the utility of the system as a long-distance network, in 1889 Bell decided to integrate local and long-distance telephony[16] by upgrading local exchanges to the transmission standards of the long-distance system. The decision, however, encouraged intercity communication at the expense of smaller, local users, conflicting with the goal of encouraging local telephone use.[17]

The model of intercity business communications is also implicit in the Bell System's decisions about where to put exchanges. There were more than 7,000 incorporated towns with populations under 10,000 in 1884, but the Bell System had established exchanges in only 52 of them. Further, in 1895, the 346 largest cities, representing only 27 percent of the U.S. population, possessed 83 percent of the nation's telephones.

Apologists for the Bell System often claim that rural areas were ignored because they were more expensive to serve. But in the 1880s and 1890s, the reverse was true. The cheapest and least technically demanding course of action would have been to establish many small, local exchanges in small and medium-sized towns. The equipment needed to provide that kind of service was fully developed and easy to mass produce. By contrast, establishing exchanges in urban centers posed numerous technical problems in switching, signaling, operation, and maintenance. Also, because of the diseconomies of growth associated with large exchanges, small-scale development would have required less capital investment, fewer workers per subscriber, and less complex management practices.

Bell was clearly responding to urban businesses' specific de-

---

16. Hibbard, Pickernell & Carty, AT&T, The New Era in Telephony 35 (address before the National Telephone Exchange Association Convention, Nov. 9, 1889), AT&T-BLA.

17. David Gabel, *Competition in a Network Industry: The Telephone Industry, 1894–1910*, J. Econ. Hist. 543 (1994).

mand for voice telephony as a substitute for, and improvement upon, the nationwide telegraph infrastructure. Bell managers would soon discover, however, that their attempt to cultivate one grand system had left open enormous, fertile expanses where hundreds of smaller ones could grow.

5

The Legal and Economic Rationales for Not Interconnecting Competitors

ALEXANDER GRAHAM BELL patented the telephone receiver in 1876. In the following years, a large and powerful business organization was built around those patents. There was an equipment manufacturing business (Western Electric); a national corporate management (known as American Bell or the Bell Telephone Company); a set of licensed local operating companies that provided local and regional service within a specific territory (for example, Michigan Bell, Central Union); and a long-distance company that connected the territories of the local operating companies (AT&T). I refer to the totality of that organization as the Bell System.

Bell's patents lapsed on January 30, 1894. Almost immediately, an independent telephone movement with its own operating companies, equipment manufacturers, publications, and trade associations took shape. By 1897, both the Bell and the organized independent interests had decided to conduct their rivalry as separate, closed systems, with the subscribers of one unable to place calls to the subscribers of the other.

Although price competition was important, it was access competition that established the distinctive economic, political, and social parameters of the contest and had the most far-reaching effects. One cannot understand the business strategies of the two interests, the rate policies and practices that were adopted, the reasons for the growth and eventual decline of competition, or the problems that ultimately had to be addressed by regulators, without reference to the fact that two mutually exclusive networks were at war with each other.

Surprisingly, not a single published work on the history of the telephone in the United States investigates the reasoning behind either side's decision to pursue access competition, or the legal context in which those decisions were made. This chapter attempts to fill that gap in the literature.

The eruption of access competition was the cumulative product of three factors. One was the business policy of the Bell System. The Bell organization had always intended to maintain absolute control over its own system and thus resisted any attempts to make it cooperate with outsiders. A second factor was the prevailing interpretation of common carrier law, which militated against legislative attempts to compel interconnection. Third, and equally important, was the development of a consensus among the independents themselves that interconnection was not a desirable goal. The independents came to see themselves as a nationwide movement to displace the Bell monopoly, not to coexist with it.

BELL POLICY TOWARD INTERCONNECTION

From 1893 to 1897, some independent exchange operators requested physical connections with Bell toll lines so that their subscribers could speak to telephone users in other cities.[1] Those early demands for interconnection took two distinct forms. Sometimes there were formal requests for the installation of trunk line connections between Bell and independent exchanges. An independent might propose to extend a line into a Bell exchange at its own expense, and offer to pay a toll or some division of toll revenue for each incoming or outgoing call its subscribers made. The independent would assure Bell that it would increase Bell's revenue.[2] In other cases, a competing independent exchange would simply subscribe to the Bell exchange and install the telephone in

---

1. "We are frequently asked by parties who have organized opposition companies . . . what arrangements they could make to connect with our toll lines." Letter from O. E. Noel, president and general manager, East Tennessee Telephone Co., to C. Jay French, general manager, American Bell Telephone Co. (Dec. 10, 1894), Box 1066, AT&T-Bell Laboratories Archives, Warren, N.J. [hereinafter AT&T-BLA].

2. The Mt. Sterling independent operator offered to let Bell build a line into his exchange and pay a small toll for the use of the line by his subscribers. Letter reproduced in *id*.

its own central office.[3] Then it would either orally relay messages between independent and Bell subscribers or, what was more significant and dangerous from Bell's point of view, physically connect the subscriber line into its own switchboard. In the first case, the demand was for a joint operating agreement that would enable Bell and the independent to exchange traffic at prescribed rates. The second tactic effectively erased the boundaries between the Bell and independent exchanges, allowing the independent to offer access to Bell subscribers without paying anything more than the regular subscription price.

The Bell System, however, did not permit its licensee companies to connect with "opposition" companies, or permit opposition companies to forward messages over their lines.[4] Bell's refusal was both predictable and logical. While joint operating agreements with the independents might have been mutually beneficial in isolated instances, their overall effect would have been to completely unravel Vail's plan of organization. In effect, interconnection would have made independent companies part of the Bell System without their having to sign a license contract. Thus, Bell would have been helping build telephone companies over which it had no financial, managerial, or technical control. Independent connecting companies could not be required to buy Western Electric equipment; nothing could guarantee that they would route their toll traffic over Bell lines; nothing could prevent them from later building their own, competing toll lines or competing exchanges. Later on, the task of technically integrating and organizing long-distance connections would have been greatly complicated. American Bell saw the license contract as the only way to maintain an integrated system under its control and integration was also the bulwark of its strategy to control the telephone business itself. Now that the patents had expired, interconnection was the only way to induce operating companies to become Bell licensees. Bell management really had

---

3. *See, e.g.,* letter from C. A. Nicholson, general manager, Central New York Telephone Co., to C. Jay French, American Bell Telephone Co. (Apr. 6, 1898): "Application is made to us by the opposition at Baldwinsville and Oneida for exchange connection, telephones to be placed in the Central Offices of the opposition companies at these points. . . . Under [the Bell] Exchange Contract can we discriminate against their customers forwarding messages to points on our trunk lines?" Box 1166, AT&T-BLA.

4. C. Jay French, Business in Connection with Opposition Enterprises (undated draft to O. E. Noel), Box 1066, AT&T-BLA.

no choice but to resist those early, casual attempts to integrate its operations with independent companies. To do otherwise would have corroded the foundations on which the entire organization was based.

There are clear economic consequences of the two approaches to interconnection. Had independents been allowed to interconnect, they would have had no need to build additional, competing toll lines. Bell and the independents would have settled into a pattern of complementarity rather than competition. Without interconnection, however, independents had to build their own facilities to match the scope of Bell's available telephone access. Refusal to interconnect was "anticompetitive" only in the sense that it prevented new companies from benefiting from the access facilities of the incumbent. In a far more meaningful sense, however, it was the refusal to connect that encouraged robust competition, because it impelled Bell's rivals to set up lines and exchanges that duplicated or surpassed Bell's, and thereby allowed for more complete competition for subscribers and traffic.

INTERCONNECTION AND COMMON CARRIER LAW

When their overtures for voluntary interconnection were spurned, some independents turned to the courts and the legislatures, using several legal precedents to try to compel interconnection.

The telephone was already regarded as a common carrier cast in the same general mold as the telegraph and railroad companies. The law regarding the relations between competing telephone companies was still unclear, however. The technical characteristics of the business differed enough to make the application of statutes and case law based on railroad and telegraph precedents less than obvious. It was true, for example, that state laws required telegraph companies to accept and deliver messages brought to them by other telegraph companies,[5] and many early telephone interconnection bills seemed

---

5. A typical nondiscrimination statute, Section 103 of the New York State Transportation Corporations Law read: "Every such [telephone] corporation shall receive dispatches from and for other . . . telephone lines or corporations . . . and on payment of the usual charges by individuals for transmitting dispatches as established by the rules and regulations of such corporation transmit the same." The use of the terms *dispatches* or *messages* in those laws shows the extent to which the telephone business was viewed as an extension of the telegraph business. In reality, telephone companies were in the business of providing circuits for real-time voice communication rather than discrete messages.

to have been drafted with those precedents in mind. But the transfer of telegraph messages did not necessitate physically linking and jointly operating the competing companies' wires, merely the willingness of one company to accept a hard-copy message from another and to transmit it at the first company's convenience. Telephonic communication, on the other hand, involved a real-time link between two parties and thus would have necessitated integrating the facilities and operations of rival companies.

Some proponents of interconnection sought to base their claims on the common carrier status of railroad, telegraph, and telephone companies. Common carriers were required to serve all members of the public without discrimination. If the concept of nondiscrimination could be stretched to include service to competing companies, it could form the legal rationale for interconnection. Rivalry between separate systems had existed for some time in both the telegraph and railroad industries, however, and the courts had drawn a fairly sharp distinction between nondiscriminatory service to the general public, an obligation that was clearly imposed by the law, and contracts with connecting companies, where special arrangements favoring one company over another were considered normal prerogatives of business management.

The most salient precedent was provided in the railroad express case, decided by the U.S. Supreme Court in 1886. The case involved "express" services, companies that contracted with railroads to provide intermediary shipping services. In an attempt to obtain what might today be called "equal access" to competing railroad facilities, various express companies sued the railroads, and the cases were tried together. The express companies were unsuccessful. In denying the companies' attempt to compel the railroads to give them through-line facilities on a nondiscriminatory basis, Chief Justice Waite distinguished between common carriers and a "common carrier of common carriers."[6] The railroads were required to be the former but not the latter; that is, they had an obligation to provide nondiscriminatory service to the public, but not necessarily to other common carriers.

The Supreme Court applied a similar distinction to the telegraph industry in 1887. Compulsory connections that allowed one

---

6. "The constitution and the laws of the states in which the [rail]roads are situated place the companies that own and operate them on the footing of common carriers, but there is nothing which in positive terms requires a

company's facilities to be occupied or used for the commercial benefit of a rival company were rejected as a "taking" of private property, prohibited by the Fifth Amendment.

Despite those favorable legal precedents, the Bell Company had no guarantees as to how the law would be interpreted in the case of telephone interconnection.

The first important challenge came from the independent National Telephone Construction Co. of Waukesha, Wisconsin, which had about seventy-five subscribers.[7] In 1895, Wisconsin Telephone Company discovered that the independent, which subscribed to Bell's long-distance service, had linked the Bell line to its switchboard so its exchange subscribers could be patched into Bell's toll network.[8] When Wisconsin Telephone threatened to remove its phone and discontinue service, National Telephone filed suit and obtained an injunction.

While the Waukesha case was pending, the Norwalk Telephone Company, an independent exchange in Ohio, requested permission of the Bell licensee, Central Union Company, to build a trunk line connecting its telephone exchange with Central Union's. Believing that the Waukesha and Norwalk situations foretold the future,[9] Bell prepared to go to court.[10]

Simultaneous to the Norwalk case, an independent exchange in Madison, Wisconsin, sued Western Union to compel it to place one of the independent's telephones in the telegraphy office, where Wisconsin Telephone (the Bell licensee) already had a telephone.[11]

---

railroad company to carry all express companies in the way that under some circumstances they may be able, without inconvenience, to carry one company." *Express Cases*, 117 U.S. 601 (1886).

7. The telephones of the Waukesha independent were reputed to be of poor quality and its service unreliable. Letter from W. A. Jackson, Wisconsin Telephone Co., to John Hudson, president, American Bell Telephone Co. (Nov. 13, 1895), Box 1298, AT&T-BLA.

8. Letter from Miller, Noyes, Miller & Wahl to American Bell Telephone Co. (Nov. 12, 1895), Box 1298, AT&T-BLA.

9. Letter from A. A. Thomas, solicitor, to H. B. Stone, president, Central Union Telephone Co. (Jan. 2, 1896), Box 1298, AT&T-BLA.

10. Letter from Melville Egleston, AT&T Legal Department, to John E. Hudson, president, American Bell Telephone Co. (Mar. 16, 1896), Box 1298, AT&T-BLA. Egleston took charge of the litigation, and on his recommendation Bell retained the Cleveland law firm of Squire, Sanders & Dempsey.

11. Dane County Telephone Co. *v.* Western Union Telegraph Co., State of Wisconsin, Circuit Court of Dane County, petition of the plaintiff, Box 1298, AT&T-BLA.

It was already well established in law that telephone companies were required to supply service to all telegraph companies who requested it. The Madison case, however, was an attempt to invert that doctrine, demanding in effect that telegraph companies be required to accept telephone service without discrimination. The AT&T counsel working on the Norwalk case recognized that the principle at stake in the Madison case was closely related to the right to compel physical connection of telephone companies:

> The telegraph company is threatened with the establishment of a rule of law which might enable not only telephone companies but also district messenger companies . . . to compel the furnishing of facilities for delivering messages to a telegraph company . . . different from those allowed to the general public; . . . and the next step, of course, is to compel actual physical connection of the lines of the two companies.[12]

American Bell was not optimistic about the outcome of either Wisconsin case. In 1882, the state legislature had passed a law requiring telephone companies to "receive and transmit without discrimination messages from and for any other company . . . upon tender or payment of the usual or customary charges therefor,"[13] a straightforward application of telegraph precedents to the telephone system. More unfavorable decisions might lead other states to pass similar laws. Bell did not want to take the Waukesha case to court, so it bought the independent, thus voiding the suit. Further, when the interconnection issue threatened to erupt into litigation in Wausau, Wisconsin, Bell offered free instruments to independent long-distance users, to preempt the demand for linking the two systems.[14]

Attempts to avoid the issue notwithstanding, Bell's lawyers prepared a strong legal defense against compulsory interconnection. They asserted, first, that its status as a common carrier required Bell to serve the general public without discrimination, but not other telephone companies,[15] as per legal precedent. That

---

12. Letter from Melville Egleston to John E. Hudson (Mar. 9, 1896), Box 1298, AT&T-BLA.

13. 1882 Law of Wisconsin, ch. 196; *cited in* David Gabel, The Evolution of a Market (1987) (unpublished Ph.D. dissertation, University of Michigan) at 341.

14. Letter from Fuller to Hudson (Nov. 30, 1895), Box 1298, AT&T-BLA.

15. "[The Bell Company] only undertakes to do business on its own lines and through its own instruments. It does not offer to connect generally with

defense, however, relied on the interpretation of statute law and thus could be superseded by new legislation. A more fundamental argument was that the requirement to connect with a rival company was an unconstitutional "taking" of private property, an argument that had two nuances. Connection involved physically entering the premises of the company, attaching wires to its switchboard, and engaging its workforce in the operations. Such intrusions did seem an invasion of one company's property rights by another, but there was another element to the argument more directly related to the unique circumstances of the telephone business. The telephone company, its lawyers asserted, had expended large sums of money and energy to construct a telephone system linking subscribers all over the state. Its competitors had built only small, local exchanges. If the exchanges were interconnected, a small exchange would be able to profit from the sale of widespread access without running the risks or assuming the burdens of building a large-scope system. To allow a competitor to benefit from the involuntary use of Bell's facilities was nothing more than the expropriation of its property. In that argument, the "property" at issue was not so much the physical facilities of the telephone company, but the access to subscribers it had created by constructing those facilities.

In 1896, that view of the interconnection issue scored some important victories. In the Madison case, the judge rejected the idea of compelling the telegraph company to accept service from an independent telephone company. Relying on precedent, he ruled that a common carrier that makes special cooperative business arrangements with another company need not extend the same arrangement indiscriminately to all other companies. The principle of nondiscrimination applied to consumers only, not to business rivals.[16] The same reasoning was used two years later in a case involving telephone interconnection in New York State.[17]

---

other companies. It does not undertake business of that character, and a common carrier is only bound to do the kind of business it holds itself out to the public as doing." Legal memorandum, Miller, Noyes, Miller & Wahl (Nov. 12, 1895), at 5, Box 1298, AT&T-BLA.

16. Opinion of Judge Siebecker, Dane County Telephone Co. *v.* Western Union Telegraph Co. (document undated; decision made Mar. 18, 1896), Box 1298, AT&T-BLA.

17. The judge held that a reasonable construction of the common carrier statute in New York did not require one telephone system to supply connections with its system to another company enabling the latter to utilize the

INDEPENDENT OPPOSITION TO INTERCONNECTION

In Norwalk, Ohio, the independents themselves suspended the litigation, not because they feared losing, but because they feared they might win. According to intelligence gathered by F. R. Colvin, a Bell agent working undercover in the independent ranks, most independent exchange operators in Ohio opposed compulsory interconnection.[18] After all, the Ohio independents had exchanges in seventy-five small towns, while Bell had only thirty-one, and most of their exchanges were connected, or were in the process of being connected, with independent toll lines. If the Norwalk company won its case, they feared the Bell Company would be able to demand and get access to those lines, which would increase the scope of Bell's access in the state and undermine the incentive for telephone users to subscribe to an independent exchange. The independents successfully pressured Norwalk Telephone to withdraw its suit, and then pursued a strategy of building exchanges and toll lines in areas not served by Central Union.

The Ohio case came to typify the attitudes of the organized independent movement. In the years to follow, numerous state independent associations passed resolutions against interconnection with the Bell System.[19] In later attempts to compel interconnection by legislation, which surfaced sporadically in various states through the 1890s and early 1900s, Bell and independent forces were usually united in their opposition and were bolstered by the U.S. Supreme Court's interpretation of the Fifth Amendment.

ACCESS COMPETITION AS PROPERTY RIGHTS DOCTRINE

The basis of that doctrine was a distinct way of applying the concept of property rights to the telephone business. The telephone companies were asserting ownership over the relations of access created by their toll lines and exchanges. For both Bell and the independents, *competition* meant separate systems supplying different subscriber universes, each vying with the other to attract

---

connected system as part of its own on payment of the nominal sum required of ordinary subscribers. SYRACUSE STANDARD, July 2, 1898, Box 1166, AT&T-BLA.

18. Letter from F. R. Colvin to Hudson (Apr. 8, 1896), Box 1298, AT&T-BLA.

19. C. A. PLEASANCE, THE SPIRIT OF INDEPENDENT TELEPHONY 81 (Independent Telephone Books 1989).

customers. The subscriber universe itself was their most important product—the valuable resource they offered to sell to the public. Competition was a matter of making that resource better than one's rival's, which meant more universal. Interconnection destroyed that form of rivalry by eliminating the differences in access universes. It thoroughly undermined the competitive advantage to be gained by attracting new subscribers, building competing exchanges, and constructing toll lines.

The Ohio independents' reaction to the Norwalk case makes it clear that they too conceived of telephone competition in those terms. Their plan was to control telephone connections to towns neglected by Bell and eventually to attract subscribers away from Bell in other areas through control of those connections. Even the independents who supported compulsory interconnection comprehended the issue in the same terms. Bell, they reasoned, was politically unpopular. It won subscribers because its lines reached places and subscribers that the independents' did not. If telephone subscribers did not have to choose between two mutually exclusive subscriber universes, but could instead obtain access to Bell toll lines and subscribers through an independent exchange, Bell would lose most of its customers. One independent spokesman predicted that with interconnection, "we can obtain at once every one of their exchange subscribers."[20]

American Bell felt the same way about its toll network linking exchanges in the larger cities. Giving independents access to its more extensive toll network would eliminate its leverage over the subscription decisions of telephone users in the local exchange. As a commodity around which property boundaries could be drawn, however, access had an unusual feature. When independent companies subscribed to a Bell exchange and then connected the Bell line into their own switchboard, they acquired the ability to sell access to Bell subscribers. Technically, there was no distinction between Bell's sale of access to a normal customer of the exchange and the sale of exchange access to a competing telephone company, which could then profit from the resale of the subscriber set Bell had created. To maintain system boundaries, a legally enforceable distinction between those two classes of users had to be drawn. From a property rights standpoint, the situation was analogous to copyright and patent protection: allowing creators to sell their

---

20. Gabel, *supra* note 13, at 346.

information without losing proprietary control of it. In prohibiting unauthorized reproduction of copyrighted material or unlicensed use of patented inventions, intellectual property law distinguishes between buyers who benefit from information itself and those who use access to information created by an initial sale to profit from its resale. Both sides' unwillingness to interconnect stemmed in part from their recognition of that unique economic characteristic of telephone access. Merging the subscriber universes of competing telephone companies via interconnection, in their view, undermined their control of the basic resource on which their business was founded: communications access.

To the Bell interests, interconnection would encourage small, parasitic companies to steal the revenues of established companies. The independent opponents of interconnection emphasized not parasitism by small companies, but interconnection's deleterious effects on their own attempts to construct alternative systems. If Bell subscribers could obtain access to independent exchanges through Bell toll lines, who would invest in and who would subscribe to an independent long-distance system? If a Bell exchange in a large city allowed its customers access to surrounding towns dominated by independents, why would the city franchise a competing exchange?

By the end of 1897, most organized independent operators were willing to take up the gauntlet thrown down by Bell's refusal to connect with them. They confidently looked upon the thousands of small communities lacking Bell exchanges and the hundreds of new independent exchanges springing up in them. In the 200 cities with dual service, they saw independent exchanges undercharging Bell companies and attracting many more new subscribers. They knew they were up against a powerful foe; their public pronouncements and trade publications exhibit the blend of strident defiance and paranoia typical of an underdog. Nonetheless, embracing access competition as their modus operandi, the independents signaled their willingness to make it an all-or-nothing battle, thus setting the course of telephone rivalry for the next fifteen years.

6

The Dynamics of Access Competition

THE REFUSAL OF THE BELL and independent telephone interests to interconnect gave the ensuing rivalry a specific form. Competition became a matter of which network provided access to the most people within a particular user's community of interest. In the more technical language of chapter 3, the networks competed on the basis of their scope, or the size of their bundle of access units. That kind of competition gave the networks strong incentives to tap new user groups, enter undeveloped areas, lower access prices, and interconnect with noncompeting networks. Caught up in that dynamic, Bell and the independents were propelled into a race to achieve universality. The dramatic expansion of telephone service did not occur because of altruistic motives, grand social visions, or government policy, but was literally forced upon the contestants by the dynamics of access competition.

This chapter recounts the progress of telephone exchange competition from 1894 until 1907. Its object is to document the link between access competition and the pursuit of universality. In accordance with this book's theme, the growth of dual service is quantified by examining previously unpublished data[1] of the num-

---

1. *See* TELEPHONE CENSUS (Government Printing Office, 1902, 1907, 1912); FCC Telephone Investigation, 1939. *See also* GERALD BROCK, THE TELECOMMUNICATIONS INDUSTRY: THE DYNAMICS OF MARKET STRUCTURE (Harvard University Press 1981); KENNETH LIPARTITO, THE BELL SYSTEM AND REGIONAL BUSINESS: THE TELEPHONE IN THE SOUTH (Johns Hopkins University/AT&T Series in Telephone History 1989). Those sources typically use the number of Bell and independent telephones in operation as the index of competition and market share.

ber of communities with competing exchanges, as well as of the gross number of Bell and independent exchanges and telephones. The presence or absence of competing exchanges in American cities is the best indicator of the growth and decline of competition. Only in cities served by both Bell and independent telephone exchanges did consumers actually have a choice of suppliers. Moreover, some independent companies connected with Bell, and therefore their telephones, though independent in manufacture, actually were united with the Bell System in the access competition.

PHASE I: FILLING THE GAPS, 1894–1898

In the first phase of the competition, the independents achieved a quick and ultimately unbreakable foothold in the marketplace by filling the vacuums left by Bell's development strategy. The geographic distribution of independent telephony, and the market segments in which they succeeded, faithfully reflected the gaps between supply and demand left by the Bell System.

From 1894 to 1898, 1,074 commercial, independent telephone companies began operation in the United States.[2] Hundreds more were started but did not survive long enough to be counted by the 1902 census. Although they are often stereotyped as rural, mom-and-pop operations, the first wave of independents was a heterogeneous lot. They were formed in cities, towns, and rural areas over the country.[3] The fate of those operations differed markedly, however. (See table 6-1.) Early attempts to occupy major cities

---

2. BUREAU OF THE CENSUS, ELECTRICAL INDUSTRIES CENSUS, table 10, 9 (1902). That statistic understates the amount of entry because it counts only telephone systems that remained in operation until 1902. Depending on the size of the community, the failure rate of independent exchanges ranged from 15 percent to 40 percent.

3. The Mercantile Electric Co. announced plans to establish a telephone exchange for bankers and brokers in downtown New York City. The New York and Eastern Telephone Co. applied for franchises in Brooklyn and New York. *See* 24 ELECTRICAL REV. 175 (Apr. 11, 1894). The Drawbaugh Telephone and Telegraph Company, the Mutual Automatic Telephone Company, and the Clamond Telephone Co. all took steps to establish themselves in Philadelphia. Between 1893 and 1898 four companies were organized to gain a competing franchise in Chicago.

Table 6-1
Dual Service by City Size, 1894–1901

	Population of City			
Entry Date	Large >50,000	Medium >20,000–50,000	Small 5,000–20,000	Total
1894				
Number	2	4	23	28
% surviving after 5 yrs.	0	50	74	68
1895–1897				
Number	16	43	161	220
% surviving after 5 yrs.	81	86	87	86
1899–1901				
Number	20	29	136	185
% surviving after 5 yrs.	95	97	96	96

Source: Chappelka (1956).

were notably unsuccessful. Most of the tiny rural farmer lines, on the other hand, came into existence five to seven years later.[4]

The first wave of independents was concentrated in the North Central part of the United States: Ohio, Indiana, Michigan, Illinois, Wisconsin, Iowa, Missouri, Nebraska, Kansas, Minnesota, North Dakota, and South Dakota. Of the 740 commercial independent systems that were started between 1894 and 1897 and survived until 1902, 424 (57.3 percent) were in those eleven states.[5]

4. Independent telephony is often associated with the small mutual companies and farmer lines that brought the telephone to rural America during the early 1900s. Although both movements were predicated on the expiration of the Bell patents and their interests often converged, their identities should not be confused. According to the 1902 census of telephones and telegraphs, 774 of the new telephone systems that began operation from 1893 to 1897 were commercial independents, while only 84 were mutual companies. After 1900, in contrast, new mutual systems sprang up at the rate of 200–300 per year. Most of the 100,000 or so independent telephones in operation by the end of 1897 were in small towns and cities, not in rural areas per se.

5. Bureau of the Census, Electrical Industries Census, table 10, 9 (1902).

The North Central region had been neglected by the Bell System for three reasons. One was its aversion to rural small towns and its concentration on cities, but Bell's bias was regional as well as urban. (See figure 6-1.) Although its grand plan was to become a national network, Bell was rooted in New England. In 1894 about 35 percent of all the telephones in the United States were in a 300-mile radius of Boston.[6] When the patents expired, AT&T's long-distance lines were just beginning to extend into the Midwest and the South.

Just as important as Bell's uneven geographical coverage was the huge gap in the market for local and regional connections left by Bell's pursuit of national service. The most successful independents concentrated on providing broader coverage of a county or a multicounty market area. They built exchanges in small towns where there were no Bell exchanges, then tied them together with short-haul toll lines. Or they built exchanges in mid-sized cities with established Bell exchanges, and supplied superior telephone access to surrounding areas that had been ignored by Bell. Their greatest success came in smaller cities that comprised the agricultural economy. While Bell had been laboring to make it possible for New York to talk to Chicago, the independents were connecting small towns with their near neighbors. A typical example was West Virginia, where new companies started exchanges in the rapidly growing towns of Grafton, Fairmont, Clarksburg, and Morgantown in 1895, all of which had populations under 6,000 and were located ten to fifteen miles apart. Although Bell had exchanges in all the locales, the independents were able to attract subscribers, according to a Bell manager, "by reason of their great extension of toll lines." "We cannot afford to cover that territory with toll lines of the character of construction which we have adopted as a standard," the manager wrote.[7] The much-vaunted superiority of the Bell long-distance system was of little help here.

That such development had the capacity to make serious inroads into Bell's business was obvious by the end of 1896. The Farmer's Telephone Co. of Massillon, Ohio, for example, constructed extensive networks of toll lines connecting rural sub-

---

6. *Exchange Statistics 1894*, AT&T-Bell Laboratories Archives, Warren, N.J. [hereinafter AT&T-BLA].

7. Letter from J. King Goodrich to C. J. French (August 26, 1896), AT&T-BLA.

Figure 6-1
Bell Telephone Licensee Companies

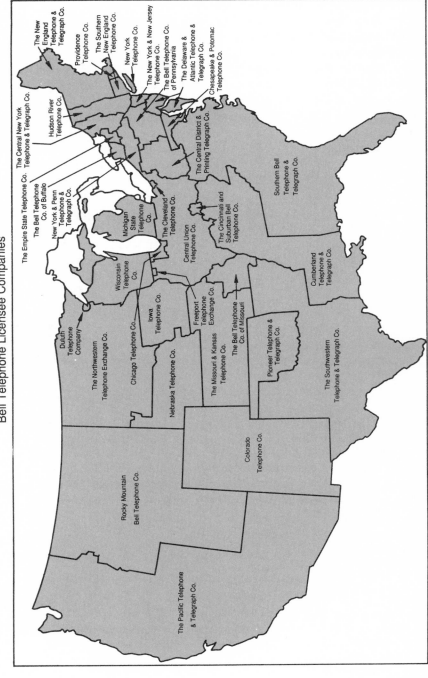

scribers to city and town exchanges and used its access control to establish a successful exchange in that city of 12,000.[8] By 1896, the 45,000 people of Fort Wayne, Indiana, were connected to more than fifty towns by the Home Telephone Company.[9] It was clearly access competition that provided the incentive to reach those areas. Indeed, in 1896, the secretary of the Ohio Independent Telephone Association wrote a letter to each independent exchange owner urging him to "hasten the construction of toll lines connecting towns so small as not to be reached by the Central Union Company."[10]

Aside from undersupplying regional connections in the country, Bell had often neglected connections between large cities and their own suburbs and tributaries. Believing that small exchanges in less populous communities could not support themselves, Bell usually just ran long-distance circuits out from a larger city and cut in one public station in each small town along the way. Such perfunctory service meant that users in those locations had to make calls from public stations; and while they could place calls to other cities in the Bell network, it was not possible for people in other cities to call them. Worse, a single circuit serving public stations in five to ten towns was a giant "party line." A call in any one of the towns along the way tied up the line for all towns along the circuit. Further, those seeking service frequently interrupted those talking.[11] Then, too, waits were long: It took an hour to get a connection from the Philadelphia suburbs to the city itself, over two hours to reach New York.[12] Bell's competitors thrived on such inadequate toll facilities and organization.

Thus, the independents did not suffer much from their lack of connections to the Bell System. On the contrary, their exclusion from Bell exchanges and toll lines encouraged them to develop a critical mass of users by constructing toll lines and new exchanges in areas underserved by Bell and organizing themselves in ways that would facilitate the interconnection of all non-Bell users. The supply of telephone facilities was so far below the demand that there was plenty of room for new subscriber universes. During the

8. 24 ELECTRICAL REV. 29 (June 13, 1894).

9. 26 ELECTRICAL REV. 35 (July 15, 1896).

10. Letter from F. R. Colvin to Hudson (Apr. 8, 1896), Box 1298, AT&T-BLA.

11. Letter from Thomas Doolittle to Hudson (June 27, 1899), Box 1330, AT&T-BLA.

12. Thomas Doolittle, *Report on Toll Matters*, to Hudson, Sept. 11, 1899.

1894–1898 period, the number of independent subscribers doubled every eighteen months. Much of that torrid rate of increase stemmed from the establishment of new exchanges. Independent exchanges that already existed, however, usually doubled in size each year for the first few years of their existence. When independent exchanges failed, and many did, it was rarely for want of subscribers. By 1902 there were 1.3 million Bell telephone subscribers, more than five times the number that had existed in 1894, but there were nearly a million users of independent telephones.

PHASE II: SYSTEM OVERLAP, 1898–1907

In the second phase of the competition, from 1898 to 1907, dual service competition was pushed from its stronghold in the mid-sized towns and previously undeveloped areas to the extremes of urban and rural America. Although, as noted in chapter 4, access competition makes perfect duplication of service impossible, it nevertheless gives competing networks an incentive to match each other's scope as closely as possible. Thus, Bell and the independents entered a period of growing system overlap. (See table 6-2.) To remain competitive with the independents, the Bell System extended its presence to small towns and rural areas, partly through new construction and partly by interconnecting with noncompeting independents. At the same time, the independents attempted to extend their access to major cities with established Bell exchanges.

From 1897 to 1904, the number of communities greater than 5,000 in population with competing exchanges shot up from 23 percent to 60 percent; it stayed over 55 percent until 1912. As dual service competition spread, price competition and service improvements in the affected cities typically doubled telephone users within a year. As that occurred, both sides raced to extend connecting service to those users. Technologies such as party lines and automatic switches, which lowered the cost of access, were rushed into operation.

Dual Service in the Cities

Early independent efforts to compete in large cities had almost always failed. A variety of snares and pitfalls awaited those who ventured directly into Bell's urban strongholds. The political maneuvering required to obtain a franchise in a major city was compli-

Table 6-2
Growth of Dual Service Competition, 1894–1907

Year	Number of Public Exchanges		Number of Telephones		Dual Service	
	Bell	Independent	Bell and Independent Connecting	Independent Nonconnecting	Number of Communities	Percentage
1894	1,409	98[a]	266,000	15,000[a]	28	2
1897	1,799	1,700[a]	415,000	100,000[a]	220	23
1902	3,005	3,400	1,401,021	969,845	449	55
1904	3,365	4,400[a]	2,399,213	1,348,000	483	60
1907	4,889	5,400	3,958,489	2,279,578	466	57

Note: Dual service points are counted only in communities with populations of 5,000 or more. Percentages are percentages of cities with populations of 5,000 or more.

a. Estimates are based on 1902 *Telephone Census*. Independent exchanges do not count rural farm lines or exchanges with incomes less than $5,000.

Sources: *Telephone Census* (1902, 1907); Chappelka (1956); *Telephony* (various issues); ABT Co. and AT&T annual reports.

cated and expensive.[13] Heavy capital investment was required to match the facilities of the Bell System. In cities, too, service was reasonably good, and complaints were usually limited to the high price of that service. Thus, Bell could undermine the demand for a new company by making rate concessions.

When the independents did manage to establish a presence in a major city, they were usually not prepared to handle the complexity of running a large exchange. Both of the independent exchanges started in 1894 in cities with populations greater than 50,000 failed within five years. The Home Telephone Company of Baltimore offered rates less than half those of Bell but became insolvent after three years. It was sold to a new company, which had to rebuild the plant and raise rates by 57 percent.[14] The same fate befell the independent exchange in Detroit.

Large urban exchanges that were the culmination of four or five years of prior development in the surrounding areas generally were the financially strongest and longest-lasting independent operating companies. Buffalo, St. Louis, Indianapolis, Kansas City, Louisville, and Minneapolis–St. Paul all followed that pattern. A competing exchange was not established in Buffalo until 1901, but in mid-1896 the *Electrical Review* reported that all the principal towns surrounding that city were connected by independent systems.[15] Kansas City did not admit an independent exchange until 1902, but in 1897, independents were thriving in many smaller towns within 150 miles.

Thus, from 1898 to 1903 a wave of new competition swept into the urban centers. It was the Bell strategy in reverse—the periphery advancing on the center.[16] By then the independents had gained more than access leverage in the countryside: They had also gained management and technical experience. Of cities over 100,000 in population, only Boston, New York, Washington, D.C., Cincinnati,

---

13. In Philadelphia the franchising of the Mutual Automatic Telephone Company was quashed when politicians were accused of exchanging their influence for stock in the company. In Brooklyn the city council franchised an independent company three times only to have the move vetoed by the mayor each time. 29 ELECTRICAL WORLD (Aug. 19, 1894).

14. 34 ELECTRICAL REV. 26 (Jan. 11, 1899).

15. 29 ELECTRICAL REV. 36 (July 15, 1896).

16. As an independent spokesman put it, where Bell had worked from the top down, the independents developed from the bottom up. HARRY MACMEAL, THE STORY OF INDEPENDENT TELEPHONY 26 (1934).

Milwaukee, and Denver managed to retain a single telephone system throughout the competitive period. Of those, only Washington and Cincinnati refused to franchise a competitor; the others authorized new entrants but the independents failed to raise the capital needed to build a competing exchange.

Quincy, Illinois, typified some of the causes behind the independents' advance into the cities. In 1894, the 500 Bell subscribers in Quincy could call one another, as well as Springfield and Peoria, but nowhere else. New, independent exchanges grew up in the surrounding areas very quickly and in 1895 the Western Illinois Telephone Company of Augusta began to construct toll lines connecting the independents in the region. In 1896, Western Illinois obtained Quincy's permission to bring its lines into a building in the city, where it set up a toll telephone. The system became very popular with local users.[17]

The convenience of the Quincy telephone line was noticed immediately by the merchants of Newark, Missouri, forty miles to the west. By issuing stock subscription and selling advance-purchase toll tickets, they raised money to build an independent line that would cross the Mississippi River and link their city to Quincy, as well as to thirty other points in Missouri. By 1899, Western Illinois Telephone operated 700 miles of toll line in six counties and maintained toll stations at fifty-nine towns. Through a submarine cable across the Mississippi River it connected with points in Missouri and Iowa; another cable across the Illinois River linked users to the farming areas around Springfield.[18]

Still, there was no independent exchange in Quincy itself, the largest city within a hundred miles. As the Bell exchange there was closed to independent connections, the only way to obtain access to the independent systems surrounding the city was to install an independent line and toll station on private business premises in Quincy. There were at least eight stations in 1903, illustrating the growing demand for independent connections.[19] Because the private lines were more expensive than a subscription to an exchange, and were becoming increasingly difficult to set up because the lines had to pass over private property to avoid the need for a franchise,

17. QUINCY HERALD, Jan. 10, 1896.

18. WESTERN ELECTRICIAN, Mar. 11, 1899.

19. THEODORE VAIL CHAPTER OF THE TELEPHONE PIONEERS OF AMERICA, THE STORY OF THE TELEPHONE IN QUINCY, AT&T Legal and Regulatory Archives, New York, N.Y.

several independents approached Quincy for a competing city exchange. The resulting debate dragged on for years.

In Quincy, as in all cities where dual service had been discussed since 1899, opponents praised Bell's "excellent service" and complained about the inconvenience of duplicating subscriptions for businesses.[20] Supporters asserted the need to obtain access to "country lines."[21] Finally, in 1904, after nearly six years and at least three separate applications to establish competing exchanges, Quincy's city council franchised the Quincy Home Telephone Co., which opened an automatic exchange system two years later. It upgraded many of the older independent toll lines, and arranged interconnection with the association of small independents. It also organized a separate company, the County Home Telephone Co., to acquire and connect independent lines in the farm areas. In the first year after the entry of Quincy Home, the presence of a competing exchange did more to stimulate new users than to take subscribers away from Bell. Both companies flourished.

In large cities, the dual service debate centered on rates, rather than access. Some cities encouraged competition as a way of controlling or reducing charges, often contrasting it with municipal rate regulation or measured service as a means to that end. They also used the threat of competition to extract rate concessions from the Bell company. Thus, an independent company was forced to make rates the basis of its franchise pitch. The outcome depended on how satisfied the local business community was with Bell.

Indianapolis provides an excellent example of how dissatisfaction with Bell fostered competition. In 1898 only 2,286 of Indianapolis' 169,000 citizens had phones, and the service was poor. A long history of disputes over rates had marred relations between the

---

20. QUINCY HERALD, Mar. 20, 1899 (reprinted editorial from CHICAGO EVENING POST): "Of what advantage will a telephone rate half as large as the present be, if one has to have two telephones to keep in touch with the business world? That is a problem which is troubling a good many people just now. Of course the answer is that in time one company or the other would be forced out."

21. "An exchange at Quincy with 200 or more of the principal business houses . . . would be of immense benefit to Quincy merchants, besides a matter of greatest convenience to the country merchants and farmers who do their trading almost exclusively in Quincy." Letter to the editor, QUINCY WEEKLY HERALD, Dec. 12, 1902, at 134.

telephone company and the citizenry, yet the company's franchise made no provisions for rate control and contained no expiration date. In that year, the city's Board of Public Works awarded a franchise to the New Telephone Company, but attached important restrictions to it. The franchise agreement fixed maximum annual rates at $40 for business and $24 for residences, 55 percent and 50 percent of the respective Bell rates. Further, the franchise would expire after twenty-five years and became void if the new company was consolidated with or purchased by a competitor.[22] That competition was conceived as a method of rate control is clear from the agreement itself, which stated that "the principal consideration for the granting of the franchise . . . is and will be the securing of a reduction of telephone rates to the citizens."[23] By January 1906, the New Telephone Company was serving 9,354 subscribers while the Bell exchange had grown to 7,670 subscribers. Thus, despite user fragmentation, a telephone subscriber in Indianapolis had access to four times more users after competition than before it.

Contrary to the trend in the rest of the country, dual service declined in the South after 1898. Due to cheap construction, unrealistically low rates, and a lack of regional cooperation and interconnection, independents in Mississippi, Louisiana, and parts of Virginia, Alabama, and Kentucky were decimated by bankruptcy and Bell acquisition after 1900.[24] The Cumberland Co. was particularly active in gobbling up financially exhausted independents, acquiring twenty noncompeting exchanges and six competing systems in Mississippi, Louisiana, and Kentucky between January 1900 and April 1901.[25]

Those failures portended financial problems that were to haunt the urban independent systems. In large exchanges, an independent promoter's calculation of the profits that could be made at lower rates had overlooked two critical considerations: depreciation and the diseconomies of growth. In the first year or two of operation, a new exchange performed well and appeared to make profits and even pay dividends. After four or five years, however, it learned

22. Patrick O'Neill, Franchising the New Telephone Company 7 (1988) (paper delivered at the Midwest Journalism Association Conference).

23. *Id.*

24. Lipartito, *supra* note 1, at 129–34.

25. Cumberland Telephone & Telegraph Co., *Acquisition of Independent Telephone Companies*, Box 1336, AT&T-BLA.

that the "profits" and "dividends" of the preceding years had not been profits at all, but should have been retained to renew the exchange's physical facilities.[26] Independents also learned that their costs increased as they added subscribers, making their initial rates inadequate. Where their rates had been locked into their franchise agreements, the problems were worse. By 1906 the independents in St. Louis, Cleveland, Indianapolis, Pittsburgh, Toledo, Madison, and many other cities had been forced to ask for rate increases of 20 to 50 percent.[27] Others began to engage in acts of financial legerdemain, such as issuing new bonds to pay for the old ones before they matured, in a desperate attempt to raise the capital needed to renew and expand. They were learning the lesson the Bell System had: Expansion demanded huge amounts of investment capital.

Access Competition and Rates

Telephone prices generally consist of two parts: a charge for access and a charge for usage. Pricing after 1894 was deliberately constructed to minimize the access cost barrier to encourage large numbers of new subscribers to join (or, in the case of Bell, to retain existing subscribers). From 1894 to 1900, the average monthly rate for local exchange service dropped by more than half. It was not unusual for Bell operating companies to temporarily set their rates at $1 per month, or even to provide service for free, in cities where an independent exchange had taken away many of their subscribers.[28] Rate reductions occurred in part because competition forced Bell to lower royalty payments on Western Electric phones, but also because competition forced companies to operate more efficiently and offer new classes of affordable service.

In nearly all cases, the independents positioned themselves as the lower-cost providers. A comparison of rates in over 471 compet-

---

26. *The Financial Side of Independent Telephony*, 11 TELEPHONY 14 (Jan. 1906) (review of FREDERICK DICKSON, TELEPHONE INVESTMENTS, AND OTHERS). Dickson, president of the Cleveland-based Cuyahoga Telephone Company, actually argued in defense of the absence of depreciation charges.

27. 12 CUMBERLAND TELEPHONE JOURNAL (1906), AT&T-BLA.

28. LIPARTITO, *supra* note 1, at 120; Richard Gabel, The Evolution of a Market: The Emergence of Regulation in the Telephone Industry of Wisconsin, 1893–1917 (1987) (unpublished Ph.D. dissertation, University of Wisconsin (Madison)).

ing exchanges by the Bell System in 1913 found that Bell's exchange rates exceeded the independents' in 90 percent of the cases.[29] In the early years that did not necessarily mean that the independents' equipment was lower quality and their service inferior. A memo from the president of the New York Telephone Company in 1902 noted that the amount of capital invested per Bell telephone was $328.20, whereas for independents the capital per phone was only $192.30. He attributed that disparity to the facts that the independent plants were newer and technologically superior to those of Bell, and that Bell had more inefficient party lines.[30]

In 1909, AT&T conducted a study that compared telephone penetration levels and rates in twelve cities without competition and twenty-seven cities with competition.[31] The study found that the average development in noncompetitive cities was only 8.2 telephones per 100 population, compared with 11.2 stations per 100 in cities with competition. The covering letter to that report states: "It seems that with competition development is somewhat greater than without. Of course part of that greater development is to be ascribed to the lower rates prevailing under competition."[32]

The need to maintain a large subscriber universe also affected the structure of the technology. Both contestants began to offer inexpensive two-party, four-party, and sometimes even eight- and ten-party lines, to increase their subscriber universe.[33] The object was to get as many subscribers onto the system as quickly and as cheaply as possible. One particularly novel attempt to broaden access was the "kitchen telephone." Kitchen telephones, which made, but did not receive calls, were to be "conveniently located for the use of the servants . . . through which to order supplies from . . . tradespeople."[34]

---

29. Bell and Independent Exchange Rates, 1912–13, Box 29, AT&T-BLA.

30. Letter from president of New York Telephone Co. to Fish (Mar. 25, 1902), AT&T-BLA.

31. Walter S. Gifford, AT&T statistician, Showing Growth in Bell and Independent Telephone Development Together with Changes in Exchange Rates in Various Cities of the United States Arranged by Five Year Periods from 1894 to 1909 (Aug. 10, 1909), AT&T-BLA.

32. C. G. DuBois, comptroller, AT&T, Effect of Competition on Development and Rates (Aug. 20, 1909), AT&T-BLA.

33. Party Line Development, 1898–99, Box 1258, AT&T-BLA.

34. *Kitchen Telephone Service*, advertising flyer, Sunset T&T Co., 1895, Box 1278, AT&T-BLA.

Dual Service in the Country

Around 1900, a new force entered the telephone competition, a development as important in its own way as the initial wave of independent competition. Huge numbers of farmers began to buy their own telephones and establish telephone systems. Farm lines were basically party lines that joined five to twenty houses. Many were built by cooperative organizations that drew on their own member-subscribers for capital and operating labor. Subscribers were expected to maintain their own part of the line, the poles on their property, and their own phone. Advice on how to construct farm lines was widely disseminated through periodicals such as the *Farm Journal*. To the large number of Americans who lived on farms, those lines were a welcome relief from isolation. Once one line was established in a farming area, "telephone contagion" struck the whole community.

Initially, each small farm line had its own organization, and all members voted on all issues. As lines proliferated throughout a region, those organizations made arrangements to interconnect their lines at someone's house, through simple serial connections run by farm wives or daughters. As telephone use spread further, these small cooperatives would often combine with others and adopt corporate, commercial forms of organization.[35]

In 1902, there were 5,979 tiny farmer lines and rural mutual systems, and another 15,598 rural lines run on a commercial basis.[36] Rural lines accounted for more than a quarter of a million telephones in the United States, about 11 percent of the total. During the next ten years, telephone penetration in the farm areas surpassed that of the urban areas.[37]

As the farm lines blossomed, they were drawn into access competition. Farmers wanted connections to markets and merchants in the cities; the telephone companies wanted to obtain a competitive edge by controlling access to rural subscribers. Independent and Bell alike took note of what came to be known as "the farm line proposition," which referred to the negotiations over which system farm lines would choose for interconnection. The once-neglected farmer became a highly sought prize.

---

35. TELEPHONE CENSUS, 1907.
36. ELECTRICAL INDUSTRIES CENSUS, 1902, table 13.
37. Claude Fischer, *The Revolution in Rural Telephony*, J. SOCIAL HIST. 5 (1987).

Rural lines are generally counted by economic historians as part of the independents' "market share," but a large percentage of them—perhaps half—had no vested interest in competing with Bell. Their goal was to bring the telephone to their areas at the lowest possible rate. They accepted the best connection terms regardless of the source. If they became dissatisfied with the toll charges imposed on them by a connecting exchange, they would frequently disconnect their line and set up their own terminus in the same town. Whereas the organized independents almost never entered into direct competition with each other, farmers had no such scruples. In some cases four different switchboards operated in the same community due to disagreements over connecting charges.[38] That type of competition so exasperated the organized independent movement that its associations tried to get manufacturers to refuse to sell equipment to independent companies that initiated competition when another independent was already adequately serving the community.[39] From a competitive standpoint, the farmers were not part of the organized independent movement, but truly independent "swing voters" who had to be courted by both sides.

It was the presence of access competition that gave the farmers their leverage over the telephone companies. Bell and many urban-based independents probably would have preferred to ignore them. But competition forced both of them to seek out the farmers and offer favorable terms for interconnection, and in some cases, for maintenance capital.

BELL'S RESPONSE TO COMPETITION

Bell embraced a variety of tactics in response to independent competition. Correspondence between the national organization and the licensee companies reveals that five basic methods were employed: the adoption of "fighting" rates, that is, temporarily lower prices for local exchange access to drive the independent

---

38. A. R. Chappelka, History of Independent Telephone Operating Companies in the United States, Memorandum on Affirmative Topic No. 10, Civil Action No. 17-49 (1956).

39. *Id.*

from the field;[40] buying out competitors; improving and extending service; interfering with the franchising of independent companies; and spreading unfavorable publicity about independent companies to scare away customers and financiers.[41]

Although evidence can be found that each of those tactics did some damage to the independents in isolated circumstances, the strategies were ultimately failures. Price wars produced nothing but financial losses for the licensee companies.[42] Rate cuts were more expensive for Bell than for its rivals because the independents' costs were generally lower.[43] Besides, rate cuts from Bell were utterly lacking in credibility, as people would not easily forget seventeen years of monopoly prices. Buying out competitors was a highly expensive proposition, too, although it was employed in a few strategic circumstances. Successful independents, however, had little incentive to sell, and by 1898 there were far too many of them for Bell purchases to make much of an impact. Blocking franchises worked in a few large cities,[44] some of them of great

---

40. For typical correspondence of that sort, *see* letter from C. E. Yost, president, Iowa Union Telephone Company, to C. J. French, American Bell (Apr. 18, 1899), AT&T-BLA; letter from E. B. Field, general manager, Colorado Telephone Company, to French (Aug. 28, 1895), AT&T-BLA. French, the national organization's person in charge of competitive tactics, advocated "fighting" rates lower than a competitor's as a temporary expedient.

41. Chappelka, *supra* note 38, discusses the variety of competitive tactics used by American Bell Telephone in the early years of competition.

42. American Bell's annual reports from 1899 to 1907 note repeatedly that competition had forced many licensee companies to reduce their rates to unremunerative levels and adversely affected their financial condition. *See* AMERICAN BELL TELEPHONE, ANNUAL REPORT 9 (1902); AMERICAN BELL TELEPHONE, ANNUAL REPORT 12 (1906). In 1902 Fish wrote to C. E. Yost, "The plan of meeting the opposition by reducing rates has, I believe, rarely if ever succeeded." *Cited in* Chappelka, *supra* note 38.

43. Mr. Jackson, president of the Central Union Company, wrote to Hudson, American Bell Telephone, in 1899 complaining that in medium-sized towns of 10,000–20,000 population the independents were charging annual flat rates of $24 (business) and $12 (residence) for single-party metallic circuit lines. "We cannot meet these rates, and cannot sell our metallic service at the present rate of $60–66 per annum in exchanges of that size." *Cited in* Chappelka, *supra* note 38.

44. Bell lobbied city governments to prevent franchising of competing companies, and if that failed, it loaded the franchises with restrictive provisions that made life difficult for the competitor. Bell's political efforts paid off

strategic importance, but the growth of independent-controlled exchanges in the surrounding areas maintained constant pressure on cities to franchise an independent. The effort by Bell's public relations agents to discredit the independents worked only in areas where people had no direct knowledge of independent telephony, such as New England and New York. In most areas, independents had a track record and support from local capital, local merchants, and local politicians. Clearly, Bell could not survive by relying on those strategies. Bell management came thus to understand that improving and extending service was the most powerful response to competition.

Toll Line and Exchange Development

As the other tactics failed, Bell managers saw that its own underdevelopment was the root of the problem of independent competition. Increasingly, they understood that Bell's main competitive advantage was its ability to offer comprehensive service within a given region. Although independent exchanges and telephones often outnumbered Bell in a given territory, Bell still had more exchanges than any individual independent company. With its coordinated business management and superior access to capital, it was in a better position than the independents to expand, interconnect, and integrate the operations of many dispersed exchanges. In effect, Bell began to try to beat the independents at their own game. The "opposition" had bested the Bell System by offering access to a larger number of local and regional points. Now Bell would expand and integrate its operations so that it could offer users an even larger bundle of regional connections than the independents. Expanding their toll lines to improve connectivity among Bell exchanges would "crush the opposition," according to one licensee company manager.[45] The president of AT&T, Frederick P. Fish, put

---

most heavily in Washington, D.C., where the influence of the Chesapeake and Potomac Company on Congress was strong enough to ensure that authority for competition was shelved in 1900. Lobbying efforts by the general manager of Bell's Colorado Telephone Company prevented a competing Denver franchise in 1901. In Scranton, Pennsylvania, Bell interests defeated three procompetition ordinances in four years. From 1896 to 1899 pro-Bell politicians in Kansas City buried several competing franchise authorizations.

45. Letter from C. J. Glidden, president, Michigan Telephone Company, to Hudson, American Bell Telephone (Jan. 28, 1899), AT&T-BLA.

it more delicately in 1903: "It is upon your toll facilities that you must depend for holding your own against the opposition."[46]

The renewed Bell emphasis on exchange and toll line development is often misunderstood as a strategy based on superior long-distance transmission technology.[47] In that view, Bell exploited its technical capabilities[48] to create ultra-long-distance connections that the independents could not match. The misconception is based on the ambiguity of the term *toll lines*. Contemporary usage referred to interexchange connections within the licensee companies' territories as toll lines, and the longer-distance, intercity lines of AT&T as long lines. The toll lines that the Bell managers saw as their salvation were not long lines, but regional connections within a 100-mile radius, which were usually supplied by the local operating companies. Indeed, Bell's toll lines utilized the same technology available to the independents.[49]

The real source of competitive advantage was comprehensive coverage of a particular region corresponding to the interest of the majority of telephone users. To be sure, the scope of access desired by different types of users varied greatly. But the best way to satisfy all possible users was to create a comprehensive, universal network.

The demand for telephone connections between points over 200 miles apart was still restricted to a tiny minority of users. No more than 5 percent of all telephone calls were to points more than

---

46. Letter from President Fish, American Bell Telephone, to G. Y. Wallace, Rocky Mountain Bell (May 25, 1903), AT&T-BLA.

47. GERALD FAULHABER, TELECOMMUNICATIONS IN TURMOIL: TECHNOLOGY AND PUBLIC POLICY 2–3 (Ballinger 1987). Faulhaber stresses the technological advantage achieved by the loading coil and that "the linchpin of Vail's strategy was to gain control of the technology."

48. *See* NEIL WASSERMAN, FROM INVENTION TO INNOVATION: LONG DISTANCE TELEPHONE TRANSMISSION AT THE TURN OF THE CENTURY (Johns Hopkins University Press 1985). Wasserman's account of the application of loading coils makes it clear that it did not play a significant role in the competitive battle.

49. Fish admitted that the company held "no controlling patents on long distance telephone apparatus or systems. [L]ong distance lines of some commercial value [could] be constructed and operated by anyone." Letter from Fish to C. H. Cutting (Apr. 3, 1903). *Cited in* Chappelka, *supra* note 38. *See also* letter from Thomas Lockwood, AT&T, to Theodore Vail (Aug. 8, 1908), AT&T-BLA.

fifty miles away.[50] For communication over longer distances, the telegraph was still the dominant and by far the most economical service. As late as 1909, a telephone businessman wrote that while ultra-long-distance telephoning "appeals most strongly to the imagination," it was "of little commercial or social importance."[51] Long-lines business was profitable, but it had always been in Bell's control; in fact, Bell's pre-1894 pursuit of that market to the exclusion of most others had left it vulnerable to competitors. The new emphasis on intensive toll line development within the licensee companies' territories was actually a sharp departure from the old Bell vision. It was, however, a logical and indeed unavoidable response to access competition.

Prodded by competition, the Bell licensee companies opened approximately 3,500 new exchanges in cities with populations under 10,000 between 1894 and 1907,[52] three times the number they had opened in the previous seventeen years. Between 1902 and 1907, Bell's wire mileage grew by 164 percent, a faster rate of expansion than the independents.[53] Between the year 1898, when the new strategy of expansion began, and the financial panic of 1907, which temporarily dried up capital resources, the Bell plant grew by an average of more than 17 percent per year, double the earlier rate. In 1899, 1900, and 1906, the annual rate of growth exceeded 22 percent.

Within the national Bell organization, Thomas B. Doolittle was the most consistent, committed advocate of responding to competition with the development of systemic connectivity. Practically from the beginning of the Bell System, Doolittle had taken a special interest in the toll line business, "not only [for its] probable earning power but as a means of protecting the business from the dangers of competition." Beginning in 1891, he and his staff studied the operating conditions of the licensee companies. For various territories, they examined traffic patterns and volume, rates, and

---

50. A graph showing the volume of toll calls as a function of distance was prepared by Doolittle for the New York and Pennsylvania Telephone Co. for 1900. For cities with exchanges, 98 percent of all calls were to points within fifty miles. For toll stations in small towns, the percentage was somewhat smaller—about 95 percent. Box 1330, AT&T-BLA.

51. Gansey Johnson, Columbus Citizens Tel. Co., 17 TELEPHONY (Jan. 2, 1909).

52. TELEPHONE CENSUS, 1907.

53. *Id.*

the operating procedures used in making up toll connections. When Doolittle began his work, the toll facilities of the licensee companies generally were poorly developed and inefficiently run. The management of the national company and that of the licensee companies were not well coordinated. Working patiently for fifteen years, he spearheaded the administrative rationalization of the interconnection process and the growth of toll connectivity in the Bell System.

Doolittle's arguments for toll line development were based on the demand interdependence of telephone service. His records of toll calling receipts convinced him that the average revenue that could be expected from a place increased as it was connected to more places. He therefore recommended extending toll lines to smaller and smaller towns.

He was an advocate of exchange as well as toll line development. He knew that when people could receive and make calls on one exchange it increased the scope of service that could be offered to users in other cities. His reports on the licensee companies from 1896 to 1902 always contained long lists of towns where small exchanges should be placed.

In promoting the development of small exchanges, Doolittle pioneered the theory and practice of "subsidizing" local exchange access with long-distance revenues. Bell would gain by establishing inexpensive exchange service in small towns, even if the exchange itself lost money on a "stand-alone" basis, he argued, because giving users in other locations access to subscribers in the smaller towns would stimulate increased use of the toll lines. That access competition produced "cross-subsidies" from toll usage to exchange access is particularly noteworthy, since economists commonly assume that such practices are a product of government rate regulation and would not exist in a competitive market.

But it was access competition, and not merely the desire to enhance toll traffic, that propelled the Bell System to extend access at lower rates to stimulate usage and expand its scope. The degree to which Bell expanded, even to the most economically unattractive rural areas, is evident in a 1907 letter from G. Y. Wallace, president of Rocky Mountain Bell, in which he claims that opening small exchanges in Utah was the "virtual undoing of Utah Independent Telephone Company."[54] Similarly, competition in the South was

---

54. Letter from G. Y. Wallace, Rocky Mountain Bell, to T. N. Vail (Nov. 7, 1907), AT&T-BLA.

overcome when Edward J. Hall, the head of Southern Bell, increased Southern Bell's capital resources by thirtyfold between 1897 and 1906 to invest in toll line construction and in upgrading local exchange circuits to make them more compatible with the toll network.

The expansion of the network increased the complexity of making connections. AT&T responded by pioneering "center checking," a method of routing, handling, and accounting for calls, which centralized the responsibility for routing and accounting for toll calls at designated exchanges. When implemented, it enabled operators to transfer toll calls headed to a specific destination, and toll center operators to get the calls to their destinations as directly and quickly as possible. Rationalizing the process of toll interconnection reduced the amount of time consumed by making a connection and resulted in great savings in plant facilities.

Rate rationalization was another important achievement of Doolittle's. He systematically simplified and reorganized the licensee companies' toll tariffs by replacing charges based on route mileage with a more uniform airline-mileage basis. Here again competition was the spur to efficiency. Doolittle's reports identify the competitive losses caused by the "border problem," the inefficiencies in interexchange service caused by Bell's division of the country into separate territories under different managements. He noted that if two towns were only fifty miles apart but were located on opposite sides of a border separating two licensee companies, someone calling between them might pay a rate for triple that distance. Independent competitors took advantage of such rate discrepancies by offering more direct, cheaper service. Doolittle brought the managers of AT&T, the licensee companies, and independent connecting companies together to establish how traffic should be routed and which company's lines should be used.

The competitive advantage derived from the Bell organization's emphasis on toll connectivity can be appreciated by contrasting Bell's systematic approach to that of the independents. Before their consolidation into regional systems, most independents relied on their state associations to coordinate toll connectivity. The lack of a central management authority continually handicapped their attempts to coordinate toll service. In November 1904, *Telephony* observed that it was the exception rather than the rule that the independents could offer competition on messages of over 100 miles. In some cases the problem was poor construction; in other cases it was roundabout routing; in still others it was inconsistent or uncoordinated operating procedures. The result was confusion, bad service, and dissatisfied customers. The problem, then, was organizational, not technological, and in particular the lack of comprehensive regional toll interconnection. The combination of Doolittle's efforts and their own mismanagement reversed the independents' incursions into the short-haul toll market. In 1902, independents handled 37 percent of the toll calls. By 1907, that had declined to 24 percent.

Sublicensing Independent Exchanges

As the wave of dual service competition continued to gather momentum, both Bell and the independents struggled to weave their exchange holdings into an integrated system offering access to as many cities and towns within 200-mile radii as possible. As part of that process, the Bell System was forced to liberalize considerably its policy of not interconnecting with independents. It began to expand its access to rural areas by "sublicensing" or interconnecting with noncompeting independent exchanges.

Conventional histories present Bell's refusal to connect with the independents as a harsh and powerful competitive tactic. More generally, antitrust economists tend to classify such "refusals to deal" as inherently monopolistic. An established system that denies access to or makes itself incompatible with its competitors is, according to that doctrine, suppressing competition. In fact, the Bell System's most powerful strategic ploy proved to be interconnecting with certain independents, a policy made in response to market pressure.

Between 1894 and 1902, the national Bell organization adhered strictly to exclusion. Independent companies could not be connected to Bell exchanges or toll lines, even when they occupied territory remote from any Bell exchange and were not competing with Bell. Bell refused to purchase equipment from independent manufacturers and refused to sell Western Electric equipment to the independents. During that time, the independents made their most rapid competitive gains. Their growth occurred because of, rather than in spite of, the noninterconnection policy. Bell was simply unable to keep up with the demand for telephone service in thousands of small towns. Its noninterconnection policy cut Bell off from the majority of telephone users in undeveloped areas, and guaranteed its competitors exclusive access to every exchange built independently of the Bell System.

By early 1901, it was clear even to the distant Boston managers that absolute exclusion of independent companies had been a costly mistake. Some managers of the licensee companies began to consider exchanging traffic with independent exchanges that did not directly compete with those of Bell. That policy was known as "sublicensing" because it involved a licensee company extending the connecting privileges of the Bell license contract to independent companies within its territory. Two licensee companies that had been particularly hard hit by competition actually had begun to implement that policy on their own.[55]

The national organization moved more slowly. Unlike other adjustments in Bell practices made in response to competition, sublicensing involved revising some of the fundamental assumptions underlying license contracts. The primary object of a license contract was to secure profits and control for the national organization while harnessing local initiative and capital. But how could the same level of control be maintained when interconnecting with independent companies? If Bell was to interconnect with noncompeting local exchanges, should it require them to lease Bell instruments, as it did of its traditional licensees? If so, what would induce those independents to lease Bell instruments when they could obtain independently manufactured telephones at a lower price? If not, how could Bell maintain uniform technical standards? Since Bell would have no ownership control over the connecting company, there was also the risk that sublicensed companies might break the connection contract later. Notwithstanding all their questions, top executives of AT&T and American Bell Telephone (ABT) knew that the time had come for some type of sublicensing. They admitted their initial mistakes:

> [If] it could have been foreseen what an extensive development of the telephone business would be required to meet the needs of the people . . . it would have been good policy on the part of the ABT Co. to have encouraged its licensees to sublicense to local people the right to furnish service in country districts and villages and towns.[56]

---

55. Letter from C. E. Yost, president, Northwestern Telephone Exchange Company, to President Fish (Sept. 12, 1902), Box 1353, AT&T-BLA.

56. Letter from Joseph Davis to President Fish (Oct. 23, 1901), AT&T-BLA.

That comment underscores the fact that universal service in the modern sense was never part of AT&T's original conception of the business. Never in their wildest dreams did the early Bell managers think that telephone service could be demanded by, and profitably extended to, as many people and places as turned out to be possible.

AT&T and American Bell Telephone decided to go ahead with sublicensing agreements that included leasing of phones. As justification, they claimed the use of other phones would lower Bell's high technical standards, even though major independent-brand telephones were equal to Bell's. But having argued earlier that independent equipment was inferior, changing its position now might make Bell look dishonest and lend support to compulsory interconnection. Then, too, Bell knew that leasing telephones was far more profitable than selling them outright.

The new policy was ratified late in 1901; henceforth, licensee companies could sublicense independent exchanges under a standard form of contract with the blessings of the national corporation. Besides using only Western Electric phones, sublicensees could not be in direct competition with a Bell exchange or connect with any toll lines other than Bell's.

Sublicensing was a powerful weapon in a battle between exclusive networks. It not only provided Bell with connections to small locations, it also removed those exchanges from the independent orbit. Sublicensing could also be used to withdraw from dual service competition without losing access to a city's telephone users.[57] In mid-sized cities where an independent exchange had established a commanding lead in subscribers, Bell would propose pulling out if the independent would agree to become a sublicensee. It offered that independent a respite from competition, access to Bell's toll lines, and a chance to raise its rates. Bell gained access to the preponderance of subscribers in the city, while relieving itself of the need to maintain a competitive facility.

The organized independents immediately recognized that sublicensing threatened to disintegrate their movement. Their publications and associations assailed the practice in the strongest terms. "You cannot be an Independent company and connect in any way with the Bell," James Hoge, president of the national independent

---

57. AMER. TEL. J. (Jan. 28, 1905).

association, wrote: "You cannot serve two masters. You must choose between the people and a greedy corporation."[58]

In 1902 the Interstate Independent Telephone Association addressed the problem.[59] It was a contentious issue for the membership: Some members unilaterally opposed interconnection; others felt that if connecting with Bell would keep a competing Bell exchange out of a city, it was good business policy.

The organization's final recommendation to its members gave slight concessions to those who wished to bar competing Bell exchanges in their jurisdictions, but strongly recommended against any form of cooperation with Bell. "Operating companies or individuals using Bell apparatus tend to 'demoralize and destroy' the independent movement and should be barred from membership in the national, interstate, or state associations. Only companies that connect their toll lines and exchanges with independent companies should be eligible for membership."[60]

The progress of sublicensing has been documented before by scholars such as Langdale (1978), but its significance in the context of access competition and its implications for standard accounts of universal service have not been fully appreciated. Despite Bell's later claims that universal service in the modern sense was its policy from the beginning, Bell ultimately obtained most of its access to small town and rural America through interconnection agreements with independent companies. More important, its decision to "reach out and touch" the rural areas was not a product of its own commitment to universal coverage, but a policy forced upon it by the exigencies of access competition.

Each of the preceding sections demonstrates how access competition promoted a universal telephone infrastructure by placing a premium on a network's scope. Had the competitors been interconnected, on the other hand, the incentives to pursue universality would have been greatly weakened. Independent competitors would have found it much easier to establish service in the urban areas

---

58. 11 TELEPHONY 314 (May 1906).

59. WESTERN ELECTRICIAN 426 (Dec. 13, 1902).

60. "We deplore individuals or companies connecting lines and exchanges with Bell licensee companies . . . as we believe that no such relation should be permitted, except, possibly, in isolated cases, which arrangement should be passed upon and authorized by the state association . . . the executive committee of the interstate association, or the advisory board of the national association." *Id.*

already developed by Bell and could have concentrated on simply undercutting Bell's price. The Bell System might never have undertaken the massive capital investments required to enlarge its exchanges in outlying areas and its network of toll lines, as those investments would not have given it a competitive advantage over the less extensive networks of the independents. Likewise, the independents would have had no incentive to construct alternative toll networks to connect independent exchanges. Incentives to restructure the technology to cheapen the cost of access would have been less powerful. Neither Bell nor the commercial independents would have been in any hurry to reach out to rural areas and small towns because it would not have mattered which system reached them first.

7

Dual Service: The Anatomy of Subscriber Fragmentation

BETWEEN 1902 and 1912, competing telephone exchanges operated in more than half of all American cities with populations larger than 5,000. When dual service peaked in 1904, it existed in 60 percent of those cities. In cities of all sizes, dual service reached its numerical apogee in 1911, when it existed in 2,290 places.

Because we all rely heavily on universal interconnection today, we tend to assume that its absence was simply a mistake—a problem crying out for a regulatory solution. But we are in no position to assess the significance of homogenized telephone access unless we know something about what things were like when it did not exist. This chapter attempts to portray the reality of dual service as it affected telephone users of the period. The first section examines the way subscribers divided themselves between the two systems in a single urban telephone exchange in 1910. The second section examines the fragmentation of intercity telephone service through both anecdotal information and maps showing regional access in Indiana in 1898, 1907, and 1912.

DUAL SERVICE AT THE EXCHANGE LEVEL

The analysis of subscriber fragmentation patterns in a dual system is especially rewarding from the standpoint of social theory. Much like the language barriers in a bilingual community, dual service divided communities by communication. Some users were confined to one of the two systems, others were "bilingual" or duplicate users. Unlike language, however, the division of the public into two telephone systems reflected consumer choice, not cultural inheritance.

How did dual service work? In 1910, the telephone was not yet the dominant mode of communication for city dwellers; only 20 percent of them had phones in their homes. The rest, if they used telephones at all, relied on public pay phones, or the free phones offered to customers by businesses such as drug stores and saloons. Virtually all large businesses had telephones, especially if they were national or interstate in scope. About 50 to 75 percent of the smaller businesses used the telephone, the rate varying widely depending on the type of business.

The Bell Laboratories Archives possess a detailed document that offers interesting insights into how dual service worked. It breaks down Louisville's 1910 telephone subscribers to 214 categories. The data show how many members of each category were Bell subscribers, how many used the independent Home Company, and how many had duplicate telephone service.[1] They yield interesting insights into the way telephone communication patterns and social structure were related to the dual telephone systems. (See table 7-1.)

At that time, Louisville was served by both the Bell-licensee Cumberland Telephone and the independent Home Telephone. There were 16,263 telephone subscribers: 60 percent residential, 40 percent business. Home Telephone had about 1,000 more subscribers than Cumberland. The aggregate duplication rate was 18 percent, with 2,923 users subscribed to both the Cumberland and Home companies. A breakdown of those subscribers shows that the duplication rate follows a hierarchy present in all social organization: some groups duplicated at very high rates and others hardly at all. A small number of large users made a disproportionate number of calls and demanded communication across a broader geographic range. Banks, railroads, hotels, and wholesale farm suppliers, for example, had very high rates of subscription and duplication. All of the businesses in that category had telephones, and 75 to 100 percent of them had dual service. Businesses with a duplication rate over 75 percent accounted for only 1.5 percent of

1. Letter from Thomas Tracy, Cumberland Telephone and Telegraph Co., to U. N. Bethell, AT&T, on the acquisition of Central Home Telephone and Telegraph (Feb. 11, 1911), Box 39, AT&T-Bell Laboratories Archives, Warren, N.J. [hereinafter AT&T-BLA].

Table 7-1
Telephone Duplication Rates, Louisville, 1910

Size of Business	Both Phones	Home Only	Bell Only	Duplication Rate (%)	Subscriber Rate (%)
Large-scale business					
Telegraph companies	4	0	0	100	100
Mill supplies	7	0	0	100	100
Gas & electric light	4	0	0	100	100
Fast freight lines	11	1	0	92	100
Railroads	21	2	2	87	100
Banks & trust companies	25	2	2	86	100
Express companies	6	1	0	85	100
Fertilizer manufacturers	8	1	1	80	100
Hotels	21	6	0	78	100
Laundries	26	7	1	76	NA
Medium-scale business					
Hay, grain & feed	34	36	3	54	NA
Druggists	83	69	3	53	100
Coal dealers	46	42	9	47	100
Insurance	65	46	36	44	NA
Dentists	35	44	3	42	63
Liquor dealers	43	56	18	37	NA
Plumbers	25	45	1	35	74
Attorneys	85	109	90	30	78
Butchers	19	47	7	26	NA
Dry goods	15	36	6	26	21
Groceries	182	466	62	25	NA
Neighborhood level					
Billiard halls	1	5	0	16	NA
Bowling alleys	1	5	0	16	NA
Carpenters	11	55	9	14	50
Barber shops	1	6	1	12	NA
Bakers	9	61	9	11	39
Saloons	64	487	19	11	87
Tailors	8	60	9	10	NA
Churches	3	12	14	10	NA
Residences	900	5,449	3,971	9	20

the total telephones in the city of Louisville, but made up 7.5 percent of all duplicate subscriptions. As those enterprises were generally large, capital-intensive, and highly dependent upon widespread communications access, a duplicate subscription was just an additional cost associated with doing business, not much different from ordering an extra telephone extension or another line from a single system.

In the middle of the hierarchy were smaller businesses who used the telephone frequently but whose markets and suppliers were primarily local. Retail businesses and professional services such as physicians, dentists, coal dealers, druggists, and attorneys duplicated at a 30 percent to 50 percent rate. For them, duplication was a larger economic commitment than it was to bigger establishments.

Home's relative dominance in Louisville made it much more likely that middle-level subscribers who used only one phone would be independent subscribers. There are, however, interesting exceptions to that rule. Whereas single-phone businesses such as coal dealers, butchers, and plumbers favored the lower-priced Home by ratios of five or six to one, Bell was almost even among lawyers and insurance agents. The disparity could be explained in a number of ways—the data by themselves being insufficient to rule out several options. One possibility is that those involved in law and finance had a greater need for long-distance connections to Cincinnati and other major cities controlled by Bell. Another explanation is that certain lawyers and insurance agents formed a community of interest with other Bell users and saw little need for connection with Home subscribers.

The final class comprises the bottom of the communications hierarchy: those who used the telephone infrequently. In addition to residential users, that category included very small businesses or solo practitioners—tailors, barbers, and physicians—and local recreational and cultural institutions, such as saloons, churches, and bowling alleys. Here the duplication rate is consistently low, averaging about 10 percent. Those duplications that did exist were usually business-related, for example, physicians who wanted access to their clients at all times. On the whole, that class of subscribers used the telephone over a limited local area and had little interest in universal access.

Once again, an uneven division of various subscriber categories suggests that subscription choices reflected other social boundaries. There is a marked bias toward the Home Company, for example, among "working class" institutions like bowling alleys, billiard halls, and saloons. The figures for residences and churches, on the other hand, are not so lopsided. That suggests that at the bottom of the hierarchy, telephone users were divided by neighborhood and/or economic status. The wealthier sections of town went for the Bell System, which had higher rates and whose advertising projected respectability, while those of more modest means responded to the independent's lower rates and, perhaps, its appeals to localism.

Unfortunately, there are no data to support that hypothesis. There is, however, anecdotal information. A field report written for Central Union Telephone states that its customers in Quincy, Illinois "[are] substantial business houses and of the better class of resident subscribers, while the Quincy Home Telephone Co. receives their greatest support from . . . those affiliated with political and labor associations."[2] In St. Joseph, Missouri, the independent exchange attracted subscribers Bell considered undesirable, either because they did not pay their bills or because they were "colored."[3] In other communities, the independent may have attracted the "better class." Which telephone company enticed which group is not as important as the fact that the division of the telephone-using public followed other political, social, and economic divisions.

Dual service, then, required large-scale, high-volume users to take out duplicate subscriptions to effect citywide commerce and have access to Louisville's institutions and services, but had little effect on other users. Dual service may have restricted social interaction, but it did not do so arbitrarily. Classes and neighborhoods voluntarily divided themselves into user communities. There was, of course, always a chance that one would not be able to call an acquaintance or a business from one's telephone exchange, but public telephones were available for such calls. There is little evidence that lack of interconnection was much of an impediment to telephone users in Louisville in 1910.

---

2. Central Union Telephone Co., form dated Dec. 3, 1909; Quincy Home Telephone Co., Regulatory History Project, AT&T Legal and Regulatory Archives, New York, N.Y.

3. *Monthly Narrative Report-St. Joseph,* May 17, 1911, Box 17, AT&T-BLA.

In cities where one of two competing exchanges controlled less than 35 percent of the city's subscribers, as many as half of those subscribers might be duplicators. In St. Joseph, Missouri, for example, Bell subscribers outnumbered Home Co. subscribers by three to one. The 1,048 duplicate subscribers represented only 12 percent of the Bell list, but accounted for 40 percent of the independent subscribers. In Philadelphia in 1907, where Bell had 95,000 subscribers and the independent only 15,000, 65 percent of the independent subscribers were duplicators. Thus, a small market share was not necessarily fatal as long as new subscribers were joining a network at a rapid pace. If a smaller system had a significant pool of "exclusives"—nonduplicating subscribers—it could attract new subscribers and make it worthwhile for business subscribers to duplicate. Once rapid growth in the overall number of subscribers stopped, however, large disparities tended to reinforce themselves over time. More and more subscribers gravitated to the dominant system and the minority exchange's base of "exclusives" began to shrink.

DUAL SERVICE AT THE INTEREXCHANGE LEVEL

Subscribers could make informed choices about their local access, but their toll connections were less predictable. The factors determining whether Bell or an independent was dominant in another community were not necessarily the same as those in their own city.

As mentioned elsewhere, and as the maps in figures 7-1, 7-2, and 7-3 demonstrate,[4] Bell expanded dramatically between 1894 and 1913 by establishing exchanges in small towns and by entering interconnection arrangements with independents. After 1906, independent exchanges that had attained a dominant share of a city's

---

4. The maps do not indicate which cities could actually be called by a Bell or independent subscriber, but it is safe to assume that either could call all or most of the other exchanges shown. Another limitation of the maps is that they do not extend to exchange communities with fewer than 5,000 residents. While there were many such communities, data about them are sparse and unreliable. For that reason, the maps underrepresent the significance of sublicensing, an activity concentrated on smaller exchanges. In addition, the communication of Bell and independent subscribers may have extended beyond the areas shown. Those limitations, however, are justified because the maps do show areas that would have been most important to subscribers.

Figure 7-1
Telephone Company Subscribers in Indiana, 1898

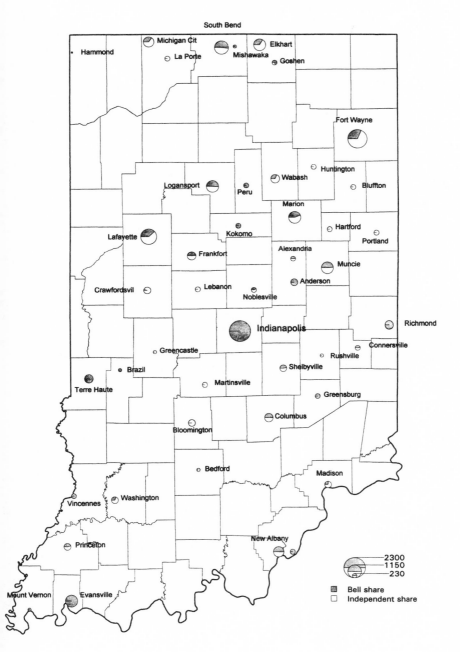

Figure 7-2
Telephone Company Subscribers in Indiana, 1907

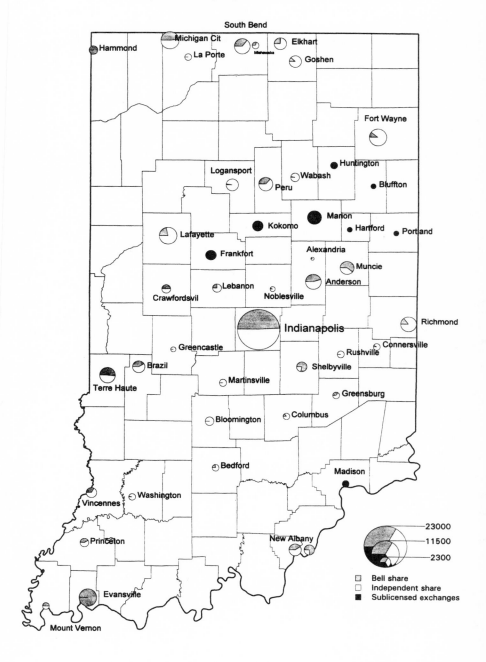

Figure 7-3
Telephone Company Subscribers in Indiana, 1912

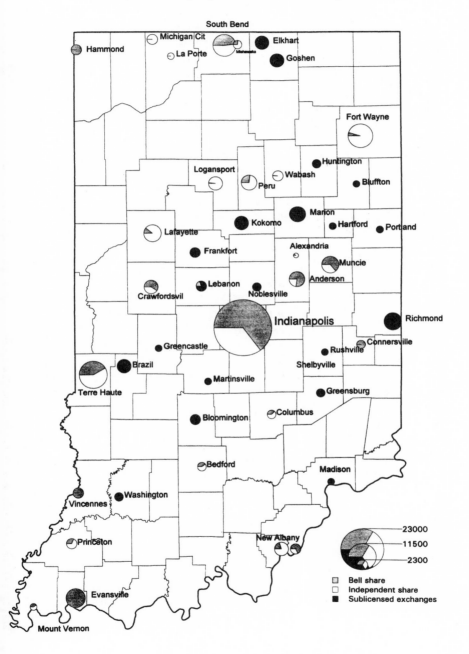

subscribers were induced to join the Bell System, thus further decreasing the scope of independent access.

What was the effect of that expansion on Bell subscribership? As the maps demonstrate, the Bell System had very little presence in Indiana's small towns before 1898. In that year, the Fort Wayne independent exchange controlled the majority of the city's telephone subscribers. Even in 1912, following a period when Bell sublicensed many local exchanges in the surrounding area, the independent still had an overwhelming lead in the number of the city's subscribers; only die-hard business subscribers used Bell. In short, Bell's expanded short- and long-distance connections were not enough to overcome the inertia associated with the independent's near-monopoly control of local exchange service in Fort Wayne.

Bell used its expansion tactics in other areas of the country as well. In New York, for example, the Utica independent exchange was cut off from connections to independents in and around Albany when Bell bought the independent in Auburn and sublicensed other exchanges that once formed part of the independent link between Utica and the cities to the east. In the Los Angeles area, independent exchanges that had beaten their Bell rivals in exchange competition were sublicensed and brought into the Bell System.

But in those places, too, the expected user convergence on Bell did not take place over a wide geographic area. Far more often, competition flourished. In Los Angeles, for example, despite the fact that Bell was connected to northern California and to other states, and that the independent had no interstate connections and little access to points north, the independent held half the city's subscribers for an extended period of time. When user convergence on a single network did take place, it was usually localized, confined either to a single city or to a geographic radius of no more than a hundred miles.

An exception in user convergence occurred in the regions surrounding New York City. Bell's monopoly control of exchange service had a stultifying effect on many independent exchanges, even those in northern New Jersey and upstate New York. That can be interpreted as evidence that the formation of large urban centers created a regionally interdependent communication pattern. We shall never know whether dual service would have been viable in the nation as a whole had there been a competing exchange in New York City. But it is clear that the absence of competition in

New York thwarted dual service competition in the surrounding areas.

Thus, while telephone communication patterns may have been increasingly interdependent at the regional and local level, the experiences in Indiana, New York, and Los Angeles demonstrate that long-distance telephone connections did not have a significant influence on the behavior of the majority of local exchange subscribers. For them, making a call to a place more than 100 miles away was a rare event. If the Bell System had the only long-distance connection to a city, an independent subscriber merely went to the Bell office or to a public toll station to make his call. While unthinkable today, in the early 1900s that was no more unusual than going to the post office to pick up a letter.

All the information presented in this chapter conflicts with the common belief that Bell's superior long-distance technology was instrumental in defeating the independents. Although patented technologies did give Bell an advantage in providing calls over distances more than 200 miles, ultra-long-distance connections were a negligible force in convergence at the local level. Only a small number of users demanded long-distance connections, and such a demand structure can sustain dual systems.

8

Universal Service: Vail's
Answer to Dual Service

By THE MIDDLE OF THE DECADE, both the telephone and competition had spread through American society widely enough to spark policy debates that transcended a particular locality. Discussions of telephone competition began to seep into national forums, much as the issue of railroad regulation had done twenty years earlier. To shape the debate to their advantage, Bell and the organized, commercial independents mounted nationwide public relations campaigns and expressed their views in magazine articles, advertisements, speeches, and books.

As noted earlier, it was then that Theodore Vail, AT&T president, began to promulgate the policy of "universal service." The term had never appeared explicitly before that time; neither had anyone inside or outside of the Bell System publicly defined such a comprehensive vision of the telephone industry and the respective roles of Bell, the independents, and the government. That being said, it is important to resist the temptation to approach Vail's universal service doctrine anachronistically. Universal service did not mean rate subsidies to make telephone service more affordable. It meant the elimination of fragmentation and the unification of telephone service under regulated local exchange monopolies. As such, it was first and foremost a response to the situation created by access competition, a response that provided the Bell System with both a critique of dual service and an appealing alternative. This chapter explores Vail's elaboration of the doctrine and the context from which it emerged.

THE PUBLIC DEBATE OVER DUAL SERVICE

Fragmentation of telephone users, particularly business users, had played a critical role in political defeats suffered by independents in large cities. Between 1905 and 1908, in cities such as New York, New Orleans, and Chicago, businessmen argued against franchising independent telephone companies: "The effect of two rival telephone systems in one city is to divide the population into two parts, without means of telephone communication with each other except at excessive cost." "Dual service compels a choice of two evils: either half service or a double price."[1] "[D]uplicate telephone systems in this city would be a calamity to all users."[2]

The independent trade press recognized that: "It is the merchants and business men of a community, newspapers, and other personal and impersonal leaders of public thought that are generally found in the forefront of the opposition to the 'nuisance of two systems' in towns where competition is first suggested."[3]

The Bell organization did everything it could to reinforce those complaints about fragmentation. One of the earliest entries in the national debate was an article in the *Atlantic* in 1905 entitled "Telephone Development in the United States," by F. W. Coburn.[4] Although there is no direct proof that Coburn was Bell-funded, the magazine was published near American Bell headquarters and took an unambiguously pro-Bell stance. The article began by recounting the extraordinary growth of telephone usage and long-distance interconnection, events Coburn claimed were made possible by expert engineers and technology. He stated that soon "a great national system will enable everybody to reach practically everybody else in the United States."

What Coburn did not admit, or did not understand, was that the goal of universal telephone coverage had been brought within reach only because of access competition. It was business rivalry, not expert engineers or technology, that had brought about the geographic scope of the telephone network. Coburn, however, denounced the very existence of independent companies as an

---

1. DELOS F. WILCOX, MUNICIPAL FRANCHISES 240 (Gervaise Press 1910).

2. *Id.* at 224–25. The Labor Federation also objected to the Bell policy of refusing to interconnect with independent exchanges outside the city.

3. AMERICAN TELEPHONY J. 238 (1906).

4. *Telephone Development in the United States*, ATLANTIC 644 (Nov. 1905).

obstacle to "that orderly development of the telephone utility upon which the engineering experts are basing their estimates."[5] The author also condemned dual service as the cause of "manifold inconveniences" and "protracted irritation on the part of citizens."

The independents did not have Bell's nationwide public relations organization, but they did not do badly. They relied on their trade press to monitor the public dialogue and used spokesmen from state and national associations to air their case in public hearings. Their national organization adopted a common symbol, and exhorted all its members to use it. In 1906, *Telephony* published a book presenting the independents' side of the controversy. *A Fight with an Octopus* was written by Paul Latzke, author of popular magazine articles romanticizing industrial success. The book extolled the independent movement as a triumph of honest, enterprising Americans over a greedy, distant corporation. *Telephony* took care to make the book "high-grade, dignified and attractive" but also inexpensive enough to reach a mass audience.[6]

Initially, the independent movement was put on the defensive by attacks on subscriber fragmentation. By 1907, however, it had developed a plausible and interesting set of counterarguments. Fragmentation notwithstanding, the rivalry for new subscribers had resulted in a net increase in telephone access for most users. Business users may have had to pay more in absolute terms for two subscriptions, but they were getting access to five to ten times as many subscribers for a price only a little higher than the rates of the monopoly period.[7] In Indianapolis, a business subscriber paid $72 per year for access to 2,286 other users in 1898. Following the entry of the New Company, a business user who subscribed to both systems paid $94 for access to 21,000 subscribers. The independents also cited indisputable evidence that competition had improved the service offered by the Bell companies.[8] Those benefits, they argued, were well worth the price of some fragmentation.

---

5. That conception of the independents' role in the industry mirrors so closely that of the Bell System itself that Coburn almost has to be viewed as a Bell propagandist.

6. 12 TELEPHONY 155 (Aug. 1906).

7. Independent Telephone Association, *Some Comments on the 1907 Annual Report of AT&T; cited in* WILCOX, *supra* note 1, at 18.

8. New York City Bureau of Franchises, *Result of Investigation of the Operation of a Dual System of Telephones in Various Cities* 8 (Nov. 21, 1906); *cited in* WILCOX, *supra* note 1.

Some independent spokesmen responded that the very redundancy about which business people complained was of great value.[9] The availability of more than one channel into an office promoted safety and reliability.

A more thought-provoking argument pointed out that business-men accepted fragmentation and duplication as a normal and unob-jectionable product of competition in other communications-related areas. An analogy was drawn between telephones and newspapers as channels for gaining access to the public. "What forces the business man to take two telephones? The same thing that forces him to advertise his goods in two newspapers in a town instead of one—to reach the people."[10] In theory, a newspaper monopoly would relieve the advertiser of the need to place duplicate ads in two or three different papers and would relieve the reading public of the inconvenience of buying and reading two or more newspa-pers. In actual practice, the competition between papers increased circulation, lowered advertising rates, and allowed businesses to reach a larger audience at a savings. Thus, while the independents recognized the advantages of universal interconnection, they did not think that it made the telephone industry exceptional.

The independents also supported competition as the best way to control rates. Eliminating fragmentation was usually associated with returning to monopoly and was the most popular argument of the independents. To many users, the inconvenience of fragmenta-tion seemed less worrisome than being subjected to rates set by a monopoly. Unification of the systems seemed like a fine idea in the abstract, but if it would result in a rate increase, many preferred to stick with dual service.

The material above makes it abundantly clear that as competi-tion reached its zenith in 1907, fragmentation of the service had

---

9. "When a subscriber says that two telephones are a nuisance, he means that the two instruments sitting on his desk are an inconvenience, they are irritating to his vision. He objects to two bells ringing simultaneously, maybe once a month or so. But two telephones on a man's desk, reaching two different companies in active competition with each other . . . are vastly beneficial to that man. His ability to reach everyone in two different manners through different sources is of immeasurable value, as is the ability to have everyone in the community reach him over two different ways." Burt Hubbell, quoted in *Chicago Hearings in Government-Bell Trust Suit*, 65 TELEPHONY 21 (Nov. 29, 1913).

10. 11 TELEPHONY (June 1906).

become the primary topic of telephone policy debate along with rates. That context is indispensable in any valid interpretation of Vail's concept of universal service.

VAIL'S DOCTRINE OF UNIVERSAL SERVICE

Vail fired the biggest salvo in the debate in AT&T's *1907 Annual Report* when he articulated for the first time the triad "One System, One Policy, Universal Service" and the philosophy underlying it. In the next seven annual reports, Vail hammered away at the theme that only an integrated monopoly offering connections among all subscribers in all locations could realize the telephone's potential.

Vail's doctrine of universal service is well documented.[11] The following statement from the *1910 Annual Report* contains the essence of Vail's conception of universal service:

> [The Bell System] believes that the telephone system should be universal, interdependent and intercommunicating, affording opportunity for any subscriber to any exchange to communicate with any other subscriber of any other exchange within the limits of speaking distance.[12]

In other words, all users of the telephone should be interconnected. As the preceding passage makes clear, Vail's rhetorical style relied on alliterative triads, the elements of which were overlapping but not entirely redundant. "One system, one policy" meant a single physical network, centrally managed and coordinated to achieve compatibility. "Universal service" meant the interconnection of all telephone exchanges and users. It did have some connotations of geographic ubiquity, but Vail's sublicensing policy made it clear that geographic coverage of remote areas was to be achieved by interconnecting with noncompeting independents, not by extending the Bell System everywhere.

Implementing his vision required eliminating access competition. Indeed, it is impossible to understand the thrust of Vail's arguments unless it is seen as a criticism of, and an alternative to, access competition. The power of Vail's ideas came from their comprehensiveness and consistency. Universal service was not a ploy cooked up for Bell's momentary advantage but a coherent set

---

11. Vail worked out the ideas promoted in the annual reports in a lengthy paper entitled *Policy of the Bell System*, Box 1080, AT&T-Bell Laboratory Archives, Warren, N.J. [hereinafter AT&T-BLA].

12. AT&T, 1910 ANNUAL REPORT 43 (1911).

of principles regarding the telephone's role in society and the proper way to develop the business. Vail's rationale for universal service had four basic components, explained below.

The "Network Externality"

The first element was that the value of telephone service grew as the number of subscribers grew:

> "A telephone without a connection at the other end of the line is . . . one of the most useless things in the world. Its value depends on the connection with other telephones—and increases with the number of connections."[13]

Vail's acute recognition of the network externality provided the basis for his criticism of access competition. Competing exchanges fragmented the telephone calling universe, thus diminishing the value of the service. Those who subscribed to one system, he said, received "a partial value [which] cannot be satisfactory," while "important users" were forced to take out duplicate subscriptions.[14] To that unwelcome predicament Vail contrasted his alternative:

> The fundamental idea of the Bell System is that the telephone service should be universal, intercommunicating, and interdependent; that there are *certain people* with whom *one communicates frequently and regularly*; there are a *certain few* with whom one *communicates occasionally*, while there are *times* when it is *most necessary to get* communication with *some other one*, who, until the *particular necessity* arose, *might have been unknown and unthought of. It is this necessity, impossible to predetermine, which makes the universal service the only perfect service*.[15] (italics in original)

Vail's clear reference here to "the universal service" as a service that provides access to "unknown and unthought of" parties makes it undeniable that universality referred to the unification of service. Indeed, his emphasis on the value of unfragmented telephone access reveals a profound understanding of the growing interdependence and impersonality of industrial society. Dual ser-

---

13. AT&T, 1908 ANNUAL REPORT 21 (1909).
14. AT&T, 1907 ANNUAL REPORT 17 (1908).
15. AT&T, 1910 ANNUAL REPORT 39 (1911).

vice was less burdensome when parties could be reasonably certain of who and where their communication partners would be. But a modern urban society, with an increasingly specialized economy adapted to the capabilities of communication and transportation between remote points, required forms of coordination and cooperation that could not be predicted in advance. That was the strongest of his arguments for integration of the telephone system.

Clearly, the network externality implies that a continuous broadening of telephone penetration would be beneficial to users. But just as clearly, Vail's reference to "universal service" in that context was not a commitment to extend service everywhere and to everyone regardless of cost. It simply meant that those who did have telephone service should be accessible to each other and not fragmented into competing exchanges. If the growth of penetration *per se* had been the primary issue, Vail's argument against competition would have lacked force, for no one disputed the rapid increases in telephone diffusion that had occurred because of competition. Moreover, everyone knew at the time that Bell's prices were higher than its opponents'.

Centralization of Control

The second pillar of Vail's argument was the claim that universal intercommunication required centralized control and coordination. Service should be provided by, or under the control of, a single firm:

> The Bell System was founded on the broad lines of "One System," "One Policy," "Universal Service," on the idea that no aggregation of isolated independent systems not under common control, however well built or equipped, could give the public the service that the interdependent, intercommunicating, universal system could give.[16]

Here again connectivity, not social ubiquity, is the basic issue being addressed. Unless a national telephone network developed under the guidance of a single firm, Vail contended, telephone users' ability to make connections with exchanges in other locations would be thwarted by uncoordination and technical incompat-

---

16. AT&T, 1909 ANNUAL REPORT 18 (1910).

ibility. Although compatibility is a precondition of social ubiquity, the two cannot be equated.

A corollary of that element of the universal service doctrine was the proposition that monopoly, and not interchange of traffic among the competing systems, was the best way to achieve universal intercommunication. Vail condemned interconnection of competitors as unfair, because it allowed smaller competitors to share in the benefits of the Bell System's larger access universe. Such competition would parasitize the larger system and amounted to legalized confiscation of its property.[17] Interconnection also would create a messy, heterogeneous telephone system that would lack the technical integrity and coordination of a single system.[18]

The Imperfection of Competition in Telephony

Third, Vail contended that competition between telephone networks is always imperfect competition. His argument was based on a clear grasp of the inherent nonhomogeneity of separate networks. Rival telephone services are never perfect substitutes for each other because both will offer access to different subscribers:

> Competition means that the same thing, or a satisfactory substitute, is offered. In this sense there can be no competing exchanges unless each exchange has the same list of subscribers, which is in itself inconceivable.[19]

Consequently, competition requires either a duplicate subscription, which Vail considered wasteful, or restricted access.[20] Clearly, in Vail's mind, competition was synonymous with access competition, and his doctrine of universal service was the alternative.

Regulation as the Alternative to Competition

Having made the case for monopoly, Vail indicated that he was willing to accept the consequences of removing his industry from competitive pressures: government regulation of rates and ser-

---

17. AT&T, 1910 ANNUAL REPORT 44–46 (1911).

18. *Id.* at 46–47.

19. *Id.* at 37.

20. AT&T, 1907 ANNUAL REPORT 17–18 (1908); AT&T, 1909 ANNUAL REPORT 22–23 (1910); AT&T, 1910 ANNUAL REPORT 37 (1911).

vice.[21] In the annual reports and in a 1913 article in *Atlantic Monthly*, Vail argued for a private monopoly monitored by an expert commission, a view that dovetailed with developments in other utility services.[22] That was an essential ingredient of the universal service doctrine because dual service retained a strong core of support among users who feared monopoly pricing. But the role of government involvement, in that conception, did not go beyond substituting for the rate and service controls of a competitive marketplace. There is not a hint of the notion that Bell and the government were joining in a partnership to extend service to everyone.

Contemporary readers can easily misinterpret Vail's references to "universality" as a commitment to social ubiquity. In fact, in 1907, after fifteen years of independent competition, Vail did make oratorical jabs in that direction, although they were notable for their vagueness. In the *1910 Annual Report* he wrote: "[the Bell System] believes that some sort of a connection with the telephone system should be within the reach of all."[23] He left unspecified just what "sort of a connection" and the meaning of "within the reach of." In all his pronouncements about universal service, that is the closest Vail ever comes to a commitment to geographic ubiquity. There is a perfectly logical reason for the vague and passing way in which Vail handled that issue. Just two years earlier, he had drastically liberalized the company's sublicensing policies to encourage interconnection with independent exchanges in remote, "unremunerative" areas so that the Bell System would not have to build and maintain new facilities. The Bell System's willingness to recognize independent systems as a permanent part of the country's telephone network was a major retreat from its earlier belief that Bell and Bell alone should control the entire industry. The breakneck expansion of the Bell System after 1900 to develop more exchanges and short-haul toll lines, another policy change forced upon it by access competition, also represented a sharp departure from its earlier vision of an exclusively urban, business-oriented national network. If Vail was now forced to admit that "some sort of a connection to the telephone system should be within the reach of all," the grudging character of that statement should not surprise us.

---

21. AT&T, 1907 Annual Report 18–19 (1908).
22. 111 Atlantic 311 (Mar. 1913).
23. AT&T, 1910 Annual Report 43 (1911).

The uniqueness of Vail's vision lay not in AT&T's alleged commitment to extend service everywhere and to everyone. At that juncture, no one disputed either the desirability or the inevitability of the telephone's rapid diffusion. Indeed, the independents far outstripped the Bell System in their commitment to extend telephone service to previously unserved areas. The growth of penetration and the affordability of service were not really the points at issue at that time. What set the Bell policy apart was its commitment to interconnect all telephone users into one big, centrally managed, nationally integrated system. The real debate was between competition and monopoly, between unification and fragmentation. Vail's doctrine of universal service represented an extremely powerful case for the latter.

Vail's vision infused the Bell System with a new coherence. "Universal service" became a competitive strategy, a political slogan, and a catchy advertising term rolled into one. In a series of full-page ads that began to appear in 1911, Bell presented itself as a nationwide system linking every community in the United States, even though it was years away from achieving that goal. "To one who has a Bell telephone at his lips," one ad declaimed, "the whole nation is within speaking distance." Another ad contrasted "Telephone Service: Universal or Limited" (see figure 8-1) and compared independent telephone systems to medieval walled cities because of their alleged lack of connections to the outside world.

Placed in historical context, Bell's commitment to universal service emerges as a coherent response to the pressures of access competition. Bell's ability to offer connections to more locations than its rival independent exchanges was its greatest competitive advantage. Instead of fighting to eliminate all independents, it would absorb them into the "universal" system by making them noncompetitive feeders through sublicensing. Above all else, universal service was the spearhead of Vail's drive to achieve political support for the elimination of competition.[24] It provided an appealing rationale for the consolidation of competing exchanges that could be used to counter growing antitrust challenges to Bell's

---

24. Bell's positioning of itself as the universal system successfully concealed its own refusal to eliminate fragmentation by interconnecting with its independent competitors. Bell strategically withheld the benefits of a unified service from the public and the independents until it had succeeded in winning support for regulated monopoly as the industry structure.

Figure 8-1
Bell System Advertisement, 1911

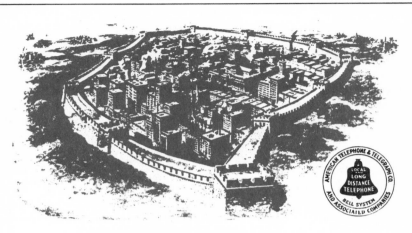

A MEDIAEVAL CONDITION

Telephone Service— Universal or Limited?

TELEPHONE users make more local than long distance calls yet to each user comes the vital demand for distant communication.

No individual can escape this necessity. It comes to all and cannot be foreseen.

No community can afford to surround itself with a sound-proof Chinese Wall and risk telephone isolation.

No American State would be willing to make its boundary line an impenetrable barrier, to prevent telephone communication with the world outside.

Each telephone subscriber, each community, each State demands to be the center of a talking circle which shall be large enough to include all possible needs of inter-communication.

In response to this universal demand the Bell Telephone System is clearing the way for universal service.

Every Bell Telephone is the Center of the System

AMERICAN TELEPHONE AND TELEGRAPH COMPANY
AND ASSOCIATED COMPANIES

32

dominance. Far from being a benevolent gift of Bell management or government regulators, the universal service concept was a deadly competitive weapon and a very effective business strategy.

The early debate over universal service did conceive of telephone penetration in broader terms. Trade journals and the popular press at the turn of the century marveled at its rapid penetration of farm areas and residences and interpreted that as a sign of the inexorable progress of the industrial age.[25] Where the 1880s and early 1890s saw the telephone as a specialized commercial device, few observers in the 1900s or 1910s would have disagreed with the assertion that eventually there would be or should be a telephone in every home. But that progress was seen as something that would occur naturally as industrialism increased wealth, lowered prices, and improved technology. Universalism in that sense posed no special policy issue and required no government action. The real policy issue was whether the telephone would develop under the guise of separate, competing systems or as a unified monopoly.

In 1907, public opinion was almost evenly divided, with dual service probably commanding more support because of its intrinsic constraints on rates. But the events of the next ten years would bring about a profound shift in public attitudes.

---

25. Commenting on the growth of residential subscribers in New York City, ELECTRICAL REVIEW wrote, "it will not be long before no moderately well appointed residence will be considered completely equipped if it is not connected to the telephone system," 31 ELECTRICAL REV. 180 (Oct. 13, 1897). For similar expressions of confidence in the inevitability of the spread of the telephone, see *The Farmer and the Telephone*, 31 ELECTRICAL REV. 126 (Sept. 15, 1897), and *Making [Social] Calls by Telephone*, 30 ELECTRICAL REV. 146 (Mar. 31, 1897).

9

The Power of Interconnection, 1908–1913

FROM 1908 TO 1913, access competition entered a critical phase—the beginning of a breakdown of system exclusivity. Access competition still placed enormous pressures on both sides to increase the scope of their networks, but the era of raw expansion was essentially over. The greatest potential for network growth came from more intensive development of toll connectivity among established exchanges and from the growth of telephone penetration within exchanges. In that context, dual service came to be perceived as a barrier to communication. To remain competitive, telephone companies had to respond to users' demands for a complementary relationship between the networks. If the scope of the telephone system was to continue to widen, the barriers between the two systems had to be destroyed. Unfortunately for the independents, their movement was far more prone to disintegration than Bell's, whose unified organization and policy made it impervious to fragmentation. The real basis of the Bell System triumph in that period came from maintaining its integrity as a system while relaxing its restrictions on allowing independents to interconnect with it. As a result, large numbers of independent exchanges connected with the Bell System and deserted the exclusive access universe of the organized independent movement.

The relationship between interconnection and network competition was the central preoccupation of that period and had two distinct aspects. One was the strategic use of interconnection in the Bell-independent rivalry. The other was the attempt of courts, legislatures, and regulatory commissions to find an appropriate public policy regarding interconnection. Should competing networks be compelled to connect? Did interconnection preserve or destroy competition? Was the strategic use of interconnection rights an anticompetitive practice or a legitimate exercise of the right of contract? Was it necessary to eliminate competition to bring about universal interconnection? Those questions moved to center stage but succeeded only in producing a welter of contradictory decisions.

THE DEVELOPMENT OF REGIONAL INDEPENDENT OPERATING COMPANIES

As discussed earlier, between 1898 and 1906, independent development was largely that of building exchanges and short-haul toll lines. After 1906, the independents began to exploit their control of exchange access to develop competitive intercity long-distance lines. While independent exchange development peaked around 1904, the independents' long-distance activity flourished from 1906 to 1911. Large regional independent operating companies, formed through mergers of several smaller companies, started long-distance subsidiaries and went about constructing access universes comparable in scope to the network of the Bell licensee companies. The independents, too, began to speak of "universality." In 1908 A. C. Lindemuth, the proprietor of the Richmond, Virginia, independent exchange, proclaimed, "For ten years we have been building exchanges. Let us now build systems." Dual service could only survive, he knew, if the independents matched the growing scope of the Bell System:

> I have adopted . . . the motto . . . "the Integrity of the Independent System and its Universal Extension." This motto implies the continuing of the present independent telephone system as a separate and distinct system, extended into all undeveloped territory whether in city or country, reorganized and strengthened into a complete and effective whole.[1]

Numerous regional independents grew up in that period, belying the stereotype of small, exclusively local operations. A typical independent operating company owned exchanges in ten to thirty key cities and signed long-term, exclusive connecting contracts

---

1. 15 TELEPHONY 267–68 (April 1908).

with independent exchanges it did not own. On the borders of their territories, independents entered into agreements with neighboring independent regionals for the interchange of traffic.

In Pennsylvania, Maryland, and West Virginia, for example, several large independent regionals competed with the Bell System. The American Union Telephone Co., centered in Harrisburg, Pennsylvania, was formed in 1906 through the merger of twelve independent companies, including the competing exchanges in Harrisburg, Altoona, Lancaster, Williamsport, and Chester. The Keystone Telephone Co. owned exchanges in and around Philadelphia, including Trenton and Camden. The Consolidated Telephone Company covered the territory to the north and west of Philadelphia, operating exchanges and toll lines connecting Allentown, Scranton, Wilkes-Barre, and Reading. The Pittsburgh and Allegheny system connected independent exchanges in the western parts of the state. The National Telephone Co. owned exchanges in Wheeling, Steubenville, and other towns in West Virginia. Each of those systems was connected to each other through an organization known as the "Eastern Traffic Association," a clearing house that accounted for and divided joint toll revenues and coordinated maintenance and operations.[2]

Comparably sized independent regionals existed in New York state, Kentucky, southern California, Washington and Oregon, and Minnesota. By 1910, independent systems extended in an unbroken line from New York to Kansas along the east-west axis. On the north-south axis, they ran from Tennessee to Minnesota. With the exception of isolated systems in Dallas, Atlanta, Mobile, and Shreveport, they were all physically connected. While those independent regionals did not have the technology or the organization to offer talking circuits over 300 miles in length, they were viable competitors for toll traffic as well as for exchange subscribers.

Independent toll service was usually lower priced than Bell's and often offered superior exchange access.[3] The incursions into toll business "not only assist the revenue of the opposition but greatly increase its prestige with the more important telephone customers," noted AT&T's Pickernell.[4] In upstate New York, the

2. *Independent Telephone Companies—Financial History*, Box 65, AT&T-Bell Laboratories Archives, Warren, N.J. [hereinafter AT&T-BLA].

3. Letter from Pickernell, AT&T, to E. J. Hall, AT&T (May 12, 1909), Box 1376, AT&T-BLA.

4. *Id.*

effect of independent toll line competition was so severe that Bell's toll earnings fell to 1 to 2 percent. AT&T suffered a "pronounced loss of business" from Buffalo to Cleveland, Pittsburgh, and Jamestown.[5]

BELL'S WAR ON INDEPENDENT CONNECTIVITY

Bell had a clearly defined goal: the elimination of dual service and the creation of a nationally interconnected monopoly administered by Bell but supervised by regulators. Monopoly would bring about universal service and relief from the low rates locked into place by the fierce competitive struggle. Universal interconnection was not the sole object; Bell also wanted to make sure that it controlled the system. To do so, it had to prevent physical connection with overlapping systems and maintain absolute control of interexchange connections. There was a place for independent companies in that scheme, but only as local feeders to the Bell System. In major cities, dual service was to be eliminated by buying out the independent and physically consolidating the exchanges. If an independent was dominant, Bell would sell out and enter into a connecting contract with the surviving exchange. Consolidation would demonstrate the benefits of a unified service while permitting the companies to raise rates to their "proper level." In smaller cities and the country, competition would be eliminated by an aggressive new sublicensing effort. Any overlapping, competing telephone systems that remained were to be isolated and squeezed out as all others were absorbed into the system.

Liberalization of Sublicensing

Vail's competitive tactics were directly aimed at the growth of connection among the independents. One of his most important countermoves was to revitalize Bell's sublicensing efforts. The independent companies who directly overlapped and competed with Bell accounted for only 40 to 45 percent of all independent telephones. The rest of the independent subscribers were in areas unoccupied by Bell. Those noncompeting independents, Vail understood, held the balance of power in the competition for universal coverage. If they could be tied into the Bell System, Bell could

---

5. *Id.*

broaden its coverage without investing in facilities or engaging in local competition. In many areas, whoever won connecting rights with the majority of the noncompeting independents would have access to the largest number of subscribers.

Bell's first sublicense contracts had limited exchanges to Bell connections and required the use of Bell telephones. That tactic prevented the independents from running away with the business in the central states, but by the beginning of 1907 it had induced just 14 percent of the independent telephones to be connected to the Bell System. To gain access to more independent systems, Vail dramatically liberalized the Bell interconnection conditions. Starting in October 1907, independent exchanges connecting with Bell no longer had to use Western Electric instruments but could use other telephones as long as they were of "first class" construction and would not impair the quality of service offered over joint lines.[6] Vail also allowed Western Electric to begin selling telephones to independent companies for the first time.[7] Letters urged the licensee companies to "pursue vigorously the policy of sublicensing" in the part of their territory that was "more or less unremunerative" or "not yet occupied."[8] Managers were warned to make sure that Bell controlled all the toll lines connecting the sublicensed exchanges.[9]

Exclusive Connecting Contracts

Bell went on to liberalize its interconnection policy in a more radical fashion. In an attempt to pry more independent subscribers away from the exclusive control of competing independents, Bell began to interconnect with independent exchanges, even if they already maintained connections with competing long-distance lines. In a few cases, Bell was even willing to connect its toll lines to an independent exchange that was directly competing with one of its own, assuming the independent had a commanding lead in the number of subscribers.[10] That tactic was used in Ohio and Indiana, where hundreds of independent exchanges had signed exclusive

---

6. Vail Circular Letter (Oct. 9, 1907), Box 1364, AT&T-BLA.

7. FCC TELEPHONE INVESTIGATION 138 (Government Printing Office 1939).

8. Vail Circular Letter (Feb. 10, 1908), Box 1364, AT&T-BLA.

9. Vail Circular Letter (Sept. 10, 1908), Box 1376, AT&T-BLA.

10. Letter from Richardson to Vail (July 3, 1908); letter from Vail to Richardson (July 7, 1908), Box 1357, AT&T-BLA.

connecting contracts with the United States Telephone Company, and amounted to soliciting the exchanges to break their contracts with UST. Nevertheless, it was an attractive option for the local exchanges, as it gave their customers access to the subscribers and cities controlled by both systems.[11] In 1908, sixteen local independent companies in Ohio and Indiana entered into connecting agreements with Bell in violation of their exclusive contract with UST.[12] UST's attempts to block those actions in the courts were unsuccessful (see section below entitled *Exclusive Connecting Contracts and the Courts*).

Armed with its new interconnection policies, Bell licensees made great efforts to attract farmer and mutual company lines. Bell promised rural telephone users service at one-fifth the rate of the independent companies.[13] The importance of sublicensing as a form of enlarging the Bell System's scope was particularly evident in the areas where strong independent toll systems were developing. In the Missouri and Kansas Co.'s territory in mid-1909, sublicensed toll lines outnumbered the Bell licensee's in mileage, and sublicensed telephones outnumbered Bell-owned telephones by two to one. The Bell licensee in the territory around St. Louis was so dependent on sublicensing for toll connections that an AT&T agent speculated that if the sublicensees should happen to break with Bell, "the Bell toll business and the Bell development would disappear, and the opposition would absolutely control most of the territory outside of St. Louis."[14]

Vail's policy of absorbing competition had a devastating impact upon the independents' attempt to build a rival system. The number of Bell-connecting independent telephones jumped from 297,218 at the beginning of 1907 to 1.2 million in only two years. By 1914,

---

11. "Our plan of having all toll lines entering our city on one switchboard has been so pleasant and satisfactory to our patrons that I think that when the court order requiring us to remove them becomes known to our patrons, I would not be surprised if some demonstrations on their part would take place expressing their disapproval of being compelled to go back to the old and unsatisfactory way of having more than one toll station in the city." Letter from William Shumaker, president, Butler (Indiana) Telephone Co., to L. N. Whitney, Central Union Co. (Dec. 1, 1908), Box 1357, AT&T-BLA.

12. Letter from J. B. Smith to J. D. Ellsworth (Dec. 5, 1908), Box 1357, AT&T-BLA.

13. 17 TELEPHONY (Mar. 27 1909).

14. Pickernell, *supra* note 3.

two-thirds of all independent telephones were connected to the Bell System. The effect of the policy is clear when those numbers are expressed as a proportion of the independent telephones not in direct competition with Bell, that is, all independents not in dual service territories. At the beginning of 1907, only 25 percent of the noncompeting independents were connected to Bell. A year later, 46 percent of them were so connected. By October 1909, 79 percent were connected to Bell.[15] By the time of the Kingsbury Commitment, 89 percent of all noncompeting independents were embraced by the Bell System's access universe. (See tables 9-1 and 9-2.)

Table 9-1
Independent Telephones Connecting with Bell, 1907–1914

	1907	1908	1909	1910	1911	1912	1913	1914
No. of independent phones (millions)	2.16	3.11	3.31	3.47	3.70	4.00	3.93	4.29
No. of Bell connecting phones (millions)	0.30	0.83	1.19	1.62	1.95	2.28	2.50	2.88
Percent connecting	14	27	36	47	53	57	64	67
Growth rate (%)	NA	178	44	36	20	17	9	15

Sources: Chappelka (1956); FCC (1938); *Telephone Censuses* (1907, 1912).

Table 9-2
Noncompeting Independent Telephones Connecting with Bell, 1907–1914

	1907	1908	1909	1910	1911	1912	1913	1914
No. of noncompeting independent phones (millions)	1.19	1.80	1.86	2.00	2.35	2.68	2.87	3.23
No. of Bell connecting phones (millions)	0.30	0.83	1.19	1.62	1.95	2.28	2.50	2.88
Percent connecting	25	46	64	81	83	85	87	89

Sources: Chappelka (1956); FCC (1939); *Telephone Censuses* (1907, 1912).

15. A. R. Chappelka, History of Independent Telephone Operating Companies in the United States, Memorandum on Affirmative Topic No. 10, Civil Action No. 17-49 (1956).

Price War in Toll Service

Bell's cooptation of noncompeting independents was supplemented by a price war against selected independent toll lines. Independent long-distance companies charged lower rates because they had lower fixed costs. Unlike Bell, they did not attempt to provide complete toll coverage of an area but concentrated their resources on high-volume routes. Bell toll lines served both "fat" and "lean" districts and installed enough capacity to handle most of the traffic. By constructing a simple economic model of those conditions, Pickernell discovered that cutting Bell rates in half to secure a larger share of the traffic would hurt an independent far more than it would hurt Bell.[16] To test his theory, Pickernell reduced rates in selected Ohio cities. The cuts increased Central Union's toll traffic by 53 percent, while reducing its revenue by only 12 percent, simultaneously devastating the toll business of United States Telephone Company.[17]

To stop the loss of its long-distance business, UST wanted both companies to restore rates to their original levels. It approached Central Union Company through the state independent association, which had come into much closer contact with the Bell licensee due to the growing number of sublicensed independent companies. A committee of the Ohio Independent Telephone Association met with Central Union and argued that the lower rates injured local sublicensees by reducing their commissions from toll traffic, a cover for the real concern about UST's loss of long-distance business. The committee asked that the state independent association be given the right to approve or disapprove of any change in toll rates made in Ohio. Bell refused that price-fixing offer.[18] As a result, UST sold its property to J. P. Morgan & Co.

Acquisitions of Competing Exchanges

The most direct blows against dual service came from Bell buyouts of competing exchanges. The policy of eliminating dual service in the larger cities through acquisition or sale progressed rapidly during that period. At the beginning of 1907, 59 percent of cities

---

16. Letter from Pickernell to Vail, Box 1376, AT&T-BLA.
17. Letter from Thayer to Vail (Nov. 18, 1909), Box 1376, AT&T-BLA.
18. Letter from Richardson to Vail (June 21, 1909), Box 65, AT&T-BLA.

with populations over 5,000 had dual exchanges. By 1913, that percentage had been reduced to 37 percent. In smaller cities, mergers of competing exchanges were often followed by the franchising and construction of a new competing exchange. In the larger cities, however, the losses were irreversible.

Independent companies were particularly susceptible to divide-and-conquer acquisitions. Their decentralization made it difficult to weather extended bouts of competition or to adhere to a common policy. Selling out to Bell offered an appealing way to escape from a variety of financial pressures: the diseconomies of growth, price wars, rate restrictions in municipal franchises, and a constant need to raise more capital. Those problems had always existed, however. What precipitated the surge of independent sellouts between 1910 and 1913 was the failure of independent attempts to build regionally interconnected systems capable of matching the scope of the Bell System. That failure was primarily the result of Bell's liberalized interconnection policy. The financial panic of 1907, which made investors less willing to put scarce capital into dual systems, also contributed. The stampede of noncompeting independents into connecting arrangements with Bell between 1907 and 1910 prompted many of the more profit-oriented independent system owners to get out while the getting was good. In 1912, the consolidation trend began to chip away at the urban strongholds of the independents. Competition was eliminated in ten of the sixty-eight cities over 50,000 in population that had dual service. In that year alone, Bell purchased 136,000 telephone stations and sold 42,650.[19]

Before 1910, Bell takeovers led to the severance of independent toll line connections.[20] After that, however, the mediation of utility commissions made mergers more orderly and protected the interests of other independent exchanges in a state whose users were dependent upon access to cities. To ensure that public reactions against severed connections did not threaten the policy of achieving a universal service monopoly through buyouts, Bell

---

19. FCC TELEPHONE INVESTIGATION 140, table 35 (Government Printing Office 1939).

20. In 1910 and 1911, independents in Adrian, Michigan, Memphis, Tennessee, and Clarksville, Tennessee, all experienced severed connections after Bell acquired independently owned toll lines in the vicinity. The practice was not so common as has been reported, however, as the independents nearly always countered with lawsuits and had political influence at the state and local levels.

announced the "Vail Commitment" in January 1912: a promise that Bell would leave all long-distance connections intact when an exchange changed hands. Acquisition would neither enlarge nor restrict the toll access of the exchanges involved.[21]

Vail had made his consolidation overtures explicit in 1910, when he offered to cooperate with the independents in thoroughly eliminating competition in the telephone business. He told the independents that the destructive warfare between them was costing the Bell Companies millions. He wanted to effect a merger that would end those losses and leave AT&T in control of most of the large cities and long-distance lines, while ceding the smaller places to the independents, where, he admitted, they operated more efficiently than Bell. He said that the merged companies could be capitalized liberally to cover any sustained losses. Vail also told them that both parties would negotiate later the specific places each would control.[22]

Between 1910 and 1913, a committee of independent leaders[23] initiated negotiations with AT&T concerning the purchase of almost every independent property. Although some of those deals were not consummated until a decade later, they were the beginnings of a Bell-independent cooperation that helped create a telephone monopoly.

INTERCONNECTION IN LAW AND PUBLIC POLICY

The law and public policy regarding interconnection, competition, and monopoly took two divergent and ultimately incompatible paths after 1907. The disturbingly rapid acquisition of competing

---

21. For a glimpse of how the Vail Commitment affected consolidations, *see* letter from J. M. B. Hoxsey, Southern Bell, to N. C. Kingsbury, AT&T (Dec. 17, 1912), Box 39, AT&T-BLA. The independent in Louisville claimed that connections to hundreds of cities in Ohio, Indiana, and Illinois had been possible before consolidation. Bell suspected that the connections, while physically possible, had never actually been made and that the independent was exploiting the terms of the Vail Commitment to acquire long-distance service over Bell lines.

22. TELEPHONY 19–23 (Nov. 29, 1913).

23. The committee consisted of Frank Woods of Lincoln, Nebraska, E. H. Moulton of Minneapolis, Theodore Gary of Missouri, H. D. Critchfield of Chicago, Arnold Kalman of St. Louis, and B. G. Hubbell of Buffalo, all owners of large independent systems.

exchanges by Bell set off antitrust alarms all over the country. Antimonopoly sentiment was at fever pitch; public fears that big businesses were strangling the market economy had led to successful prosecutions of the Northern Securities Company and to the dissolution of both Standard Oil and the American Tobacco Company in 1911. Congress passed a new, broader antitrust law, the Clayton Act, in 1914. Other institutional responses at the state and local level, however, pointed in an altogether different direction. Municipalities weary of dual service began to favor consolidation or connection of competing exchanges. State governments began to create utility commissions with the authority to regulate telephone companies, or empowered existing railroad commissions to do so. The majority of states also passed laws authorizing those commissions to compel the telephone companies to connect their lines. The commissions upheld regulation as a substitute for competition and often encouraged monopoly. The desire to preserve market competition mingled uncomfortably with an impulse to unify the system. As the courts, commissions, cities, and telephone companies groped for a solution to the "telephone situation," it did not become evident that those two approaches worked at cross purposes until the Kingsbury Commitment, made at the end of 1913, transfigured the contradiction into a national policy.

Antitrust Law

The organized independents knew that competition could not be sustained without dual exchanges in as many cities as possible. The weapons they used to fight Bell acquisitions were state and national antitrust laws.[24] When the national independent association heard of Bell's intentions to merge independent and Bell properties in 1908, it formed a litigation committee and raised thousands of dollars from independent companies and associations.[25] The committee urged the attorneys general of Michigan, Nebraska, Kansas, and Missouri to block Bell purchases of independent companies. A 1908 merger in Marion, Ohio, was also countered by a lawsuit under the Valentine Act, a state antitrust law. In Kentucky, merger negotiations between Bell and the Louisville-based independent

---

24. A. C. Lindemuth, 15 TELEPHONY (June 1908).

25. Minutes of the Executive Committee of the International Independent Telephone Association (May 7, 1908), AT&T-BLA.

were called off because the state constitution prohibited the consolidation of competing common carriers. Prodded by complaints from Postal Telegraph Company, Mississippi sued AT&T for integrating its operations with Western Union; the state charged that AT&T was trying to monopolize the telegraph business.[26]

Federal antitrust proceedings were initiated in 1912, when the U.S. attorney for the Portland, Oregon, district filed a suit under the Sherman Act, charging Bell with an attempt to monopolize the telephone business in the Pacific Northwest. At the local level, consolidations were opposed by those who feared they would lead to a rate increase or a deterioration of service. Advocates of that position had no trouble finding evidence that Bell rates in noncompetitive cities were higher than those in cities with competition. As consolidation was rumored in Kansas City, the *Kansas City Post* waged an effective newspaper war against the merger, noting that while Bell had promised residential rates of $36 a year, the residential rate in monopolized cities of comparable size was $42 or $48 a year. "If the Bell Company charges from $42 to $48 a year for residence phones in other cities, won't it find excuses to do the same thing here if competition is removed?" the paper asked.[27] In many quarters there was still a willingness to rely on the traditional method of competition to control rates and service.

Exclusive Connecting Contracts and the Courts

The dispute over exclusive connecting contracts illustrates the complexity of the relationship among interconnection, competition, and monopoly. From the viewpoint of a local exchange, an exclusive connecting contract prevented competition by tying all of its long-distance traffic to one carrier. From a subscriber's viewpoint, exclusivity destroyed his ability to choose long-distance carriers and made him accept a system with less than universal coverage. To the embattled independent regional systems, however, exclusive access to independent exchanges was their chief competitive advantage against Bell. Opening up their connecting exchanges to Bell subscribers destroyed their ability to compete with a much larger system. Protecting consumers' and local exchanges' right to choose

---

26. 64 TELEPHONY 32 (1913).
27. KANSAS CITY POST, Oct. 21 and 22, 1911, Box 17, AT&T-BLA.

toll carriers would accomplish little if enforcing that right left only one carrier in the field.

The United States Telephone Company lawsuit against Bell for connecting with its contracting exchanges was the testing ground for those issues. It went first to the Ohio Court of Common Pleas, which treated the case as a simple breach of contract. The court upheld the independent long-distance company and ordered the exchanges to sever their connections with Bell toll lines. Bell continued the practice, however, and UST was forced to litigate the case on broader grounds. It sued Bell under the state antitrust laws, charging that Bell's new policy was an attempt to drive UST out of business and monopolize the trade.[28] The 1909 decision of the Ohio Supreme Court, however, found not Bell, but the United States Company, guilty of monopolistic practices. The court invalidated UST's ninety-nine-year exclusive contracts because they gave the independent long-distance company a "monopoly" of the local exchange's long-distance business.

In a lively and incisive review of the application of common carrier principles to the telephone, the court dismissed the precedent of the railroad express cases, which had previously shielded telephone companies from interconnecting with other companies. The practical demands of railroad operation were completely different from those attending the making of telephone connections, the court said. While it was physically impossible, as well as unsafe, to allow railroad companies to run trains over another company's tracks without the second company's cooperation and consent, the interconnection of telephone companies did not pose the same problems.

> Conceivably, 20 long-distance companies might be connected with the local exchange with the same simplicity and with the same absence of confusion which we find in relation to the local subscriber's lines, and there is no more physical difficulty . . . in connecting a subscriber with one of the 20 long-distance lines than in connecting a subscriber with another local subscriber served by the same exchange.[29]

As common carriers, telephone companies were required to provide service to all who applied without discrimination, and a

---

28. United States Telephone Co. *v.* Central Union Co., 171 F.130 (1909).
29. *Id.* at 143.

long-distance company should be treated no differently from any other subscriber. Since the operations required to link subscribers to the lines of a long-distance company were the same as those required to set up a connection with any other subscriber, the company's common carrier obligation could and should be extended to long-distance companies. The U.S. Supreme Court's earlier doctrine that "common carriers" had no obligation to be "common carriers of common carriers" was no longer valid.

The procompetitive intent of the decision is clear from its basis in antitrust law and its reference to the possibility of "20 long-distance companies" serving a single exchange. Indeed, its reasoning was exactly the same as that underlying the "equal access" provisions of the 1982 Modification of Final Judgment, which paved the way for long-distance competition in the 1980s. In theory, as well as in the perceived version of telephone history, larger networks are supposed to benefit from the refusal to connect and smaller competitors are supposed to favor joining their system to the larger one. In 1909, however, the dominant network was seeking to interconnect with companies bound to its competitors. The Ohio Supreme Court decision allowing it to do so was correctly seen as a setback to the cause of independent long-distance competition.

Competition suffered because the court decision interfered with the competing independents' ability to coalesce a critical mass of subscribers and exchanges outside of the Bell System. Joseph Ware, secretary of the national association, expressed the prevailing view among independents:

> Judge Tayler fails to grasp . . . that, excepting the Independent companies are connected together into one system there can be no competition in the telephone business.[30]

Competition in the telephone business revolved around the scope of access. A few large independent companies were attempting to construct regional access universes that would be competitive with Bell's. In any given region of the country, Bell controlled a far greater number of exchanges than any individual rival. Thus, the many small, scattered independent exchanges held the balance of power. Bell had guaranteed access to a larger number of exchanges to begin with; allowing it to break exclusive contracts

---

30. Joseph B. Ware, secretary, International Independent Telephone Association, 17 TELEPHONY (May 29, 1909).

binding the small independents to competitive long-distance networks would place "50 percent of the Independent force in the
doubtful column," a Nebraska independent wrote.[31] He went on
to say:

> If our faction [the independents] were made up of one organiza-
> tion some uniformity of methods could be followed, but to
> compel an interchange of service under present conditions
> means elimination of competition in favor of the larger organiza-
> tion and nothing else. . . .
> The second point which the judge fails to grasp is, that there
> is no competition where long distance lines are connected into
> one exchange—where one operator can put messages over all
> lines. The benefits to the public which come from competition
> . . . can only be obtained successfully by having competitive
> systems, rather than variously owned lines into each exchange,
> with one long-distance company—the Bell. He overlooks the
> fact that the Bell company has, or had, a competing local
> exchange in each of the towns where connection was made
> with a local company having contract relations with the U.S.
> Telephone Co., and that, co-incident with the connection of the
> Bell toll lines to the local independent exchange, local competi-
> tion was eliminated.[32]

The independents were asserting that nondiscriminatory interconnection was fundamentally incompatible with competition. If
Bell could gain access to local subscribers through an independent
exchange, it would not operate a competitive exchange. If there
were competing long-distance lines terminating in a monopoly local
exchange, an exchange operator would route long-distance calls
over his own company's lines rather than those of a competitor.

The tendency to apply concepts of nondiscrimination to the
telephone business in such a way as to require competing companies to exchange traffic appeared in other important legal decisions
of the period, and represented one strand of thinking.[33] The Su-

31. *The Necessity of Independent Long Distance Service to Independent
Local Companies*, 17 TELEPHONY 98 (Jan. 23, 1909).

32. *Id.*

33. The Supreme Court of Indiana required two competing exchanges
in West Lebanon to restore their connections after one of the companies
discontinued them. Goodwine *v.* Cadwallader, 172 Ind. 619, 87 N.E. 644
(1909), 89 N.E. 319 (1909). The court rejected the claim that the notion of
common carriage as applied to a telephone company required indiscriminate

preme Court of New York, on the other hand, upheld the validity of exclusive contracts on the grounds that it preserved competition.[34]

Physical Connection Laws

A different approach to the problem was taking shape at the state level. Twenty-eight states passed laws creating regulatory commissions or giving existing railroad commissions jurisdiction over the telephone companies between 1909 and 1913.[35] Twenty-six states passed laws authorizing some form of compulsory physical connection between telephone companies from 1904 to 1913, inclusive.[36] In 1910 the Interstate Commerce Commission was given the authority to regulate telephone companies as common carriers. Armed with their new powers to regulate entry, mergers, and connections, the utility commissions began to push the telephone system toward a monopolistic structure.

Compulsory physical connection legislation was the most important arena for working out the public policy regarding dual

---

service to competitors. In doing so it restated the rationale of the express cases, noting that the effect of such interconnection would be parasitic or confiscatory (at 648). But the opinion went on to hold that a telephone exchange that agreed to interconnect with one system in its area was obliged to offer the same privileges and terms to all other exchanges—a departure from, if not a direct contradiction of, the railroad precedents. *See also* Medina County Farmers Tel. Co. *v.* Medina Tel. Co., 30 Ohio Dec. Rep. 500 (1911), which relies on the nondiscrimination precedent of Cadwallader and cites U.S. Tel. Co. *v.* Central Union.

34. Supreme Court of New York, Wayne Monroe Tel. Co. *v.* Ontario Tel. Co., 112 N.Y. Supp. 424: "There is no stronger inducement to the managers of a public service corporation to serve the public well than a healthy apprehension that a rival concern will do so. It is sometimes argued that the presence of two telephone systems in a given district is a disadvantage to the community, which is best served by one system reaching all subscribers; but one system will never be made to reach all subscribers as cheaply as would otherwise be the case if the possibility of competition is destroyed."

35. Jeffrey Cohen, *The Telephone Problem and the Road to Telephone Regulation in the United States, 1876–1917,* 3 J. POL. HIST. 42 (1991).

36. South Carolina (1904), Georgia (1907), Oklahoma (1907), Texas (1907), Maryland (1910), Kansas (1911), Michigan (1911), Ohio (1911), South Dakota (1911), Washington (1911), Wisconsin (1911), Arizona (1912), California (1912), Kentucky (1912), New Mexico (1912), Oregon (1912), Colorado (1913), Florida (1913), Idaho (1913), Illinois (1913), Indiana (1913), Maine (1913), Missouri (1913), Montana (1913), Nebraska (1913), and Pennsylvania (1913).

systems. Contrary to common assumptions, the passage of those laws did not end access competition, but merely empowered a utility commission to order connections when petitioned to do so by the telephone users of a specific locality. Rulings required hearings and a finding of public interest, convenience, and necessity by the commission, and thus could be applied only on a case-by-case basis. The laws were almost never used to connect urban exchanges engaged in direct competition with each other; more often, they were applied to broaden interexchange access. The restricted scope of their application was attributable to the widespread belief that merging subscriber sets would eliminate competition, do economic harm to one of the two telephone systems, or do both. Because there was as yet no public consensus on the issue of monopoly, the commissions concentrated on cases where dual service restricted communication between different cities.

The flood of physical connection legislation from 1910 to 1913 reflected a change of heart among some of the independents. There had always been public demands for connecting the separate networks, but the combination of Bell and independent opposition had prevented action. By 1910 some independents were beginning to back away from access competition. Those who embraced that view did not see interconnection as a means of preserving competition, but were generally the same independents who worked out consolidations or divisions of territory with Bell. Others saw interconnection as a way to minimize Bell competition at the local level by giving their exchanges access to Bell toll lines.

The physical connection provision of Wisconsin's state utility law was defeated in 1907, when the independents opposed it, but passed in 1911, after they had given up hope of establishing an exchange in Milwaukee and the state association had become dormant.[37] Frank Woods, president of the National Independent Telephone Association, openly embraced the "universal service" concept and advocated laws compelling the interchange of service between all companies under the supervision of the Interstate Commerce Commission.[38] Two years later, Woods worked out a

---

37. David Gabel, The Evolution of a Market: The Emergence of Regulation in the Telephone Industry of Wisconsin, 1893–1917 349 (1987) (unpublished Ph.D. dissertation) (University of Wisconsin (Madison)).

38. HARRY B. MACMEAL, THE STORY OF INDEPENDENT TELEPHONY 183 (Independent Pioneer Telephone Association 1934).

consolidation with Bell that eliminated dual service in most of southeastern Nebraska. In 1911, the NITA national convention followed Woods's lead and passed a resolution for compulsory connection and state and national regulation.[39]

The issue of interconnection and cooperation with Bell split the independents, however. A splinter independent association led by the owners of the competing systems in New York, Pennsylvania, and West Virginia was formed in January 1913. One of its leaders, Burt Hubbell, explained that the new association "shall be composed of members who represent telephone companies not owned or controlled by the AT&T, directly or indirectly."[40]

Municipal governments also were agitating for the elimination of fragmentation. In 1908, the Cleveland City Council declared dual service a "nuisance" and instructed its committee on telephones and telegraphs to investigate the feasibility of compelling the Bell and Cuyahoga exchanges to interconnect. A civic committee in another former independent stronghold, Indianapolis, also recommended a return to one system after an investigation of the telephone situation. Kansas City experienced political agitation to connect or consolidate its systems.[41] In all cities, however, support for the elimination of dual service was tempered by fears that doing so would lead to a rate increase.

Compulsory interconnection laws were vociferously opposed by Bell and by the hard-core independents led by Hubbell. Although their motives were different, their arguments about the competitive effects were often parallel. Physical interconnection posed a problem for Bell in that the company publicly advocated universal service but was unwilling to bring that goal about by connecting with competing systems. It had to argue that universal service could best be achieved by one system, and it prepared a detailed memo outlining its case,[42] the arguments of which were presented in Vail's attacks on interconnection in Bell's annual reports.

The Bell memo contrasted the standardization, coordination,

---

39. *Id.* at 186.

40. *Id.* at 196.

41. *Bells May Talk to Homes*, KANSAS CITY STAR, Mar. 6, 1911.

42. Physical Connection (a syllabus and brief on the question of statutorily compelled connection of telephone lines owned by different companies) (Apr. 25, 1907), AT&T-BLA.

and high quality that could be achieved under a monopoly with the chaotic and uncontrolled conditions that would result from nondiscriminatory connection with multiple independently owned, overlapping systems. It also attempted to argue that independently manufactured telephones would not work with the Bell System as well as Bell telephones, although the validity of that point suffers from Bell's sublicensing of thousands of non-Bell systems.

A more significant argument was that competition between connected networks was inherently imperfect and even parasitic. If a Bell exchange in a dual service city had fewer subscribers than its opponent and Bell was forced to connect its toll lines with its competitor, the independent subscribers could benefit from Bell toll access without subscribing to Bell. Bell would lose all its exchange subscribers to the larger local company:

> "If toll lines were forced to connect with competitors, any fellow who feels aggrieved because his call did not reach him promptly when his mother-in-law had cramp colic . . . can and probably will build a competing line between your most profitable points, hitch onto you at each end, and make you take his calls to all other points on your lines . . . and you will hold the bag, and eventually lose out entirely."[43]

In economic terms, that can be summarized as an argument that interconnection made networks complements rather than competitors. Bell's defenders also made an appropriability argument: Bell laid out telephone facilities to cover an entire district. Even though some parts of that system were not profitable in isolation, interconnection could make the system profitable as a whole. Interconnection laws would allow another company to serve only the profitable areas while benefiting from Bell's access to the "lean" areas.

The independents' motive in opposing compulsory interconnection was to preserve dual systems rather than to eliminate them. A unified, fully interconnected telephone system, they believed, could not possibly be a truly competitive one. They advanced two reasons for that view: first, there was a tension, if not an outright contradiction, between competitive rivalry and the kind of interfirm cooperation needed to set up telephone connections jointly; second, the whole competitive process in telephony was driven by

---

43. 17 TELEPHONY 129 (Jan. 30, 1909).

access differentials that would disappear once the systems were interconnected.

Establishing a telephone connection over the facilities of two or more companies involved linking their lines at the same time to form an unbroken channel. The workers of the two companies had to cooperate rapidly and efficiently, and their methods had to be compatible. The independents did not deny that was possible. They did point out that the cooperation required was so intricate that companies involved in it could hardly maintain their status as competitors.

Business firms sufficiently receptive to exchanging traffic could just as easily divide the market, fix prices, and cease to compete. By the same token, integrating operations involved a degree of mutual trust and openness that hardly seemed compatible with business rivalry. Whichever firm controlled a local exchange, for example, would be in a position to discriminate between toll lines of long-distance companies when it routed traffic, or could engage in preferential treatment of its own subscribers at the expense of the other's. A columnist in the *Telephony* said of making connections over Bell toll lines: "It would be easy to detect discrimination if Bell operators refused to record your calls. But the switchboard having lots of business, some calls will have to wait. Do you think the Bell calls would wait? No! But do you doubt that your calls would wait? They would wait."[44] The independent defenders of dual systems also believed, like Bell, that dissolving the access differences between the networks eliminated real competition.

There was at least one advocate of connecting with competing companies within the Bell System. B. E. Sunny, the head of Chicago Telephone, believed that Bell would benefit from voluntarily entering into connecting arrangements. In 1910, he wrote a memo proposing to operate lines connecting the independent exchanges in Indianapolis, Grand Rapids, Racine, and Aurora to the Bell System, an arrangement that would give independent subscribers in those cities access to Chicago, Cincinnati, and Milwaukee. Sunny pointed out that the proposal would have numerous advantages: It would preempt the growing demand for physical connection legislation, allowing Bell to connect on its own terms; it would eliminate the need to grant franchises to competing companies in cities currently monopolized by Bell; it would greatly

---

44. 13 TELEPHONY 98 (Feb. 1907).

increase Bell's toll business, or at least allow it to find out what effects interconnection would have on its traffic; and it would reveal to Bell the identity of independent long-distance users, allowing it to solicit them to subscribe exclusively to Bell's service, which would do away with the costs of transferring calls between two systems. The only disadvantage Sunny recognized was that it might lead to the loss of exchange subscribers in cities where Bell rates were higher.[45] Despite its apparent advantages, Bell did not implement his proposal, fearing that interconnection would perpetuate dual systems and ease the pressure for consolidation. It may, however, have been a model for the interconnection arrangements of the Kingsbury Commitment (see chapter 11).

Case Studies in the Application of Interconnection Laws

Three landmark cases in California, Wisconsin, and Oregon highlight the different facets of the interconnection issue—the attitudes of users toward nonconnected networks, the effects that the telephone companies believed connection would have on their economic viability, and the attitudes of regulators toward competition.

Glen and Tehama Counties, California. In 1912, two rural independent telephone systems in northern California filed complaints calling for physical connection. The Glen and Tehama County Telephone companies had started operations five years earlier in the predominantly rural counties. Before their formation, the Bell System had established exchanges only in cities, had minimal toll lines, and used obsolete equipment; the new companies had built exchanges and modern toll lines throughout their counties. Following the standard pattern of access competition, Bell was forced to install modern switchboards, construct extensive toll lines, and sublicense farmer lines to remain competitive. That competition had produced a high level of duplicate subscriptions. Bell held the majority of users, but only 30 percent of the Bell-connected telephones were leased from Bell; the rest were sublicensed phones owned by farmers. The California Railroad Commission decided that connecting the two systems was an appropriate solution be-

---

45. Memo dated circa February 1910. B. E. Sunny collection, manuscripts, 1879–1920, AT&T Legal and Regulatory Archives, New York, N.Y.

cause the independents offered superior local service while the Bell System had more extensive toll access.[46]

In addition, the utility commissioners saw interconnection as a means of eliminating duplicate subscriptions and overlapping exchanges. Their ruling pointedly did not disagree with Bell's contention that it would lose most of its exchange subscribers if telephone users could gain access to its toll lines without subscribing to its local exchanges. Like Bell, the commissioners thought of the telephone as a natural monopoly. That Bell had been forced to extend and improve its service by the new entrants was interpreted by the commission not as evidence for the benefits of competition but as an indication that a monopoly could and should have been doing better.[47]

Wisconsin. In 1912, Frank Winter, a businessman in LaCrosse, Wisconsin, petitioned the Wisconsin Railroad Commission to connect the toll lines of the town's two competing systems: Wisconsin Telephone (Bell), which had 1,400 subscribers, and the independent LaCrosse Telephone, which had 4,200. Both companies had toll facilities offering connections throughout the state, but Wisconsin Telephone's lines extended to many places not reached by LaCrosse. Only 8 percent of the telephone users had duplicate subscriptions, and twelve to fifteen large businesses had private branch exchanges connected to the toll lines of both companies. When calls for people not on the Bell exchange came into the city, messengers brought the desired parties to a Bell station. Winter requested connecting only the toll lines of the two systems, leaving the division of local exchange service intact. He argued that the arrangement would be more convenient and would benefit the Bell company by increasing its toll business.[48]

---

46. The commission's decision is reprinted in 64 TELEPHONY (Mar. 1, 1913).

47. "A reduction of rates . . . and improvement of service under competition is an indication of one of two things, either that the rates are too high and the service not good enough before the competition arose, or that the rates are made too low and the service too good for the price under the stress of the competition. The former result could and should have been brought about without competition; the second result cannot be permanently maintained even under competition unless the utility according too low a rate is charging too high a rate elsewhere." *Id.*

48. 64 TELEPHONY 25–29 (May 17, 1913). *See also* Gabel, *supra* note 37, at 360–68.

Wisconsin Telephone opposed the request with its usual arguments. Interconnection would result in the loss of most of its exchange subscribers. If users could obtain access to Bell toll lines without a subscription to Bell's exchange, they would migrate to the larger independent exchange to obtain universal local service in addition to Bell's widespread toll line service. To support its contention, it introduced evidence from Canada, where interconnection had been ordered in eight cities and Bell's growth in subscribers had been reversed while its local competitors grew.[49]

The Wisconsin regulators ordered the connection made. Unlike the California commission, however, they took seriously the question of confiscation of property. "It is evident that the only inducement to subscribe to the Bell System is the fact that thereby the subscriber is connected with a telephone system covering the entire country." To compensate for economic damage to Bell's exchange, the commission imposed a surcharge on users of Bell toll lines who did not subscribe to the Bell exchange. "A subscriber who has not installed the telephones of both exchanges is not entitled to the toll service of both exchanges without paying an additional charge," it said.[50] In 1914, the Wisconsin Railroad Commission issued another physical connection order pertaining to the city of Janesville. In that case, the connection order included both local exchange and toll service.[51] In LaCrosse, Bell's fears proved to be true—local subscribers gradually deserted the Bell exchange over the next four years until the exchange was closed. In Janesville, however, market shares stabilized, but the exchanges were eventually consolidated anyway.

Portland, Oregon. Portland, Oregon, in 1913 was a dual service city with about 40,000 Bell telephones, 13,600 Home telephones, and 7,000 duplicate subscribers. The Hotel Oregon had Home phones in all its 400 guest rooms, and forty-five Bell phones in public places throughout the hotel. Thus, hotel guests had to go to the lobby or hallways to call Bell subscribers in the city, or to receive an incoming Bell call. Interconnection would have been easy; the two switchboards were in the same room. Home was

49. Gabel, *supra* note 37, at 632–63.

50. 64 TELEPHONY (May 17, 1913).

51. David Gabel, *Competition in a Network Industry: The Telephone Industry, 1894–1910*, J. ECON. HIST. 543 (1994).

willing, but Bell refused. It offered, instead, to install Bell phones in all the guest rooms, an expensive proposition for hotel management. On the motion of the hotel's owners, the case was brought to the Oregon Railroad Commission. The commission ordered the telephone companies to connect their hotel switchboards and exchange traffic and charge three-and-a-half cents for each transferred call.

There were other important physical connection cases in Hamilton, Ohio, and Grand Ledge, Michigan. In each case, connection was ordered, but the decision was appealed. As in the exclusive-connecting-contract cases, state supreme courts' decisions conflicted with each other. The Supreme Court of Indiana ruled against compulsory physical connection in 1909.[52] The Supreme Court of California overturned the California Railroad Commission's interconnection order in 1913, calling it "confiscatory." The Wisconsin Supreme Court upheld its state commission in 1916.[53]

Regulation as a Substitute for Competition

Regulatory commissions often promoted consolidations as well as interconnection. In 1911, only three months after the bill creating the Ohio Utility Commission became law, state officials began meeting with representatives of the Bell company to discuss plans for the elimination of dual service throughout the state. In 1912 the Bell and independent telephone companies in southeastern Nebraska worked out a consolidation in which Bell achieved a monopoly in some territories and the independent a monopoly in the others. The deal was made with the aid and approval of the state commission. The Michigan commission presided over the consolidation of the competing exchanges in Detroit in 1912 and helped to assure the remaining independent companies that the change would not impair their access to the city.[54]

When the regulators and their supporters attempted to push for legislation against dual service, however, they were rarely successful. Bills that explicitly prevented competition or permitted mergers between competing companies were defeated in Wiscon-

---

52. 18 TELEPHONY 159 (Aug. 7, 1909).

53. Wisconsin Telephone Co. *v.* Railroad Commission of Wisconsin, 162 W.R. 383 (1916).

54. MACMEAL, *supra* note 38, at 194.

sin, Illinois, and Ohio in 1909 and 1910. Another merger bill with the support of both Bell and the Morgan interests (which controlled the big independent system in the state) was introduced in Ohio, but failed to pass. A similar bill was vetoed by the governor of Nebraska in 1911. While the creation of one system had the support of regulators, it was still controversial with the general public.

The vitality and novelty of the issue of interconnection can be measured by the contradictory nature of the responses it evoked. Exclusive connecting contracts had been declared to be both anti-competitive and the salvation of competition. Their legality had been upheld by one state supreme court and overturned by others. Consolidation of competing telephone companies was being prosecuted under state and federal antitrust laws but actively encouraged by state utility commissions. The commissions could effect consolidations, but bills explicitly authorizing them were usually defeated. Physical interconnection was a desirable goal, but so was competition, and the two did not seem to be compatible. Compelling physical connection was authorized by law in many states but had been declared confiscatory and illegal by some state courts.

10

Saving Dual Service: The Kingsbury Commitment

By THE END OF 1913, Vail's attempt to unify the telephone system had generated a whirlwind of controversy. AT&T was mired in lawsuits regarding rates or antitrust issues in almost every state. The federal government had initiated antitrust litigation against Bell in the Pacific Northwest. A stockholder of the Central Union company was suing AT&T for conspiring to bankrupt the licensee company to subject it to an inexpensive takeover by AT&T. More threatening still, AT&T's pursuit of a single system had fueled agitation for government ownership of the telephone system, and Congress was drafting a bill to nationalize long-distance telephone lines.

Bell's attempt to acquire and consolidate the Morgan-owned independent properties in Ohio brought matters to a head. After extensive negotiations with state and federal authorities, it learned that the consolidations would be considered a violation of the Sherman Act. To extract itself from litigation and abate the threat of government ownership, Bell was forced to back away from its pursuit of a unified system. Its vehicle for doing so was the "Kingsbury Commitment" of December 19, 1913, so named because it was expressed in a letter from AT&T vice president Nathan C. Kingsbury to the Department of Justice. The letter eliminated, for the time being, the threat of federal antitrust prosecution and stilled some of the demands for government ownership.

The Kingsbury letter committed AT&T to three things:

- AT&T agreed to divest itself of its controlling stock holdings in its Western Union Telegraph Company, despite the important

economies of scope gained from joint operation of telephone and telegraph lines;
- AT&T agreed to stop acquiring competing independent exchanges, thus preserving dual service in the 1,234 cities and towns where Bell and an independent divided the market; and
- AT&T offered to open up its long-distance lines to independent exchanges under certain conditions.

The interconnection provisions of the commitment applied only to exchanges that were more than fifty miles apart. Thus, the agreement attempted to preserve a divided, competitive service at the local level while depriving AT&T of the competitive advantage it obtained by tying long-distance access to local exchange service.[1]

Contemporaries viewed the Kingsbury Commitment as a near-complete victory for the view that competition rather than monopoly should be the norm in the telephone industry. The independents referred to the commitment as a "gift from Santa Claus Bell"[2] and congratulated themselves on what seemed to be "the acceptance of the principle of competition in the conduct of [the telephone] business."[3] Indeed, to this day the Kingsbury Commitment is renowned within the telecommunications industry as a historical milestone. It is hard to understand why. Although the spinoff of Western Union was accomplished, the commitment had no impact whatsoever on toll interconnection. Within three years of its ban on acquisitions, Bell, the independents, and state and federal governments were engaged in a mutually agreeable process of consolidating their properties. Only seven years later, its restrictions on buyouts were officially eliminated by a new federal law. The Kingsbury Commitment was neither a milestone nor a turning point, merely a brief pause on the road to regulated monopoly.

THE KINGSBURY COMMITMENT
AND TOLL INTERCONNECTION

The Kingsbury Commitment is often misinterpreted as a sweeping interconnection agreement that effectively ended the fragmentation

---

1. The complete text of the Kingsbury Commitment is published in AT&T's 1913 ANNUAL REPORT 24–26 (1914).
2. 65 TELEPHONY 1 (Dec. 27, 1913).
3. Comments of E. B. Fisher, president, Independent Telephone Association of America, 65 TELEPHONY 20 (Dec. 27, 1913).

brought about by Bell and independent competition. It was nothing of the kind. Its primary intention was to leave dual service competition intact at the exchange level. Thus, it did not permit connection of Bell and independent exchanges that were sited within a fifty-mile radius of each other. As noted before, 95 percent of all telephone calls at that time were to points within fifty-mile radii. More important, there is no evidence that any sizable independent company availed itself of the opportunity to establish long-distance connections with AT&T under its terms. Bell's own statistics on the number of telephone subscribers connected to itself through independent companies show no quantum leaps in 1914 or 1915. On the contrary, the rate of increase in the number of connecting stations, which had advanced rapidly the sublicensing craze of 1908 to 1912, declined steadily from 1913 to 1916. The number of independent stations connected to the Bell System increased by 8 percent from 1912 to 1913, by 4 percent from 1914 to 1915, and by only 3 percent from 1915 to 1916.[4] Additional sublicensing of small exchanges in outlying areas, rather than the Kingsbury Commitment, accounts for those rates of growth.

The reason for the commitment's lack of impact on interconnection becomes apparent as soon as its actual provisions are examined. The commitment was carefully crafted to preserve Bell's competitive advantage, and its terms were far from generous. To make long-distance connections over the Bell System, an independent had to build its own lines to the nearest Bell exchange and pay the regular toll charges, as well as a ten-cent fee for every call handled. The idea of imposing a surcharge on the exchange of traffic between competing systems had been employed by many utility commissions as a way around the appropriability argument and court restrictions on confiscation. But the physical connection agreements ordered by utility commissions usually established a surcharge one-third to one-half that size. The agreement also stipulated that an entire toll circuit should be over Bell facilities and under the control of Bell operators. Independent long-distance lines, in other words, could not be used to make up any part of the circuit, except to get a call to the nearest Bell switchboard in cases where there were no Bell lines. That excluded independent long-distance companies from the entire market for long-distance traffic

---

4. FEDERAL COMMUNICATIONS COMMISSION, TELEPHONE INVESTIGATION 129, table 32 (Government Printing Office 1939).

flowing from independent to Bell telephones. More restrictively still, the agreement permitted independent subscribers only to terminate calls in Bell exchanges; it did not allow Bell subscribers to place calls to users on independent systems.

Although those terms of trade benefited only Bell, most independents viewed the commitment as a victory. They thought it would be the first step in a bargaining process that would eventually yield favorable terms. Some, however, saw the commitment as "absurd" and "insane."[5]

J. C. Kelsey, a columnist in *Telephony*, correctly characterized the commitment as the last in a series of three steps taken by Bell to deprive the independents of their exclusive control of portions of the telephone business. The sublicensing contracts had opened up a significant number of independent exchanges to Bell connections without allowing competing independents access to Bell exchanges. The decision to sell Bell-manufactured telephones to independent companies had eroded the independent manufacturers' exclusive control of independent operating company purchases without permitting any Bell companies to buy independently manufactured equipment. Now, said Kelsey, the Kingsbury Commitment opened up to Bell parts of the long-distance business heretofore exclusively controlled by independents, without any reciprocal concessions: "[Bell] has offered to share your exclusive customers' business with you. Surely, another typically generous act."[6]

In another letter to the Justice Department, Kingsbury made clear the nonreciprocal nature of the commitment: "The Bell System cannot, under the terms of that contract, open up an independent system to its subscribers."[7]

Any existing optimism about improving toll interconnection arrangements was dashed when major independents entered into post-Kingsbury Commitment negotiations. AT&T would make no concessions to reciprocity.[8] Complaints to the Justice Department and complaints by the independents' national association charging

---

5. TELEPHONY 29 (Jan. 17, 1914).

6. J. C. Kelsey, *Some New Year Thoughts*, TELEPHONY (Jan. 10, 1914).

7. Letter from N. C. Kingsbury to G. Carroll Todd (Oct. 1, 1914), section 7, papers of the attorney general, National Archives.

8. Letter from N. C. Kingsbury to B. G. Hubbell (Oct. 1, 1914); letter from Hubbell to Kingsbury (Oct. 8, 1914), AT&T Legal and Regulatory Archives, New York, N.Y.

that Bell was not living up to the spirit of the agreement had no effect.[9]

THE BAN ON ACQUISITIONS

The Kingsbury Commitment's moratorium on acquisitions was far more important than its lopsided, ineffectual interconnection proposal. The suspension left intact many large independent operating companies, rooted in major cities and possessed of significant levels of toll interconnection. At the time of the agreement, there were 1,234 communities in which Bell competed with an independent exchange and 630 communities in which a Bell-connected independent competed with other independent exchanges. Dual service thus remained in 1,864 places, 13 percent of the total number of communities with exchanges in the United States.[10]

The moratorium on consolidations, however, was at odds with other forces propelling the telephone system toward monopoly. The growing desire of users for universal access, state utility commissions' determination to supplant competition with regulation, and World War I–induced centralization all pointed toward unification of the network. The Kingsbury Commitment thus was a hiatus in the march toward monopoly rather than a victory for the competitive principle. For the next five years, the commitment impeded consolidations while the political, economic, and social forces favoring them continued to build.

The forces undermining the commitment are evident in a host of Bell archives files pertaining to acquisitions of independents after 1912.[11] In many cases, the commitment was the only obstacle to a proposed merger in which an independent was willing to sell, Bell wanted to buy, city and state authorities approved the deal, and voters had expressed their desire to unify service. Faced with

9. HARRY B. MACMEAL, THE STORY OF INDEPENDENT TELEPHONY 221 (Independent Pioneer Telephone Association 1934).

10. *Id.* at 208.

11. Letter from Kingsbury to George W. Wickersham, attorney general (Mar. 3, 1913), Box 32, AT&T-BLA. Attached memo contains a list of twenty-nine acquisitions in Nebraska, Iowa, and Minnesota that "have been postponed or abandoned on account of Vail's letter of August 6th [1912]." For other postponed acquisitions, see Continental (1910), Box 65, AT&T-BLA; Indianapolis (1907–1915), Box 36, AT&T-BLA; St. Louis, Missouri, Box 16; Missouri and Kansas (1909–1919), Boxes 17, 18, AT&T-Bell Laboratories Archives, Warren, N.J. [hereinafter AT&T-BLA].

such a situation, the independent telephone interests or local government officials would often ask federal antitrust authorities to sanction a deal. The Justice Department let it be known that it would raise no objection to such consolidations as long as dual service was eliminated by swapping territories, not by takeovers. Although that option left Bell in exclusive control of one territory and an independent in exclusive control of the other (and thus eliminated competition) Bell and the independents stayed in control of roughly the same number of telephones as before. Invariably, the key argument used to justify consolidations—not only by Bell, but by independents, government officials, and users—was that unification of the telephone service was more desirable than a divided service. Thus, within a few years of the Kingsbury Commitment a number of major consolidations of telephone service took place. Kansas City, Los Angeles, Memphis, and many smaller places traded dual service for universal service. Two of those consolidations are examined in detail in the next chapter.

The government's acquiescence in the piecemeal elimination of dual service is a critical element in understanding why the United States ended up with a telephone monopoly. Historical interpretations that stress economic predation by the Bell System (or Bell-inspired manipulations of the political process) ignore the fact that at that critical juncture in telephone history, major independent operating companies had survived, and both federal and state governments possessed all the tools they needed to prevent monopolization of the industry. Antitrust laws, at both state and federal levels, could have prevented consolidation had they been applied. Opposition from any well-organized and reasonably influential interest group could have stopped the process of waiving the Kingsbury Commitment.[12] But opposition rarely materialized. More often than not, voters, city councils, and statewide referenda weighed in on the side of universal service and consolidation.

The antitrust-inspired Kingsbury Commitment was a shrewd tactical move by AT&T, in that it deflected antitrust pressures but did not undermine the company's superior position in access competition. The erosion of the ban on acquisitions was the product

---

12. In Kansas City, for example, the newspapers waged a successful editorial campaign against consolidation in 1911 (Box 17, AT&T-BLA), while in Shreveport, Louisiana, labor interests defeated a resolution favoring consolidation.

of a legal and regulatory system that had not yet come to grips with the fact that its desire for an integrated telephone system was completely at odds with its commitment to the preservation of normal market competition. The only positive accomplishment of the Kingsbury Commitment was to bring Bell's acquisition of independent systems to a halt for four years, giving the telephone companies, utility commissions, city and state governments, and federal antitrust officials the breathing room needed to work out a coherent policy regarding telephone monopoly, competition, and interconnection.

11

The Subtle Politics and Economics of Unification, 1914–1921

THE PERIOD BETWEEN the Kingsbury Commitment and the Communications Act of 1934 is something of an empty space in telephone historiography. Those accounts that do exist tend to imply that the regulated monopoly system was basically in place from 1914 on. In the wake of Bell's agreement to stop acquisitions, however, more than 1,800 cities, many of them large, still had unconnected, competing exchanges. Those systems had weathered the storm of acquisitions and interconnection from 1908 to 1913 and showed no signs of going out of business. Dual service was still an important factor in the American telephone industry.

Nevertheless, within three years of the Kingsbury Commitment a series of great unifications of independent and Bell telephone systems began in major cities. Many were concluded by 1918, well before a 1921 federal law nullified the Kingsbury Commitment. It is important to examine what motivated that process. It is also important to examine that unification of service from an economic standpoint to evaluate the sources of efficiency in telephone monopoly.

Unifying telephone service could be accomplished primarily in two ways: interconnection, wherein the competing systems exchanged traffic, or consolidation, where one system bought another and moved all customers to the buyer's system. (A third, rarely selected option was a municipal takeover of the telephone system.)

While the public and municipal governments generally looked favorably on unifying telephone service, support for consolidation could evaporate if it was accompanied by a rate increase, which was, of course, Bell's primary goal. Thus, Bell developed a careful approach to consolidations. It promised universal service to develop public support for change and would not move forward until it had at least the tacit consent of users and all relevant local authorities. Because it could skirt the Kingsbury Commitment if it did not come out of a consolidation with a larger share of telephones, Bell would offer to trade territories with independents with which it wished to consolidate. Given strong local support, and the fact that Bell was losing as many telephones as it was gaining, antitrust officials usually approved Bell's consolidations. The following two case studies illustrate the machinations of telephone consolidations.

CONSOLIDATION IN BUFFALO, NEW YORK

The Buffalo-based Federal Telephone Co. was run by Burt G. Hubbell and had an ownership interest in thirty-five independent exchanges in western New York, including the systems of Buffalo, Rochester, and Jamestown. The Jamestown independent exchange had more subscribers than its rival Bell exchange; the Rochester exchange was roughly equal to its competitor, while Bell's subscriber list in Buffalo outnumbered the independent by nearly three to one.

In 1916, Hubbell observed a tendency among subscribers served by two exchanges to gravitate toward the larger of the two systems. His Buffalo exchange was having a hard time attracting new subscribers, and the size of its list was decreasing. User convergence was taking place in Buffalo. But that convergence at the local level was leading to greater fragmentation at the interexchange level. According to Hubbell, "the natural tendency of the public to patronize the company with the largest number of subscribers . . . has led to a segregation into telephone districts in each of which one of the two competitors has usually acquired a great predominance of subscribers." As a result, large numbers of users in western New York were unable to communicate with each other by telephone.[1]

That such convergence was driven by demand-side economies of scope, rather than by the superiority of Bell's service, is clear.

---

1. Letter from B. G. Hubbell to U.S. attorney general (Aug. 30, 1916), Box 25, AT&T-Bell Laboratories Archives, Warren, N.J. [hereinafter AT&T-BLA].

In a memo to the U.S. attorney general seeking approval for a consolidation, Hubbell pointed out that Federal Telephone had used every means at its disposal to reverse the downward trend in Buffalo. It had waged an advertising campaign touting competition, local control, and lower rates, as well as purchased and installed an automatic switching system, but had failed to reverse the migration of subscribers to the Bell System. Hubbell concluded that the public felt its best interests would be served by a unified telephone system under state control.[2]

New York Telephone Company pursued the consolidation in the cautious manner described earlier. During the consolidation, it worked closely with the Buffalo Chamber of Commerce to secure its approval of the rate changes it wanted to make. It insisted that the majority of telephone users express their approval of the consolidation by petition or a local referendum before the companies applied to the attorney general for a waiver of the Kingsbury Commitment.[3] Bell skirted the prohibition of the Kingsbury Commitment against the acquisition of competing independents by proposing to trade territories with its former competitor. In this case, Bell acquired control of the Buffalo area while the independents gained a monopoly over Rochester and Jamestown and vicinity.

The Buffalo Chamber of Commerce approved the consolidation after a special committee conducted a detailed investigation of telephone rates in the city. The committee concluded:

> No permanent and satisfactory telephone situation can be established which contemplates the division of our people into two separate groups. General inter-communication is the essential requirement for adequate and complete telephone service, especially for business men.[4]

The Chamber of Commerce report proposed to completely overhaul the telephone rate structure upon consolidation. The report claimed that neither telephone company was making an

---

2. *Id.*

3. Federal Tel. & Tel. Co., Rochester Tel. Co., Home Telephone Co. of Jamestown, New York Telephone Co., An Analysis of the Present Unsatisfactory Telephone Conditions Now Existing in Western New York and a Plan for Remedying Them (Oct. 5, 1917), Box 25, AT&T-BLA.

4. Buffalo Chamber of Commerce, Telephone Committee's Report (May 5, 1916) at 10.

adequate return under existing conditions and that either could, if it so requested, obtain approval for a rate increase from the Public Service Commission. That, it claimed, "would prove an added burden to the telephone users of this city, and particularly to those who use both services." As an alternative to rate increases under continued dual service, the report proposed a system of measured rates and a move away from party-line service. Consolidation would reduce operating expenses, while the proposed rate changes, the committee asserted, would reduce rates for most subscriber groups and would justly assign a larger share of the costs to those who used the telephone the most. In assessing the impact of the rate change, the committee relied almost entirely on information provided by New York Telephone.

The structure of the proposed rates yields important clues about who wanted universal service and who was expected to pay for it. One effect of the new rates was to dramatically increase the charges of the 1,000 or so large business users at the top of the hierarchy. One such user, the Postal Telegraph-Cable Co., entered an emphatic protest with the city council, pointing out that the company's payments for telephone service would triple under the proposed rates.[5] The Postal Company circulated its own petition for continued competition to counter the Bell–Chamber of Commerce petition favoring merger. The leaflet carried a list contrasting the rates of cities with and without competition.[6]

The Chamber of Commerce report tried to show that the change would not affect residential and small user rates. But it is fairly certain that the rates of users on the bottom of the hierarchy were being subtly increased, too. All business party lines were to be eliminated, and half the business subscribers of both companies were served on a party-line basis. The lowest of the new measured service rates allowed a business subscriber to make only about two calls a day without incurring extra charges. Four-party residential lines, formerly priced at $24 per year, were to be put on a measured basis, while individual and two-party residential lines were to be

---

5. Postal Telegraph-Cable Co., *Telephone Merger* (August 28, 1916) (pamphlet addressed to the City Council of Buffalo, New York).

6. The Postal Telegraph Company had been an opponent of AT&T ever since the latter's acquisition of Western Union in 1909. It opposed consolidations because it feared that the telephone giant would use its market power in the telephone arena to dominate the telegraph industry.

offered on a flat-rate basis at much higher rates. Although the four-party residential line preserved the old monthly rate, it now came with a limit of 600 messages per year, beyond which there would be an additional charge of four cents per call. If each person on a four-party line made only one call a day, the four parties would exceed that limit by 840 calls and would incur extra charges of $33.60 per year.

The discouragement of party lines was a predictable characteristic of a telephone system that no longer had to compete on the dimension of access. Party lines had flourished during the competitive period because each network wanted to get as many subscribers as possible onto its system at the lowest possible cost. As competition waned, the telephone companies took access for granted and concentrated on maximizing their revenues from usage.

If the consolidation increased rates for users at the top and bottom of the hierarchy, it probably saved money for business users located somewhere in the middle, if they were single-line users before. Savings would be especially pronounced for businesses with a moderate level of calling that had paid for two subscriptions before. Consolidation gave them universal access at a price about the same as and possibly lower than the price of a subscription to a single system before the change.

CONSOLIDATION IN SOUTHERN CALIFORNIA

The political response to dual service in Southern California was particularly revealing. By 1916 the Bell and independent systems had split the telephone business of the region almost exactly in half. Bell's Pacific Telephone and Telegraph Co. had eleven exchanges serving 67,000 stations in the area. Its toll lines offered connections to most of the Bell exchanges west of the Rockies and AT&T connections to the rest of the United States. The independent Home Telephone and Telegraph Co. operated fourteen local exchanges and one toll exchange using automatic switching equipment. In 1916 the Home Co. had 60,300 subscribers and toll connections to many other independent exchanges in Southern California, although it offered no interstate connections. Despite the fact that the Los Angeles city council had imposed artificially low rates on both companies that forced them to operate at a loss,

both systems were financially sound and in good physical condition.[7]

Yet, as the telephone saturated the area, political agitation
against dual service and for some form of unification took hold.
Organized demands for change began around 1910, when the city
created its own municipal public utilities board. Three remedies
were discussed: compulsory interconnection of the competing exchanges; municipal ownership of the telephone system; and consolidation into a privately owned but publicly regulated monopoly.
The first option, which appeared to leave both competition and the
existing companies intact, was the most popular. In April 1910 the
Municipal League of Los Angeles asked the Board of Public Utilities to investigate the feasibility of establishing a method of interconnecting the two rival telephone systems.

As the board prepared its report, the business community
increased its opposition to dual service. In 1912 the Southern
California Hotel Men's Association created a committee to prepare
a plan to eliminate the use of both telephones in hotels.[8] The hotel
association's approach to the problem boiled down to an attempt
to coordinate users to select one telephone system over the other
as a bloc. The same year a group calling itself the Telephone
Reform Association initiated a campaign against dual service and
for consolidation.[9] By 1914 the association had changed its name to
the One Phone League and claimed 1,200 members. There was no
doubt that the policy of interconnecting the two companies enjoyed
widespread public support. A municipal referendum on June 1,
1915, saw 63,194 voters express their preference for compulsory
interchange of service, while only 14,921 voted against it. Also in
1915 the Socialist Party put a referendum on the ballot authorizing
the city to take over and operate the telephone system. The
proposition was defeated with 20,000 votes in favor and 30,000
votes against.

---

7. A letter from Henry Robinson to N. C. Kingsbury (July 27, 1915) noted
the improved financial condition of the Home Co. and urged Kingsbury to
consummate a merger before the market value of the independent company's
shares improved and its stockholders began to oppose a merger (Box 18,
AT&T-BLA).

8. Los Angeles Times, June 22, 1912.

9. For a complete chronology of the political opposition to dual service in
Los Angeles, *see Summary of Information Furnished to the Department of
Justice in Connection with Los Angeles Telephone Consolidation Case* (March
23, 1917), Box 18, AT&T-BLA.

A survey taken by an economics student at the University of Southern California in 1916 asked telephone users, "Are you ever troubled about not being able to get people by telephone because they have the other service?" The survey interviewed fifty businessmen, fifty professional men, and fifty housewives. The majority of each group responded in the affirmative: businessmen (100 percent), professional men (96 percent), and housewives (66 percent).[10] The unanimity with which business users opposed dual service is striking. It is reasonable to assume that most of the businessmen were "troubled" not because they were *unable* to get people by telephone—many of them would have been duplicate subscribers, after all—but because they objected to the additional expense of subscribing to both systems. The corresponding lack of unanimity among housewives is equally striking. Although a large majority of them answered yes to the question, one in every three of them was willing to say that she was troubled not at all by an inability to reach half the telephone subscribers in the region. That is even more remarkable when we keep in mind that very few residential users were duplicate subscribers, so that they, unlike the business and professional users, really were unable to reach subscribers on the other system. The demand for homogenization was widespread, but the most vigorous calls for it came from the upper and middle levels of the communications hierarchy.

The Los Angeles Board of Public Utilities issued its report on the subject of interconnection on April 28, 1914.[11] The report had been conducted by the utility department's chief engineer, James Barker, and was viewed by all concerned as an objective and impartial study. The Barker report effectively destroyed compulsory interconnection as an option by showing how expensive it would be to build and operate the facilities required to transmit, switch, and record calls between the two systems. The expense of joint service was increased by the technical incompatibility of the two systems. Bell relied on manual and the Home Co. on machine switching, and both operated at different voltages. The main problem, however, was the sheer size of the two systems. Compulsory

---

10. Lloyd Heck Marvin, The Telephone Situation in Los Angeles (plate II) (January 7, 1916) (unpublished master's thesis, University of Southern California).

11. The text of the Barker report (April 1914) is printed in the 1914 ANNUAL REPORT OF THE CALIFORNIA RAILROAD COMMISSION 62 (1915) AT&T Legal and Regulatory Archives, New York, N.Y.

interconnection had never been carried out on a scale involving more than 100,000 telephone subscribers before. The places in which it had been tried, such as Janesville and La Crosse in Wisconsin, or Pasadena in California, had only a few thousand subscribers and one central office for each company.

To connect the two large regional systems in Southern California, Barker observed, required either full-mesh interconnection between the Home Company's and the Pacific Company's central offices by direct trunk lines or by establishing a tandem switching center. The first option would require duplicating the existing trunking equipment of each company and making extensive changes in the switchboards. The second would require about $400,000 in capital investment and another $500,000 to $600,000 per year in expenses. The latter figure represented about one-third of the total annual operating revenues of both companies combined. Barker concluded:

> [t]he best plan for obtaining the desired results is, in my opinion, through a consolidation of the two systems. By this means all duplication and unnecessary investments are avoided and operating and overhead costs are reduced to a minimum, and in the end the patrons will be given a better service and at the lowest rates commensurate with the necessary investment.[12]

After the Barker report, consolidation became the most popular strategy for unification because the voters repudiated municipal acquisition. The Bell Company's franchise expired in November 1916, and the city seized on that opportunity to require a consolidation by refusing to grant the company's request for a renewal. The product of the merger, the Southern California Telephone Company, was Bell-owned. It began operation on May 1, 1917. The three-sided struggle over rates among the city's telephone users, regulators, and telephone companies continued, but the question of dual versus universal service had been settled.

COMPLETING THE TRANSITION

In retrospect, it is clear that telephone consolidations were not motivated by Bell's ability to achieve supply-side economies of scale or scope, nor did they result in rate decreases. Pressures for

---

12. *Id.*

mergers came from both the demand and the supply side, but the cases of Buffalo and Los Angeles make it clear that no change could have been effected without the support of users.

From the demand side, consolidations were supported because they unified the service. Users in the middle of the communications hierarchy wanted the benefits of unified telephone access without the expense of a duplicate subscription. The case of Buffalo shows that even without consolidation, users were showing a tendency to converge on a single network.

From the supply side, the mergers were motivated by a desire to eliminate competition and clear the way for a rate increase. The ferocious access competition of the preceding fifteen to twenty years had demanded constant expansion of facilities, which tended to increase costs, while placing severe restraint on rates. Bell looked upon the elimination of dual service as an opportunity to recover those losses.

In large cities such as Buffalo and Louisville, public policy was consumed with the problem of what to do with established competitors. Given the heavy capital requirements and the entrenched position of existing firms, there was little threat that a new company would enter. That was not true of small towns and rural areas, however. There telephone competition continued with the vigor of the early 1900s until the state utility commissions actively suppressed it.[13]

Ohio affords a revealing example. State law authorized the utility commission to prevent telephone companies from "invading the territory" of another company without a certificate of public interest, convenience, and necessity from the commission. When small telephone companies came to the commission to obtain permission to compete with an existing company, however, the commission refused whenever it had the authority to do so. A judge ruled that "multiplicity of telephone systems" and the confinement of telephone service to "one well regulated company" was "the whole intention of the [utilities] Act."[14]

When one small-town company attempted to enter the territory

---

13. The April 24, 1909, TELEPHONY reported that the independent telephone companies of New York opposed commission regulation "because of the prejudice of that body against competition in public utilities."

14. Clinton Telephone Co. *v*. New Burlington Telephone Co., Ohio Public Utilities Commission, Sept. 1912.

of a neighboring company because of the latter's failure to maintain its facilities in proper working condition, the commission denied that neglect was a legitimate reason for competition. The filing of a complaint before the commission, it said, could compel any company to improve its facilities. In other words, the commission was determined to substitute regulatory remedies for problems of service and rates formerly addressed by means of competition. That evidence suggests that while dual service was still economically viable in many parts of the country, its elimination was mandated politically by the victory of the regulated monopoly paradigm. Once the telephone industry had been classified as a natural monopoly, regulation would substitute for the market.

After the end of World War I, there were still competing exchanges in 1,000 locations, including twelve major cities. Further consolidations were blocked by the Kingsbury Commitment and the Clayton Antitrust Act.[15] The telephone companies' inability to consolidate, they claimed, made it impossible for them to raise money to rebuild their systems. In a movement that had the active support of both Bell and independent interests, Congress amended the Transportation Act to permit the consolidation of dual telephone systems with the approval of the Interstate Commerce Commission. In introducing the Willis-Graham Act of 1921, Representative Graham stated:

> [It is] better policy to have one telephone system in a community that serves all the people, even though it may be at an advanced rate, properly regulated by State boards or commissions, than it is to have two competing telephone systems. There is nothing more exasperating, nothing that annoys the ordinary business man or the ordinary person more than to have two competing local telephone systems, so that he must have in his house and in his office two telephones, on neither one of which he can get all the people he wants to be in communication with.[16]

The passage of the Willis-Graham Act gave the imprimatur of the U.S. Congress to the elimination of the last vestiges of competition. It cleared the way for final major telephone consolidations.

---

15. Section 7 of the Clayton Antitrust Act prohibited mergers that created a monopoly.

16. CONGRESSIONAL RECORD 1966 (June 1, 1921).

12

The Legacy of Access Competition

BY THE MID-1920s, the remnants of access competition had been eliminated. The political and ideological victory of the regulated monopoly paradigm, advanced under the banner of universal service, was so complete that the accomplishments of that period have been eclipsed. Nevertheless, the twenty-five year bout of dual service competition left an indelible impression on the American telephone network. The geographic scope of the network and popular adoption of telephones had been pushed to surprisingly modern levels.

Our picture of the popularity of the telephone by 1920 has been distorted somewhat by the modern emphasis on telephone penetration ratios as the indicator of telephone development. At the end of the dual service era, household penetration was about 30 percent and the simple penetration ratio (the number of telephones in service per 100 population) was only 13 percent. In most developed countries with universal service today, the penetration ratio is about 45 to 55 percent. Those bare numbers overlook two important facts about the dual service era, however. One is that by 1920 the U.S. telephone network was geographically universal; it reached virtually all settled areas with public exchanges and lines. The other is that there were major regional variations in penetration. Many parts of the United States—particularly those where independent competition was strongest—had already achieved household penetration levels above 50 percent.

THE GEOGRAPHIC SCOPE OF THE
TELEPHONE NETWORK BY 1920

Access competition did not put a telephone in every home, but according to the available statistical sources, it did put a telephone exchange or line in practically every community. By 1920, the physical infrastructure for supporting universal telephone service was essentially in place. By "physical infrastructure," I mean public telephone exchanges linked by trunk lines to the national network. The presence of an exchange is the best indicator of geographical coverage, because it is the most important factor determining whether access was available in a given location.

The 1920 census documents 15,692 incorporated places of all sizes in the United States.[1] According to AT&T records, there were 19,550 places with a telephone exchange in November 1917.[2] The 1917 telephone census counted 12,294 telephone exchanges with annual incomes over $5,000. The remaining 3,858 exchanges were probably serving small rural communities. For the 40 percent of the U.S. population who in 1920 still lived in unincorporated areas, there were 30,317 rural lines as of 1912.[3]

Undoubtedly, some remote parts of the country were un-reached by telephone lines or exchanges, but no other country or region achieved a comparable degree of continent-wide coverage so rapidly. Indeed, the number of public telephone exchanges in the United States has changed only marginally since 1917. (In fact, growth in exchanges slowed noticeably after 1907, when the phase of system overlap ended.) Fifteen years later, in 1932, the number of exchanges had increased by only 3 percent. In 1990, 15,227 telephone central offices in the continental United States reported to the Federal Communications Commission. That is significantly less than the 19,550 total counted by AT&T in 1917, but about 3,000 more than the 12,294 exchanges with an average annual income greater than $5,000 reported in the 1917 Telephone Census. The comparison between 1917 and 1990 statistics is of necessity rough and imprecise. Telephone companies under a certain size do not

---

1. U. S. BUREAU OF THE CENSUS, POPULATION 1920, table 31, Distribution of Population in Groups of Cities Classified According to Size, and in Rural Territory: 1890–1920.

2. Memorandum from the acting statistician, Jan. 9, 1918, Box 13, AT&T-Bell Laboratories Archives, Warren, N.J.

3. TELEPHONE CENSUS OF 1912, table 18 (1915).

report to the FCC, but the reporting criteria have changed since the 1920s. Some of the additional exchanges counted in 1990 may have existed in 1917 but were owned by companies too small to count. The lack of precision does not detract much from the essential observation: Despite the huge growth in population, users, penetration levels, and traffic between 1920 and 1990, the number of telephone central offices has changed relatively little. The geographic extension of the American telephone network came during the years of access competition.

TELEPHONE PENETRATION BY 1920

Access competition also produced major changes in the quantity and type of users. Penetration expanded to the highest levels in the world, although the picture is complex. Some parts of the country actually began to approach the ideal of universal household penetration; for other regions, notably the South, that goal remained distant.

By 1920, 38.7 percent of American farms had telephones, whereas only 30 percent of all American households did. That disproportionate rural adoption of the telephone occurred for several reasons. Communication was more valuable to rural inhabitants. It was easier for city dwellers to rely on public telephone stations or other forms of communication. Telephone service was more expensive in cities because of the larger scope of local exchange service. Then, too, cities had a greater proportion of poorer, immigrant populations. No one, however, contemplating the development of the telephone business in the 1880s or 1890s would have predicted a smaller percentage of penetration in the cities. Only the spontaneous, "disorderly" phenomenon of access competition allowed the full scope of rural demand to emerge.

State-by-state statistics for 1920 reveal extremely wide variations in telephone penetration. In the North Central states, farms were close to universal penetration: farms in Ohio, Indiana, Illinois, Kansas, and Nebraska had subscription rates between 60 and 80 percent; 86 percent of the farms in Iowa had telephones. Of the ten states with the lowest farm penetration, eight were Southern. The four lowest states—South Carolina, Louisiana, Florida, and Georgia—had levels of telephone penetration scarcely one-tenth that of the North Central states.

That result can be explained only partly by variations in

wealth. A linear regression between average farm value by state and the state's telephone penetration among farmers yields a moderate but statistically significant correlation coefficient (R^2) of .29.[4] Independent competition is a weaker but also statistically significant factor. States with higher levels of rural telephone penetration tend also to be those in which a high proportion of the users were served by independents in 1907 (R^2 = .13).[5] The huge size of the regional disparity, however, suggests that other important cultural and socioeconomic differences were at work. Statistical analysis of telephone penetration in the 1980s and 1990s yields a much stronger correlation between wealth and variation in penetration levels. Further consideration of that puzzle is outside the scope of this work.

Another sense in which access competition pushed the United States toward universal service is the extension of telephone service to homes. Before the entry of the independents, the telephone had been primarily a business tool; the ratio of business to residential subscriptions was about 9 to 1. The years between 1900 and 1910 saw the number of residential telephone subscriptions surpass the number of business telephones in most cities with an exchange. The growth of residential subscribership reflected access competition's relentless drive to increase the value of networks by increasing their scope, as well as falling prices for equipment.

Household diffusion of the telephone was more extensive in smaller cities. While the average for the country as a whole in 1920 was about one telephone for every three households, there were many communities in the United States that had telephones in more than half of their households as early as 1910.

By 1920, the competitive period had created the kind of geographic and social penetration capable of supporting the modern notion of universal-service-as-social-ubiquity. The social role of the telephone had been utterly transformed. Later, the policy expectations applied to the telephone by government legislators and regulators began to reflect that new social role. But it is important to understand the sequence: Market processes made the telephone a popular and geographically ubiquitous item first; government policy to extend and support that notion came second.

---

4. R^2 = .29044, F = 17.6, significance of F = .0001.
5. R^2 = .13148, F = 6.5, significance of F = .0144.

13

The Reincarnation of Universal Service

THE UNIFICATION OF TELEPHONE SERVICE by the middle of the 1920s put an end to the first-generation debate over universal service. But the term made a highly visible comeback in the mid-1970s, sparking a debate still underway. The return of "universal service" as a policy touchstone gave the term a new meaning. As noted in chapter 2, an entire historical mythology has grown up around the new definition.

Accurate or not, that change in the popular meaning of the term is an important part of the history of telecommunications in the United States. This chapter analyzes that change and shows how it emerged from the debates over the introduction of competition in long-distance markets in the 1970s. The chapter retraces relevant developments in regulation from 1920 to the mid-1970s, including the development of separations by federal and state regulators and the passage of the 1934 Communications Act. In the process, it refutes the historical misconceptions created by the shift in the meaning of the term.

THE SECOND-GENERATION UNIVERSAL SERVICE CONCEPT

Contemporary readers will have no difficulty recognizing the definition of universal service that prevails today: universal service is comprehensive household telephone penetration—a "telephone in every home." Universal service policy has become synonymous with regulating rates to make telephone service more affordable to consumers. Cross-subsidies do that. Long-distance users are overcharged to subsidize local service. Urban customers pay more so rural customers can pay less.

If that new definition represented only a change in government policy made with full historical knowledge, it would pose no problem. It does not, however. The new linkages among universal service, household penetration, and regulated monopoly were parts of a politically motivated attempt to salvage the fortunes of the regulated monopoly system in the 1970s. The new definition brought with it a sweeping revision of the history of the telephone system—a revision that fabricated the legislative origins of universal service policy and exaggerated the role of regulated monopoly in making telephone service affordable and available to most Americans.

In the mythology associated with the new conception, the competitive era's contribution to the development of the infrastructure is ignored, and the earlier universal service debate is forgotten. The origins of universal service policy were instead traced to the 1934 Communications Act, specifically to the wording of the act's preamble:

> to make available, so far as possible, to all the people of the United States, a rapid, efficient, Nation-wide, and world-wide wire and radio communication service with adequate facilities at reasonable charges.[1]

In the revisionist view, regulators and telephone monopolies acting together exploited the characteristics of the regulated monopoly system to bring about widespread household access to telephone service. Generally, the separations and settlements process, which allocates part of the revenues generated by the long-distance network to the support of the local network, is identified as the mechanism by which that policy goal was accomplished. In its more romantic formulations, the modern construction of universal service implies that without such measures telephone service would never have been affordable to the bulk of the population.[2]

---

1. 47 U.S.C. § 151.

2. *See, e.g.*, John Browning, *Universal Service: An Idea Whose Time Has Passed*, 3 WIRED 102 (Sept. 1994): "This is the story of the noblest idea in the history of technology: universal telecommunications service. Universal service brought America into the information age. It put telephones into every home (well, about 94 percent of them) and wove telephone lines through the fabric of American life. . . . Universal service was made a guiding principle of American telecom regulation in 1934."

Of course, Vail was using the term "universal service" almost three decades before, and he meant nothing like the meaning of the preamble to the Telecommunications Act of 1934. That fact did not deter the revision of the term, however. Instead, those who bothered to read Vail's pronouncements simply projected the new meaning into them. Thus, many historians, especially those directly associated with the Bell System, contend that universal service in the modern sense was an objective of AT&T from the very beginning.[3] They view the gradual but steady increase in household penetration after 1920 as evidence of Bell's commitment to widespread household penetration. Those historians would refuse to recognize any qualitative distinction between the term's usage now and Vail's usage in the early 1900s.

With the new mythology of universal service sketched out, we can now review the postregulation era developments to assess their historical accuracy. The narrative that follows will make three arguments: that the separations process was not actively used to subsidize local service until the late 1960s and the 1970s, and that its impact on the growth of penetration was minor; that the 1934 Communications Act did not articulate a national universal service policy; and that the redefinition of universal service actually took place in the mid-1970s as part of the regulated monopoly system's attempt to defend itself against long-distance competition.

UNIVERSAL SERVICE AND THE PROBLEM
OF SEPARATING THE RATE BASE

The initial application of rate regulation to the telephone industry in the 1920s posed complex problems in economics. Rate base regulation demands that the rates charged by a telephone company for a particular service be based on the book costs of the physical plant used, plus expenses and a reasonable rate of return. It assumes, in other words, a scientific link between the cost of the facilities used and the price charged. Applying that logic to telephone service is no simple matter. A telephone system supplies millions of possible connections to its users. In chapter 3, I argued that each connection is a separate service. But subscribers use the

---

3. ALVIN VON AUW, HERITAGE AND DESTINY: REFLECTIONS ON THE BELL SYSTEM IN TRANSITION (Praeger 1983); PETER TEMIN & LOUIS GALAMBOS, THE FALL OF THE BELL SYSTEM (Cambridge University Press 1987).

same telephone, local access line, and central office switch for all of those outputs. How should the costs of those facilities be apportioned among services so that regulators can determine what the "proper" rates should be?

The first-generation concept of universal service supported a holistic approach to that problem. It focused on sustaining the telephone network as a system and not as a collection of discrete components. Access competition had forced the telephone companies to extend their networks into "lean" territories to preserve the competitive value of their systems. Regulators wanted to ensure that with the end of competition, service to remote or less profitable areas would continue. Thus, the application of utility regulation to the telephone companies brought with it "obligation to serve" requirements, or restrictions on a firm's freedom to exit from markets.[4] Naturally, the telephone companies wanted to ensure that the method of rate regulation allowed them to profitably sustain the scope of service regulators required of them. As a result, both regulators and the local telephone companies supported methods that based rates upon sustaining the telephone system as a whole.

Although the holistic approach to the rate base involved some averaging of costs, those were not perceived as subsidies but as a method of determining reasonable rates in a way that took into account the demand interdependence of telephone service. The principle that users paid rates not simply to recover the cost of the physical facilities they used, but rates that sustained the system as a whole, became known in the industry as "value of service" pricing. Value of service pricing is a logical expression of the first-generation universal service concept, because it attempts to recover the value of the network externality. Indeed, as chapter 6 showed, the pressures of access competition had induced the telephone companies to adopt similar policies on their own, before regulation.

The holistic approach, however, could be applied uniformly only within a single regulatory jurisdiction. When telephone calls crossed state boundaries, the rate base had to be divided into separate parts to distinguish between federal and state regulatory authority. That became known as the problem of jurisdictional separations.

---

4. *See, e.g.,* some of the cases cited in Alan Stone, Public Service Liberalism: Telecommunications and Transitions in Public Policy (Princeton University Press 1991).

In the 1920s, debate over jurisdictional separations took the specific form of how to separate the costs and revenue requirements of local-exchange service and long-distance service. There were two basic theories about how that should be done. One, the so-called board-to-board method, held that the rates for local service should recover all of the costs of the local exchange plant. Long-distance rates should recover only those additional costs required to supply facilities connecting the switchboards of local exchanges. The other principle was known as the station-to-station method, which held that because local exchange facilities were used in establishing a long-distance call, some of the costs of the local exchange plant and service should be recovered from long-distance rates. It traced costs from one telephone (station) to the other. That method was more complex in that the costs of the local network had to be divided or allocated among state and interstate services.

The Bell System supported board-to-board accounting—and for a very good reason. At that time, state regulation of rates was fairly stringent, whereas federal rate regulation was practically nonexistent. The long-distance business was increasingly profitable, while the Bell System viewed the consolidation of local service as an opportunity to raise what it viewed as the unremunerative rates foisted upon it by fifteen years of competition.[5] Brock has observed that "when there is differential regulation, the monopolist has an incentive to maximize the allocation of costs to the tightly regulated jurisdiction to justify higher regulated prices, while minimizing costs to the unregulated jurisdiction to capture [unregulated levels of] profit."[6] If AT&T could shift more of the allocated costs to the state jurisdiction, it could justify local rate increases and clear the way for higher long-distance profits.[7] State regulators, of course, had quite different incentives. Ratifying local rate increases made them look bad before their constituents, so they supported the station-to-station method.

For modern-day observers it is tempting to read a second-generation universal service promotion policy into that debate.

---

5. See chapter 11 for evidence of that.

6. GERALD BROCK, TELECOMMUNICATIONS POLICY FOR THE INFORMATION AGE (Harvard University Press 1994); *see also* TEMIN & GALAMBOS, *supra* note 3, at 20–22.

7. That fact by itself belies the claim that AT&T was then interested in promoting the modern concept of universal service.

Under the board-to-board method, local exchange access rates would be relatively higher and long-distance rates relatively lower. Under the station-to-station method, long-distance users pay more to support the local exchange plant. The station-to-station method can thus be seen as a means of using long-distance revenues to make local service more affordable. In fact, the debate over separations principles did take that form starting in the early 1950s. But from the 1920s until the end of World War II, the debate had no such implications.

That is apparent from the U.S. Supreme Court decisions that sanctioned the station-to-station principle, *Smith* v. *Illinois Bell* (1930) and *Lindheimer* v. *Illinois Bell* (1933).[8] The issue before the court was whether the rates imposed on the Chicago Telephone Company by the Illinois state commission were "confiscatory" under the Fourteenth Amendment. The Bell interests based their argument on board-to-board accounting methods. The Supreme Court rejected their method. It ruled that separation of interstate and intrastate plant "is essential to the appropriate recognition of the competent governmental authority in each field of regulation." Some part of the local exchange plant should be "apportioned" to interstate service, the court ruled, otherwise "the exchange property . . . will bear an undue burden." There is no indication that regulators were attempting to keep exchange rates low to stimulate telephone penetration, or that the regulators or the Supreme Court recognized subsidization of exchange access to promote universal service as a valid criterion in ratemaking. In fact, such considerations would definitely have been considered illegal. The "just and reasonable" rates mandated by regulation required establishing a link, as scientific as possible, between actual costs and the rates charged to customers. Rates that did not adequately compensate the telephone companies or that were designed to transfer wealth from one person to another could be challenged as confiscatory.

The courts and regulators were grappling with the issue of how to define the costs of a multiproduct firm, not pursuing a social welfare policy. Even if that had been their intention, the impact of separations practices on local rates would have been minimal. According to Gabel, the separations concepts prevailing in the 1920s and early 1930s would have relieved exchange property of

---

8. Smith *v.* Illinois Bell Tel. Co., 282 U.S. 133 (1930); Lindheimer *v.* Illinois Bell Tel. Co., 292 U.S. 151 (1933).

only 2 or 3 percent of the investment burden.[9] Even more important, the station-to-station principle, though sanctioned by the
Supreme Court in 1930, was not actually implemented on a nationwide basis until 1949. Thus, the growth of telephone penetration
from 1920 to 1950 cannot be attributed to the effects of that policy,
whatever its motives.

THE COMMUNICATIONS ACT OF 1934

The Communications Act of 1934 was passed after the House
Committee on Interstate and Foreign Commerce spent more than a
year investigating the communications industry. The congressional
committee probed not only AT&T but also independent telephone
holding companies, the telegraph industry, RCA, and the new
broadcasting networks. The committee suspected that the large
holding companies controlling communications were rife with financial abuses. AT&T attracted particular notice because, despite
its status as a monopoly, it operated free of effective regulation,
particularly at the interstate level. Its ability to move assets and
accounts between the federal and state jurisdictions in a way that
could manipulate the regulatory process was particularly troublesome to Congress. "The American Telephone and Telegraph Company," the committee's special counsel wrote, "is more powerful
and skilled than any state government with which it has to deal."[10]
The Interstate Commerce Commission should be relieved of regulatory authority over telephones, the committee believed, because it
was preoccupied with railroad regulation and thus lacked the resources to oversee the large and growing communications field.

In a report accompanying the draft bill, the committee described its purposes as: a codification of existing federal legislation
regulating communications; a transfer of jurisdictions from several
departments, boards, and commissions to a new communications
commission; and a postponement for further action after further
study and observation of some of the more difficult and controversial subjects.[11]

---

9. RICHARD GABEL, THE DEVELOPMENT OF SEPARATIONS CONCEPTS IN
THE TELEPHONE INDUSTRY 17 (Michigan State University Public Utilities
Studies 1967).

10. *Preliminary Report on Communication Companies* (submitted by Sam
Rayburn pursuant to H.R. 59 and House Joint Resolution 572, 72d Cong., Apr.
18, 1934), 73d Cong., H. Rept. No. 1273.

11. *Id.* at xxix.

From that it is clear that the Communications Act of 1934 was essentially a consolidation of federal regulatory authority over the burgeoning new telecommunications field. It was not the starting point of a new policy or a new approach to regulation, but the beginning of real regulation at the federal level.

"Universal service," in either its modern or classical sense, did not appear in the deliberations. Congressional records contain no mention of telephone penetration levels. There are no data in the reports purporting to show that an unacceptable number of people was unreached by the telephone network or unable to afford service. There is not even a discussion of the problem of jurisdictional separations. There are, instead, thousands of pages of materials analyzing the telephone and telegraph companies' capital structures, shareholders, ownership, and voting control, as well as interlocking directorates.

What, then, are we to make of the act's preamble, often cited as the mandate for the second-generation approach to universal service promotion? A complete citation of the preamble provides the basis for a more realistic understanding of its meaning:

> For the purpose of regulating interstate and foreign commerce in communication by wire and radio so as to make available, so far as possible, to all the people of the United States a rapid, efficient, Nation-wide, and world-wide wire and radio communication service with adequate facilities at reasonable charges, for the purpose of the national defense, for the purpose of promoting safety of life and property through the use of wire and radio communication, and for centralizing authority heretofore granted by law to several agencies and by granting additional authority with respect to interstate and foreign commerce in wire and radio communication, there is hereby created a commission to be known as the "Federal Communications Commission," which shall be constituted as hereinafter provided, and which shall execute and enforce the provisions of the Act.

The preamble contains a grab bag of extremely broad purposes, such as protecting national security and the safety of life and property, as well as a standard regulatory commission charge to ensure adequate facilities at reasonable charges. The absence of any concern with telephone penetration or separations principles, or of any specific provisions addressing those issues, suggests that that aspect of the law is merely a list of all the good things that come about from telecommunications.

But the most direct refutation of those who see a cryptic universal service policy in those two little lines of the preamble cited earlier comes from the behavior of the Federal Communications Commission itself. It did not immediately shift revenues from the federal jurisdiction to state jurisdictions to subsidize local service. On the contrary, between 1935 and 1945, the FCC succeeded in extracting a series of long-distance rate reductions from AT&T. The FCC had no interest in reducing local service rates via separations because that would have jeopardized its ability to deliver rate decreases in its own jurisdiction.

As the FCC was reducing interstate long-distance rates, the Bell System and other telephone companies were asking for, and often receiving, increases in state exchange rates and intrastate long-distance rates. The resulting disparity between state and interstate telephone rate trends was embarrassing to state regulators. Federal regulators seemed to be more effective, more able to "deliver the goods," than state regulators.

In reaction to the FCC's decreases in AT&T's interstate long-distance rates, state regulators eventually unified in support of the station-to-station principle, which would shift some of the intrastate costs to the federal jurisdiction, thereby preventing another interstate rate decrease and eliminating the pressure for more state rate increases.[12] At that time, AT&T also accepted the station-to-station principle because it could be used to counteract pressure for lower interstate long-distance rates.[13] By 1944, AT&T, state regulators, and the FCC were working together to develop a common approach to separations.

A comprehensive agreement about how to divide exchange and toll plants did not come until 1947 with the adoption of the first uniform *Separations Manual* by the National Association of Regulatory Utility Commissioners (NARUC) and the FCC. The Bell companies did not actually file intrastate tariffs that reflected the new cost separations methods until 1950.[14] Thus, the station-to-station method of separating costs was not fully operational at the national level until thirty years after the end of dual service. Despite the absence of any specific policy to promote or subsidize

---

12. *Id.* at 27–45.

13. TEMIN & GALAMBOS, *supra* note 3, at 22–25.

14. *See* CAROL WEINHAUS & ANTHONY OETTINGER, BEHIND THE TELE-PHONE DEBATES (Ablex 1988) for a detailed history and description of separations and settlements procedures.

local service, household penetration grew steadily from 1920 to 1950, faltering only for a few years during the depths of the Great Depression.

CROSS-SUBSIDIES AND LOCAL TELEPHONE SERVICE

After 1950, the formula used by regulators to allocate part of the costs of the local network to the long-distance rate base was based on "subscriber line use" (SLU), or the average proportion of minutes a subscriber's telephone line was used for state and interstate calls. In 1950 interstate SLU was less than 3 percent, so the impact of the station-to-station method on local rates was still minimal. Politicians and state regulators, however, were quick to realize the potential of separations to shift the cost burden among more or less favored constituencies. In 1951, as the FCC began a new inquiry into interstate rates, AT&T, with NARUC's support, proposed an alteration of the *Separations Manual* that would shift more of a local telephone plant into the interstate rate base.[15] The FCC opposed that plan on the grounds that it would lead to a situation in which "services subject to federal jurisdiction would, in effect, be subsidizing services beyond that jurisdiction."[16] The FCC's resistance was overcome, however, by the strenuous intervention of Senator Ernest W. McFarland of Arizona, the chairman of the Senate Subcommittee on Communications, who scolded the FCC for its willingness to shift the load from large national corporations to the "average housewife and professional man who do not indulge in a great deal of long distance."[17]

Thus, in 1952 and 1953 the interstate (long-distance) contribution to local exchange plant increased from 3 percent to 5 percent. The first step toward the use of long-distance revenues to subsidize local service had been taken.

A number of interpretive issues must be underscored here. First, the Federal Communications Commission actively opposed

---

15. TEMIN & GALAMBOS, *supra* note 3, at 24.
16. Letter from Paul A. Walker, FCC, to Matt L. McWhorter (Oct. 18, 1950).
17. Letter from Ernest W. McFarland to Paul A. Walker, Jan. 30, 1951, *cited in* TEMIN AND GALAMBOS, *supra* note 3, at 25.

the expansion of cross-subsidization. Second, neither NARUC nor Senator McFarland cited the preamble, or any other section of the Communications Act, in making the case for shifting the burden. Instead, NARUC was concerned about the growing disparity between state and interstate rates. And the senator did not argue that the "average housewife and business or professional man" would be unable to afford telephone service unless the burden was shifted.

Indeed, while the precedent was important, the impact of the 1952 separations change on local rates was still small. From 1952 to 1965, the percentage of local plant cost allocated to the interstate jurisdiction grew from 5 percent to 7 percent, while interstate SLU grew from 2.5 percent to 4 percent (see figure 13-1). As that occurred, the average monthly charge for residential telephone service, in constant 1980 dollars, actually increased from $14.25 in 1952 to $15.86 in 1955. In fact, average residential telephone service rates remained higher than their 1952 levels until 1965. While one could argue that rates would have gone up faster without the changes, it appears that no drastic subsidy was involved, particularly when compared with post-1970 changes. Despite that, household penetration continued to grow rapidly.

Full-fledged exploitation of the separations process to subsidize local service did not really begin until 1965. From 1952 to 1965 only 3 percent of the costs over and above SLU were shifted from the state to the interstate jurisdiction. During the seventeen years from 1965 to 1982, an additional 20 percent was so shifted.[18] From 1965 to 1969, the real average monthly charge for residential service dropped by $2. By 1982, it was almost half of what it had been in 1965. The adoption of the Ozark Plan in 1970 facilitated that process.[19] Although the Ozark Plan's separations were based in part on measures of relative use, its formulas effectively multiplied interstate minutes by a factor of three to establish the amount of local plant to be recovered from the interstate revenues. That led to a continuous and automatic increase in the cross-subsidy from 1971 on.

---

18. In 1965, as part of the Denver Plan, state and federal regulators increased the interstate allocation by nearly 3 percent. Only four years later, a new separations plan put forth by the FCC increased the interstate allocation by another 5 percent.

19. *See* WEINHAUS & OETTINGER 83–103 (1988) for a description and analysis of the Ozark Plan.

Figure 13-1

Percentage of Subscriber Plant Costs Allocated to Interstate Service

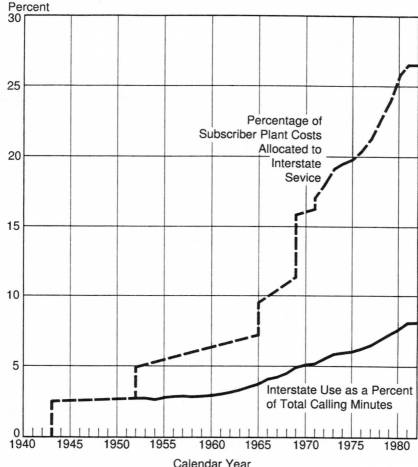

Source: AT&T data

The pressures to do that were simultaneously ideological, political, and regulatory. Consumer groups in the activist 1960s were pressuring utility commissions for lower rates.[20] Regulatory analysts were becoming aware of the social policy possibilities of the separations system. In 1967, for example, economist Richard

20. Horwitz notes that state regulators' support for the Ozark Plan was partly a response to pressure from public interest groups to keep residential

Gabel charged that the separations principles used by regulators penalized exchange ratepayers:

> Alternative separations treatment could reduce the costs of local exchange service and, eventually, exchange rates, making possible a universal development of exchange services.[21]

Most important, perhaps, was the desire to avoid upheavals. Regulators and telephone companies were faced with a precipitous drop in long-distance costs and a steep increase in the costs of labor-intensive local services. By shifting costs from the state to the interstate jurisdiction, regulators would avoid the kind of rapid price dislocations that would undoubtedly create political headaches.

Ironically, that move to exploit the social policy possibilities of the separations and settlements process came at a time when the justification for such a subsidy was weak, as at least 85 percent of all American households already had telephone service.[22]

Simple chronology thus defeats any attempt to attribute the growth of household penetration to a universal service policy formulated by the Communications Act and implemented by regulators and telephone companies. The use of rate regulation to lower the cost of local access was never part of the law but was a set of practices that evolved out of the debate over the proper way to separate the rate base into regulatory jurisdictions. And the policy kicked in at a time when the vast majority of American households already had telephone service.

THE RETROACTIVE REDEFINITION OF UNIVERSAL SERVICE

How did the obviously untrue myth that the Communications Act of 1934 fostered a national universal service policy take hold? The answer is that a major redefinition of universal service occurred in the 1970s, when long-distance competition began to threaten the

rates low. ROBERT B. HORWITZ, THE IRONY OF REGULATORY REFORM 235 (Oxford University Press 1989).

21. GABEL, *supra* note 9, at 5.

22. The FCC's STATISTICS OF COMMUNICATIONS COMMON CARRIERS for the year ended Dec. 31, 1965, reported that 85 percent of all American households had telephone service; the STATISTICS for 1970 reported that 92 percent of all households had telephones. Because the method used to measure household penetration at that time is thought to have overstated the actual amount, I have deducted 5 percent from each estimate, which yields a household penetration percentage of 87 for 1970 and 80 for 1965.

new separations practices adopted by federal and state regulators. By targeting long-distance routes for selective entry, competition struck at the heart of rate-regulated monopoly. Long-distance services had been assigned higher costs due to the new separations methodology embodied in the Ozark Plan. New long-distance networks such as MCI and Sprint were not required to allocate a portion of their costs to local service; they simply ordered local business lines from AT&T at the normal (subsidized) rates to gain access to local users. They therefore had a built-in cost advantage over AT&T.

The political challenge that represented forced AT&T and state regulators to develop an explicit rationale for regulated monopoly and its system of separations and settlements. In that struggle, the concept of universal service was redefined in a way that linked it to the practices of regulated monopoly. Regulated monopoly and its separations practices were retroactively credited with making telephone service universally available and affordable.

Three milestones in that reconstruction can be clearly identified. One was a speech before NARUC in late 1973 by AT&T chief executive officer John B. DeButts. The second was a report submitted to Congress by Eugene V. Rostow on behalf of AT&T in 1975. The third was the Bell System's proposal in 1976 to reform the 1934 Communications Act to preserve regulated monopoly.

By the early 1970s, the FCC's incremental opening of AT&T's markets to competition had provoked a crisis in telecommunications policy. The Bell System felt itself besieged on many fronts, confronted with an ambiguous and shifting set of rules. One strategy was to gradually accommodate itself to the new order; another was to stand its ground and fight for the old order. In 1973 DeButts chose the latter option. In a speech before NARUC he took a stance against competition and in favor of traditional public service regulation. His speech, entitled "An Unusual Obligation," harkened to the earliest years of regulation in the 1920s and invoked the special social contract between a regulator and a regulated firm.

That attempt to provoke a public dialogue was next extended into the legislative arena. Bell began to promote congressional action to protect itself from new competition. Eugene V. Rostow, the chairman of President Johnson's 1968 Task Force on Communications Policy, was retained by AT&T to support its legislative efforts. In 1975, he submitted testimony to Congress entitled "The Case for Congressional Action to Safeguard the Telephone Network as a Universal and Optimized System.''[23] That testimony first aired the specious claim that a monopoly system devoted to universal service was part of the mandate of the 1934 Communications Act.

Bell, however, considered the existing Communications Act far too weak a foundation for its case, so it prepared an amendment, the Consumer Communications Reform Act of 1976, the so-called Bell bill.[24] According to Temin and Galambos, the bill bluntly stated that existing rate structure, by which it meant primarily separations, had promoted universal service.[25]

We have only to look at the context of those events to understand why Bell was trying to persuade Congress to preserve the traditional monopoly structure. The Justice Department had just filed the antitrust suit that eventually led to the breakup of AT&T. And MCI had invaded switched long-distance with its *Execunet* service in 1975, a development that threatened to subvert the whole station-to-station approach to separations.

During the battle over the Bell bill and the ensuing years of antitrust proceedings, "universal service" became a political weapon for defenders of regulated monopoly and lost its historical meaning. Although AT&T's political objectives did eventually fail, its historical revisionism was an overwhelming success. The confusion between the contemporary and historical usages of "universal service" has made it difficult for modern scholars and policymakers to appreciate the significance of the earlier "universal service" period. And the contemporary meaning has unfairly eclipsed the contribution of access competition to the development of a ubiquitous telephone infrastructure.

---

23. Eugene V. Rostow, The Case for Congressional Action to Safeguard the Telephone Network as a Universal and Optimized System (paper based on the memorandum prepared for AT&T for use in the Nov. 1975 hearings before the Subcommittee on Communications of the House Committee on Interstate and Foreign Commerce).

24. The proposed Consumer Communications Act of 1976 quickly acquired the "Bell bill" label because of AT&T's sponsorship and all-out lobbying effort on its behalf.

25. TEMIN & GALAMBOS, *supra* note 3, at 119.

14

Universal Service in the 1990s

UNIVERSAL SERVICE REMAINS a focal point of telecommunications policy in the 1990s, not only in the United States, but in every other country that has begun to liberalize or deregulate its telecommunications industry. The new policy dialogue revolves around four questions. First, how much do the universal service obligations of incumbent telephone companies cost? Second, how can those costs be financed in a competitive environment? Third, what kind of technical and pricing arrangements should be made to interconnect incumbent telephone companies with the new, competing networks? Finally, should the service bundle designated as "universal service" be redefined to take into account new technologies, and if so, how?[1]

In the United States, debate over those issues reached a milestone when the U.S. Congress passed the Telecommunications Act of 1996.[2] The new law is the first comprehensive revision of the Communications Act of 1934 and culminates twenty years of legislative struggle over how to adapt federal law to the new

---

1. So far that aspect of the debate has been confined to the United States, whereas the first two have been actively debated in every country that has liberalized its industry. For samples of the U.S. debate over new definitions of universal service, see the transcripts of hearings of the NTIA Universal Service Working Group, chaired by Larry Irving, assistant secretary for communications of the Commerce Department, held in Albuquerque, New Mexico, December 13, 1993, Los Angeles, California, February 16, 1994, and Indianapolis, Indiana, July 12, 1994.

2. Telecommunications Act of 1996, Pub. L. 104-104, 110 Stat. 56 (Feb. 8, 1986) [hereinafter *Telecommunications Act*].

realities of telecommunications. In effect, the new law codifies the perceived wisdom about interconnection, competition, and universal service in telecommunications. Because one of the chief purposes of this book is to mount a historically grounded challenge to that orthodoxy, the new law provides the perfect foil for a critique that links the historical and contemporary policy debates over universal service.

The first section of this chapter analyzes the universal service section of the law and shows how it is meant to codify the second-generation universal service policy. A critique of the assumptions of that portion of the act follows. The second section concentrates on the law's interconnection provisions and shows why "procompetitive" interconnection policies are responsible for the perceived crisis in universal service support. That section also links historical experience with interconnection and competition to current controversies over access pricing and interconnection.

THE CREATION OF A NEW ENTITLEMENT: ANALYSIS OF THE NEW UNIVERSAL SERVICE LEGISLATION

The first generation of universal service policy (1907–1921) aimed at unifying service so that all telephone subscribers could speak to each other. During the crisis of the Bell System in the mid-1970s, universal service was redefined as an industry-government commitment to put a telephone in every home. That second-generation universal service policy invented a mandate from the 1934 Communications Act and claimed credit for making telephone service available and affordable to nearly all Americans. Both claims, as we have seen, are myths.[3]

Nevertheless, the idea that America's basic communications law contained a commitment to something called "universal service" stuck. And that is what is so eerily fascinating about the Telecommunications Act of 1996. In a weirdly posthumous political victory, the mythology of universal service created by the old order has become the law of the land.

---

3. *See* L. J. PERL, RESIDENTIAL DEMAND FOR TELEPHONE SERVICE (National Economic Research Associates 1983); Alexander C. Larson, Thomas J. Makarewicz & Calvin S. Monson, *The Effect of Subscriber Line Charges on Residential Telephone Bills*, 13 TELECOM. POL. 337 (1989); Jerry A. Hausman, T. Tardiff & A. Belinfante, *The Effects of the Breakup of AT&T on Telephone Penetration in the United States*, 83 AM. ECON. REV. 178 (1993).

The Telecommunications Act of 1996 has an entire section devoted to universal service.[4] According to a committee report accompanying the draft bill, the goal of the new section is

> to clearly articulate the policy of Congress that universal service is a cornerstone of the Nation's communications system. This new section is intended to make explicit the current implicit authority of the FCC and the States to require common carriers to provide universal service.[5]

That statement comes close to revealing that there was no prior explicit legislative authority for universal service.

Subsection (b) of section 254 requires the FCC to define "universal service" based on recommendations from the public, Congress, and a joint board of state and federal regulators. The language makes it clear that universal service obligations need no longer be confined to traditional telephone service. Universal service is to be an "evolving level of telecommunications services," and the definition must take into account advances in telecommunications and information technology.[6] The FCC must include, at a minimum, any telecommunications service to which a substantial majority of residential customers subscribe. It must also revise and update the definition periodically.

Further, the law specifically provides that "quality services should be available at just, reasonable, and affordable rates."[7] The FCC must, therefore, decide what is "affordable" and supply subsidies to any providers whose costs of providing the designated service exceed the affordability targets. Here again, the new legisla-

---

4. *Telecommunications Act, supra* note 2, § 254.

5. Committee Report on the Telecommunications Competition and Deregulation Act of 1995 (Lawrence Pressler, chairman, Senate Committee on Commerce, Science, and Transportation) to June E. O'Neill, director, Congressional Budget Office (March 28, 1995).

6. The bill lists the following principles regarding which services should be eligible to be included under the rubric of universal service. Eligible telecommunications services must be essential to education, public health, or public safety. They must have, through the operation of market choices by customers, been subscribed to by a substantial majority of residential customers. In addition, they must be deployed in public telecommunications networks by telecommunications carriers. Finally, they must be consistent with the public interest, convenience, and necessity. *Telecommunications Act, supra* note 2, § 254(c).

7. *Id*. § 254(b) (universal service principles).

tion codifies the mythology of universal service. "Affordability" was a post hoc rationale for the rate regulations and cross-subsidies of the AT&T monopoly during the 1970s. But the original system of utility regulation was intended to make sure that "just and reasonable" rates were those based on demonstrated costs plus a fair return to capital, not on whether specific groups could afford them. The addition of the word "affordable" to the new law, therefore, is highly significant; it gives regulators an explicit mandate to depart from cost standards in rate setting.

Financial contributions to the preservation and advancement of universal service will be provided by "all telecommunications carriers providing interstate telecommunications services."[8] Only carriers designated under the new section 214(e) will be eligible to receive universal service support. Section 254(e) also requires that all universal service support be "explicit." Those sections of the law are intended to improve the postdivestiture system of universal service support by making subsidies transparent and competitively neutral. As the previous chapter explained, the post-1984 system of universal service support still relies almost entirely on having long-distance rates subsidize local service rates. The long-distance carriers feel that it not only distorts the market, but imposes upon them a competitive disadvantage as they begin to compete directly with local exchange providers. Depending on how they are implemented, those aspects of the law could improve the efficiency and fairness of the support system. But they also greatly expand the scope of universal service policy. Under the second-generation policy, universal service subsidies were confined to basic telephone service, and both the cost obligations and the supports were internalized within franchised monopolies. The new law requires a constantly updated definition of universal service, and to support that definition the FCC is authorized to extend regulatory taxation to all telecommunications service providers. That could have far-reaching implications for the development of information and communications markets. If, to cite just one example, Internet service

---

8. *Id.* § 254(d). The commission is given specific authority to exempt a telecommunications carrier or class of telecommunications carriers from that requirement if their contribution would be *de minimis*—if the administrative cost of collecting contributions from a carrier would exceed the contribution that carrier would otherwise have to make under the formula for contributions selected by the commission.

providers were classified as telecommunications carriers because some of their users install voice communication software, they could be required to pay fees to support universal service.

The law also mandates geographic equality in the provision of advanced services.[9] All consumers should have access to telecommunications and information services "reasonably comparable" to those available in urban areas, at rates "reasonably comparable to those of urban areas." Those aspects of the law appear to have been derived from highly publicized concerns about "electronic redlining"—the fear that telecommunication companies might deliberately ignore certain regions or neighborhoods as they construct the information superhighway. That kind of requirement regarding the rollout of new services and technologies is unprecedented in U.S. communications law and regulation.

Section 254(g) of the new law codifies the policies of geographic rate averaging and rate integration of interexchange services to ensure that subscribers in rural and high-cost areas continue to receive both intrastate and interstate long-distance services at rates no higher than those paid by urban subscribers.[10] Actual costs have more to do with route density than distance, but in the transition to competition and deregulation, rural telephone companies and rural legislators have opposed tenaciously any attempt to permit the deaveraging of long distance rates, using "universal service" as their rationale. Indeed, federal regulations already required long-distance carriers to average long-distance rates, while allowing for certain exceptions.[11]

The pattern of explicitly authorizing subsidies that were only implicit under the regulated monopoly regime is taken to new and unprecedented lengths where the act enumerates provisions

---

9. Access to advanced telecommunications and information services should be provided in all regions of the nation. *Id.* § 254(b).

10. *Id.* § 254(g).

11. Brock shows how the AT&T Hi-Lo private line tariff of 1973, which based rates on route density rather than distance, was a response to MCI's competition. *See* GERALD BROCK, TELECOMMUNICATIONS POLICY FOR THE INFORMATION AGE (Harvard University Press 1994). The policies supporting rate averaging are contained in Integration of Rates and Services for the Provision of Communications by Authorized Common Carriers between the United States Mainland and the Offshore Points of Hawaii, Alaska, and Puerto Rico/Virgin Islands, 61 F.C.C.2d 380 (1976).

intended to subsidize telecommunications access and usage by schools, health care facilities, and libraries. Schools and libraries will receive whatever is designated "universal service" at discounted rates.[12] Here the concept of affordability makes another appearance, being designated as the standard for determining how much of a discount will be required. In subsection (b), where seven basic principles to be used by the FCC in defining universal service policy are enumerated, the sixth principle provides that "elementary and secondary school classrooms, health care providers, and libraries should have access to advanced telecommunication and information services."[13] The FCC has not yet determined what "advanced services" are, but the specification that access should be provided in each classroom, rather than in one or more points in a school building, is an expansive vision.[14] Low-income consumers are also identified as one of the act's beneficiaries.

To summarize, the new universal service section is notable for two major reasons. First, the law effectively codifies the universal service mythology created in the 1970s by the regulated monopoly system. Despite the claims of Congress and the president that the rewrite makes U.S. law "catch up with the future,"[15] the new law buys heavily into that philosophical holdover from the regulated monopoly era. It attempts to preserve the geographic cross-subsidies of the old system and assumes that a standard level of new telecommunications service will never become universal unless the federal government designates it as such and subsidizes it. Second, the new law moves beyond the old universal service mythology to explicitly embrace the manipulation of telecommunications policies

---

12. *Telecommunications Act, supra* note 2, § 254 (g)(1)(B).

13. That is elaborated in *id.* § 254(h)(2)(A).

14. A taste of what is in store for the industry was provided by testimony from the Council of Chief State School Officers before the Joint Board. The board was urged to make "unbundled broadband switching and transmission capacity capable of delivering high-quality video; and classroom and library access, including high-speed, broadband circuits to the building demarcation point, and inside wiring to all classrooms" the standard for advanced services. Testimony of Gordon Amsbach, executive director, Council of Chief State School Officers, before the Federal-State Joint Board on CC Dkt. No. 96-45, Universal Services for Elementary and Secondary Education and Libraries, April 12, 1996.

15. President William J. Clinton, *quoted in* E. Andrews, *Communications Bill Signed, and the Battle Begins Anew*, N.Y. TIMES, Feb. 9, 1996.

and rates to favor designated constituencies. Concepts of affordability and subsidization, which in the past were only *post hoc*
rationalizations for regulatory practices, are now explicit parts of
the law. Telecommunications service has become a new enti-
tlement.

Critique of Section 254

Most policy debate about the universal service section of the new
telecommunications law is concerned with technicalities, such as
what shall be included under the definition of universal service and
the specific mechanisms to be used to fund it.[16] While those issues
are important, they are peripheral to the basic policy assumptions
on which section 254 is based. Those assumptions fall into four
broad classifications. First, it is inappropriate to rely exclusively
on market mechanisms to promote the diffusion of basic and
advanced telecommunications services. Second, local telecommunications access must be subsidized if it is to become universally
affordable. Third, it is both possible and desirable to designate a
particular type of service as the "universal" service. Finally, it
is possible to reconcile the goal of a competitive, deregulated
telecommunications marketplace with universal service subsidies.
Those assumptions went virtually unquestioned during the drafting
of the new legislation, yet all of them are open to serious challenge.

The Facts about Phonelessness. One of the key assumptions of the
second-generation universal policy was that the price of local
telephone access should be the critical area of policy intervention.
The main reason to shift cost recovery from the state to the
interstate jurisdiction, regulators claimed, was to make service
more affordable to more people. Thus, the affordability of telephone service was equated with the price of the monthly line rental.
The new legislation emerged from the same philosophy. It proposes
to designate a core set of services as "essential" and use intrain-
dustry subsidies to make sure the monthly rate for those services
is set at "affordable" levels. The only difference is that the new
law attempts to make the subsidization process more explicit and

---

16. *See* reply comments of AT&T Corp., In the Matter of Federal-State
Joint Board on Universal Service, CC Dkt. No. 96-45 (May 7, 1996).

to distribute the burden of subsidization in a "competitively neutral" manner.

A recent spate of empirical research on disconnection and phoneless households, however, has completely destroyed the rationale for that approach to universal service policy. Between 1993 and 1995, four different studies of households without telephone service were conducted.[17] All four found that the monthly price of basic local service is not the most important factor affecting the affordability of telephone service. Marginal users are driven off or prevented from joining the network by a combination of the following factors: unpaid bills or bad credit records relating to toll calls; deposits and installation fees; and call control issues. Of those, a household's inability to pay usage-related costs is usually the most important. The studies estimate that anywhere from two-thirds to three-fourths of all households without telephone service have had service in the past but were unable to keep it.[18]

As utility regulators have become more aware of the importance of usage bills on telephone penetration they have begun to look more closely at the telephone companies' disconnection policies and practices.[19] As the features and capabilities of the public network increase, the risk that some consumers will spend beyond their means also increases, so service providers must protect themselves against uncollectible bills or bad credit risks in some way. The key issue in universal service policy, then, is how to

---

17. Chesapeake and Potomac Telephone Company's Submission of Telephone Penetration Studies, Formal Case No. 850 (filed October 4, 1993); Field Research Corporation, *Affordability of Telephone Service—A Survey of Customers and Noncustomers*, 1993 (study funded by GTE-California and Pacific Bell, mandated by the California Public Utilities Commission); Milton Mueller & Jorge R. Schement, *Universal Service from the Bottom Up: A Profile of Telecommunications Access in Camden, New Jersey*, 12 INFORMATION SOCIETY 3 (April 1996); John Horrigan & Lodis Rhodes, The Evolution of Universal Service in Texas (September 1995) (working paper, LBJ School of Public Affairs).

18. In the California study, 65 percent of all phoneless households had had telephone service in the past but were unable to keep it for that reason. In the Texas study, 77 percent had had telephone service, and 54 percent had had it within the past three years. In the Camden study, two-thirds of the respondents without phones had had service but had been disconnected.

19. Notice of Proposed Rulemaking, In the Matter of Amendment of the Commissions Rules and Policies to Increase Subscribership and Usage of the Public Switched Network, CC Dkt. 95-115 (July 20, 1995).

maximize access while minimizing credit risk. In such an environment, totally new approaches to whether, when, and how to subsidize must be devised. Despite all the toil and trouble it will take to implement it, the old, second-generation policy of access subsidies is largely irrelevant.

Heterogeneous Access and the Market's Role in Promoting Affordability. There is an even more fundamental problem with the second-generation policy in the contemporary environment. Telephone service was once simple and homogeneous. The new legislation assumes that the new telecommunications access will also be simple and homogeneous, as evidenced in the law's requirement that anything subscribed to by a substantial majority of Americans must incur universal obligations. It is also apparent in the legislation's requirement that "advanced services" be available everywhere. Much has been written about how to define the "new" universal service.[20] How much bandwidth and what features and functions will it involve? Will it include Internet and other data communications, cable as well as telephony, wireless as well as wireline? At bottom, the whole dialogue is a futile attempt to pour the old wine of regulated monopoly telecommunications into the new bottles of a digital marketplace. It assumes that a digital broadband network will, like the telephone system of the past, reach into every home with a uniform grade of service, allowing the population to be neatly categorized into those who can afford that level of service (the "information haves") and those who cannot (the "information have-nots").

One of the few safe predictions we can make about the future of information technology is that such a simple dichotomous out-

---

20. *See* W. G. Lavey, *Universal Telecommunications Infrastructure for Information Services*, 42 FED. COMM. L. J. 151 (1990); S. Hadden, *Technologies of Universal Service, in* UNIVERSAL TELEPHONE SERVICE: READY FOR THE 21st CENTURY? 53 (Institute for Information Studies 1991); NTIA, THE NTIA INFRASTRUCTURE REPORT: TELECOMMUNICATIONS IN THE AGE OF INFORMATION (Government Printing Office 1990). For an interesting critique of attempts to develop an a priori definition of universal service, *see* H. Sawhney, *Universal Service: Prosaic Motives and Great Ideals, in* TOWARD A COMPETITIVE TELECOMMUNICATIONS INDUSTRY: SELECTED PAPERS FROM THE 1994 TELECOMMUNICATIONS POLICY RESEARCH CONFERENCE 205 (Gerald Brock ed., Lawrence Erlbaum Associates 1995).

come will not happen. The new telecommunications infrastructure will not be a digitized, broadband version of the old one. The idea of "basic service" will soon be obsolete, if it is not already, because communications access is taking an ever-wider variety of forms. There is a broad spectrum of access types and a very broad range of information transmitting and processing capabilities. Access can be provided, for example, by a two-way pager, a debit card, a traditional telephone, a fixed or mobile computer in the home, or a terminal in a public space. Functions can be precisely tailored to specific market segments; customization, not uniformity, is the rule. That is most evident in wireless communications, where the market is generating a bewildering variety of terminals, interfaces, access methods, and service grades.

In its rush to codify the second-generation concept of universal service, the new law overlooks what is, from the standpoint of truly universal telecommunications, the most promising feature of the new competitive marketplace: the enhanced ability to tailor the price and capability of service to specific user needs and socioeconomic constraints. No single form of telecommunications access can be classified as absolutely necessary for all people. If the FCC attempts to define and subsidize a "universal" service, the commission will simply waste a vast amount of resources on suboptimal solutions. Further, it may discourage the market from discovering and supplying the solutions that are optimal for various groups.[21]

Explicit Funding and Competitive Neutrality. Two key objectives of the new universal service section are to make subsidies "explicit" rather than "implicit" and to ensure that universal service support payments are competitively neutral. In other words, subsidies should be readily quantifiable and their distribution clearly accounted for, rather than buried within regulations and complex cost allocation procedures. The collection and distribution of subsidies, moreover, should not favor one competitor or one type

---

21. The case of Juno Online Services, L.P., provides an interesting example of how far behind the market the new legislation already is. Juno offers free electronic mail service using advertiser support. Users get an account, an e-mail address, and unlimited usage at no cost, but a portion of their computer screen displays advertising.

of technology, but should allow the most efficient company or technology to be used. Economists who are normally critics of cross-subsidies and distorted rates can make their peace with a universal service program that meets those criteria.

The pre-1996 system of universal service subsidies was neither explicit nor competitively neutral. Traffic-sensitive elements of the network (long-distance access) were taxed to support non-traffic-sensitive elements such as the local loop. One study estimated that implicit subsidies, combining urban-to-rural transfers, business-to-residential transfers, and long-distance-to-local transfers, totaled $15.3 billion dollars a year, whereas the explicit subsidies of the Universal Service Fund and other sources totaled only $2.5 billion.[22] The prior system favored incumbent local exchange carriers' (LECs) wireline networks. By keeping the rates of incumbent LECs artificially low, regulations made it unattractive for long-distance carriers or new technologies such as wireless personal communication networks to compete in local access markets.

The new universal service legislation requires the FCC to identify an affordable rate and then to calculate the costs of serving a particular area. If the cost of service exceeds the affordable rate, then a subsidy equal to the difference between the two will be made available. Under the new legislation, any telecommunications service provider, not just incumbent LECs, is eligible to receive that subsidy if it serves customers in an area qualifying for subsidization.[23]

In that respect the new law's intentions were good. A complete overhaul of the universal service support system that succeeded in making all subsidies transparent and competitively neutral would benefit everyone (except, perhaps, incumbent LECs who are irretrievably inefficient). But that goal is fundamentally incompatible with many other aspects of the law. In all likelihood, transparency and competitive neutrality will remain elusive goals.

To begin with, the law requires the FCC to include some services within the definition of universal service and exclude

---

22. Wayne Leighton, *Telecommunication Subsidies: Reach Out and Fund Someone (Whether You Want to or Not)* (Citizens for a Sound Economy Issues and Answers Series 1995).

23. Small rural telephone companies, however, have been exempted from the portability requirement. That was done to protect them from competition for the very large subsidies they often receive.

others. That by itself is an important breach of competitive neutrality. An enormous range of telecommunication and information services, such as cable television, on-line information services, paging services, and voice mail, will probably never be subsidized. Subsidies are also limited to a special class of carriers. The law specifies that the distribution of universal service subsidies be nondiscriminatory. That is important for competitive neutrality, because it means that both new entrants and incumbents can compete for subsidies. But the law exempts small rural telephone companies from that requirement. Since a large portion of the high-cost telephone lines are served by those companies, that aspect of the law seriously undermines the goal of competitive neutrality.

In short, the new universal service mechanisms keep the FCC in the business of classifying technology and applying different rules to different categories—an activity that has proven to be a source of never-ending headaches ever since it tried to draw a line between telephones and computers in the 1960s. As technology shifts and new services start to undercut the market share of older firms and services, we can expect to see rancorous debates about which companies are eligible to pay out and receive universal service subsidies. If such debates result in a "competitively neutral" outcome, that will be nothing short of a miracle. If the FCC was really interested in competitive neutrality, it would simply step out of the way and let market choices determine the diffusion of services.

INTERCONNECTION OF COMPETING NETWORKS

The issue of interconnecting competing networks has emerged as the preeminent telecommunications policy problem of the present day, just as it was in the early 1900s.[24] The prevailing view of the role of interconnection in telecommunications competition, however, turns the older viewpoint on its head. Where Bell and the

24. *See* WERNER NEU & KARL-HEINZ NEUMANN, INTERCONNECTION AGREEMENTS IN TELECOMMUNICATIONS (Wissenschaftliches Institut fur Kommunikationsdienste Working Paper No. 106, 1993); MILTON MUELLER, NEW ZEALAND TELECOMMUNICATIONS AND THE PROBLEM OF INTERCONNECTING COMPETING NETWORKS (Reason Foundation Policy Study No. 177 1994); Martin Cave, *Interconnection, Separate Accounting, and the Development of Competition in UK Telecommunications* (Institute of Economic Affairs Lectures on Regulation 1993).

independents actively competed on the basis of their scope, current policy strives to ensure that no network can derive a competitive advantage from its "bottleneck" control of access. Contemporary policy favors unbundling network elements, nondiscriminatory pricing based on incremental costs, and equalization of technological conditions among competing networks. The rest of this section describes the new approach to interconnection policy and assesses it in the light of the historical experience.

The modern approach to interconnection policy developed gradually during the 1970s and 1980s. It started with terminal equipment deregulation[25] and gained momentum during regulatory experience with long-distance competition.[26] Both were perceived as successful experiments with unbundling the elements of what had been an integrated telephone network under the end-to-end control of monopolies. After 1985, regulators and new entrants pushed for extending the concepts of unbundling and nondiscriminatory pricing even further, into the elements of the local exchange.[27] The new policy doctrine regarding interconnection purports to give us the best of all possible worlds. "Open access" fosters competition, but without the fragmentation of the dual service era; it permits unified service, but without monopoly or even, perhaps, much regulation. It almost sounds too good to be true. It probably is.

Interconnection and the Telecommunications Act of 1996

The Telecommunications Act of 1996 codifies the new approach to interconnection policy. The basic principles of what had been an evolving set of policies and practices implemented by regulators at state and federal levels are now written into law. There are still numerous regulatory details to be resolved and some room for

---

25. Deregulation of end-user equipment established a standardized interface between customer premises equipment and a public network, paving the way for vigorous competition in PBX and telephone set markets.

26. The struggle between AT&T and new common carriers over the terms and conditions of toll interconnection gave birth to concepts of "equal access," a combination of dialing parity and nondiscriminatory pricing of long-distance access to the local exchange.

27. *See, e.g.*, Filing and Review of Open Network Architecture Plans, 4 F.C.C. Rec. 1 (1989).

variation across states, but the principles of unbundled access and nondiscriminatory pricing are fixed.

Part II of the 1996 Act, "Development of Competitive Markets," deals most extensively with interconnection. Section 251 enumerates the obligations of local exchange carriers regarding interconnection. Those include a general obligation to interconnect and a prohibition against installing network features, functions, or capabilities that contradict the principles of "nondiscriminatory accessibility by the broadest number of users and vendors of communications products and services," or that impair "the ability of users and information providers to seamlessly and transparently transmit and receive information between and across telecommunications networks."[28] That aspect of the new law could be seen as a modern-day restatement of the first-generation universal service policy, but the attempt to maintain classical universal service in an environment of multiple, competing networks leads to a very different approach to interconnection terms and conditions.

Thus, section 251 prevents all local exchange carriers from prohibiting or limiting the resale of their telecommunications services. Number portability and dialing parity must be provided to competing providers of telephone exchange service and long-distance service. All competing providers must have nondiscriminatory access to telephone numbers, operator services, directory assistance, and directory listing, with no unreasonable dialing delays. The section also regulates access to poles, ducts, conduits, and rights of way and imposes a duty to establish reciprocal compensation arrangements for the transport and termination of telecommunications traffic. The object is to make the scope, and to some extent the performance, of any network equivalent from the standpoint of the end user.

The local exchange carriers described as "incumbents"—the established monopoly carriers—have an additional set of obligations, designed to level the playing field. Incumbent LECs are required to provide "nondiscriminatory access to network elements on an unbundled basis" at any "technically feasible" point. Rates, terms, and conditions of interconnection must be "just, reasonable, and nondiscriminatory."[29] Incumbent LECs must offer for resale at discounted ("wholesale") rates any telecommunications service

---

28. *Telecommunications Act, supra* note 2, § 256(a)(1)–(2).
29. *Id.* § 251 (c)(3).

that they provide at retail to other subscribers.[30] They must issue public notices of any changes in their network that would affect its ability to operate with other networks. They must allow competing operators to install ("collocate") equipment necessary for interconnection or access to unbundled network elements at an incumbent's central switching office.[31] Those obligations are intended to diminish any competitive advantage a LEC might obtain from its current control of subscriber access, thereby eliminating the need for its competitors to duplicate its infrastructure to compete effectively.

The principle of open and nondiscriminatory interconnection is fairly easy to articulate. The difficult part is determining how much telecommunication carriers should pay one another for fulfilling those obligations. On that subject, the law offers some broad guidelines, but leaves much to the discretion of state and federal regulatory commissions. "Just and reasonable" rates for interconnection and network elements are defined in Section 252(d) as "based on cost,"[32] "nondiscriminatory," and "includ[ing] a reasonable profit." Charges for transport and termination of traffic are "just and reasonable" if they "provide for the mutual and reciprocal recovery by each carrier of costs associated with transport and termination." State commissions must approve any interconnection agreements adopted through negotiation or arbitration and may reject them if they discriminate against a telecommunications carrier not a party to the agreement, or if the agreement is not consistent with "the public interest, convenience, and necessity."

By unbundling the network and eliminating all discriminatory pricing, the new interconnection policy encourages radical deaveraging of rates. Each individual component of a network will be priced on a stand-alone basis. Cross-subsidies will be shaken out of the network entirely. That goal, however, directly contradicts the legislation's call for universal service subsidies and rate averaging in section 254. Indeed, section 254 appears to be designed to prevent precisely the kind of radical restructuring of prices that the new approach to interconnection appears to make inevitable. That

---

30. *Id.* § 251 (c)(4).

31. *Id.* § 251 (c)(6). The incumbent carrier may provide for "virtual" collocation if the local exchange carrier demonstrates to a state commission that physical collocation is not practical for technical reasons or because of space limitations.

32. The new law specifically excludes using rate-of-return or other rate-base proceedings to determine cost. *Id.* § 252 (d)(1)(A)(i).

contradictory logic and policy, however, has a compelling political rationale. In delivering open access interconnection, the new legislation was responding to the demands of powerful business interests in the telecommunications industry who view LECs in general and the regional Bell operating companies in particular as bottleneck monopolies. In drafting the universal service section, Congress was responding to a different constituency: rural telephone companies, public interest groups, schools, hospitals, libraries, and end users.

Historical Comparisons

Much can be learned by comparing the interconnection policy of the early competitive era with contemporary policies, not to argue that the older views are perfectly correct or directly applicable to the current situation. Such a comparison illuminates some of the economic and regulatory issues inherent in the modern approach to interconnection policy.

History provides some interesting counterexamples to the prevailing wisdom about interconnection and competition. We have seen that the Bell System's refusal to deal with its competitors did not foreclose competition. Despite its seventeen-year head start and its superior capital resources, the Bell System could not destroy the growth of the independents. Of course, that growth occurred in a market with plenty of room for additional development.

Current doctrine assumes that unbundling and interconnection among competitors is always conducive to consumer choice. Historically, however, facilities-based competition in the local exchange market was discouraged and sometimes eliminated by interconnection. Bell's sublicensing of independent exchanges was the most damaging blow to the independent movement, as it removed much of the incentive to develop an alternative infrastructure. That experience also contradicts the modern assumption that dominant incumbents have no incentive to interconnect with smaller competitors. Without any prodding from regulators, Bell progressively liberalized its interconnection terms and conditions from 1901 to 1912 to prevent an alternative system from developing.

Most economists believe that intranetwork cross-subsidies or transfers of revenues would not exist in a competitive market. That belief is also contradicted by the historical evidence. Under a regime of access competition telephone networks often sustained their large scope by averaging rates and costs. Intrasystem averaging seemed to be sustainable as long as the competing systems were not interconnected. During the competitive era, the Bell System established many small exchanges in outlying areas and sustained them in part through toll usage revenues.

Nondiscriminatory Pricing and Appropriability. Perhaps the most crucial distinction between the old and new policies involves the issue of discrimination. The regulatory policies of the 1990s and the new telecommunications act require nondiscriminatory interconnection among competing networks. The policy is intended to eliminate any competitive advantage a network might gain from controlling access to subscribers. Access competition in the early 1900s, on the other hand, was based on the right of networks to discriminate between the terms and conditions they offered to end users and competitors. The belief then was that competing networks ought to enjoy some reward for enlarging their scope and that suppliers could rightfully exclude competitors from enjoying those fruits. Earlier in this book I referred to that as the appropriability issue.

By now it should be evident that the incentives associated with appropriability played a major role in the development of the American telephone system. Competition between the Bell System and the independents between 1894 and 1920 was structured as a system rivalry between unconnected local exchanges and toll networks. That gave both competitors a powerful incentive to make their networks as universal as possible. Current interconnection policies appear to have the opposite effect. Unbundling and nondiscriminatory interconnection will encourage radical deaveraging of rates, pushing up costs for many marginal subscribers, while allowing new entrants to concentrate on the most profitable network segments and locations.

The salience of the appropriability problem hinges upon what the new networks pay for access to the incumbent. If the price of access compensates an incumbent adequately for its large scope, then interconnection with a competitor does not harm the incumbent. If the price a competing network pays is no different from that of any ordinary user, then parasitism may in fact occur.

The modern approach to access pricing in telecommunications does not recognize the existence of an appropriability problem. It is more concerned with the survival of small competitors in the face of what it sees as the overwhelming advantages of larger, incumbent networks. Such a policy does have important advantages: It eases the entry of new firms into the marketplace, thereby putting pressure on an incumbent to improve its service and rationalize its prices. Those advantages apply, even if the new networks are not actually more efficient than older ones. In the long run, however, the appropriability and universal service problems inherent in such an approach cannot be ignored, particularly when competition enters local access as well as long-distance markets. Thus, the modern approach to interconnection really has not avoided or superseded the concerns about appropriability expressed in the early 1900s.

Recognition of that fact is indicated by the growing debate over "efficient component-pricing" as the theoretical basis for access pricing. The efficient component-pricing rule was developed by economists William J. Baumol and Robert D. Willig, initially in the context of railroad regulation.[33] In that pricing methodology, competing networks pay incremental costs plus an opportunity cost, representing the profit that the incumbent loses by extending service to a competitor rather than serving the end user directly. The Baumol-Willig pricing rule correctly recognizes a legitimate basis for discriminating between the price charged to a competitor and that charged an end user. In a market where final service prices are governed by competition, network service providers would in fact attempt to recover any foregone profits that could be derived from serving an end user directly before selling a component to a competitor. The problem with the Baumol-Willig rule, however, is that the final service price of an incumbent monopoly is not set by market competition. In such circumstances a substantial part of an incumbent's "opportunity costs" consists of lost monopoly rents.[34] The only way to avoid compensating an incumbent for its loss of monopoly profits is to impose cost-based regulation upon that incumbent. But that type of regulation has enormous problems of

---

33. Clear Communications, Ltd. *v.* Telecom Corp. of New Zealand, slip op. (H.C. Dec. 22, 1992), rev'd slip op. (C.A. Dec. 28, 1993), [1995] 1 N.Z.L.R. 385, 404–05 (Oct. 19, 1994, Judgment of the Lords of the Judicial Committee of the Privy Council). For a discussion of the efficient component-pricing rule, *see* WILLIAM J. BAUMOL & J. GREGORY SIDAK, TOWARD COMPETITION IN LOCAL TELEPHONY (MIT Press & AEI Press 1994).

34. 11 YALE JOURNAL ON REGULATION (1994) contains several articles supporting and criticizing the efficient component-pricing rule.

its own and, moreover, does not move the telecommunications industry any closer to deregulated competition.

Whatever the merits of the Baumol-Willig proposal, an access pricing regime capable of supporting universal service cannot require telephone companies to make access available to competitors at a price that reflects only the incremental costs of the facilities used.

Unbundling. Unbundling is the mantra of current policy. Its hopes for a completely open, deregulated telecommunications marketplace are pinned to the process of separating the components of the public network so that consumers can assemble the services they want and need and so that no supplier can use its power in one service area to control another.

This book has provided the outline of a theoretical critique of that policy. Chapter 3 argued that networks by their very nature are enormous bundles of heterogeneous access units. Consumers benefit from a service provider's ability to deliver multiple services over a single access facility. Economies of scope, on both the demand side and the supply side, are the very basis of network efficiencies. Those facts have two important implications for contemporary policy.

First, if networks are bundles, then a policy that equates bundling with restrictions on competition is bound to find anticompetitive behavior everywhere. Such a policy will be perpetually at war with the very basis of network efficiencies. We need a much clearer standard for determining when bundling constitutes a barrier to competition than is currently available. Moreover, such a standard needs to take into account the positive social value that can be derived when networks compete on the basis of the size of their service bundle, as the Bell System and the independents did in the early 1900s.

Second, although breaking apart the components of a network does give users more choice and control over the nature of the bundle, it entails costs as well as benefits. Every act of unbundling creates additional transactions costs for users. A consumer of telecommunication network services and functions who must assemble various elements herself is faced with decisions that require costly information and time. On the supply side, unbundling may also sacrifice economies of scope.

It is instructive to compare the economic effects of modern

network unbundling with those of dual service competition. In the dual service era, the costs of integration were entirely shifted to users, who had to buy duplicate access facilities. In the modern approach, those costs are internalized by the public network. Duplications of facilities still exist—they have just become invisible to the users and the costs are distributed among users in unaccounted-for ways. For example, the existence of competing but interconnected local exchanges requires additional signal processing and transport facilities to handle traffic between the systems. Those facilities would not, in principle, be necessary in an optimized single system. The implementation of equal access arrangements and number portability also requires heavy investments in transport, signal processing, and switching capabilities that would not be necessary otherwise. Whether that regime is more efficient than an alternative such as dual service is outside the scope of this book. We do, however, need to pay closer attention to the trade-offs involved in mandated unbundling. The current doctrine may impose upon consumers and suppliers an economically inefficient level of unbundling.

The Future of Regulation

Open access is supposed to pave the way for market competition in telecommunications. But the current approach to interconnection has not done away with regulation. Far from it: equal access and "fair" interconnection pricing have generally increased regulatory intervention in the industry. If incumbent networks hold insurmountable "bottleneck" control over access, then unregulated market transactions cannot be relied upon to set prices. If regulators are to fill the gap, long deliberations about the identification of costs are required. The arcane debates about pricing must also be supplemented by complex forms of intervention in the technical structure of the network. Interconnection of competing operators is seldom possible through the purchase of preexisting types of service from an incumbent. It usually involves new forms of access and interoperability for which no established market or prices exist. Thus, regulators have been forced to reach deeply into the structure of the public network to create, by fiat, an intermediate market for telecommunications access. The implementation of equal access, for example, required the creation of artificially defined territories known as local access and transport areas (LATAs) and the restriction of local exchange telephone companies to those territories. At the local exchange level, nondiscriminatory interconnection requires that regulators take control of numbering plans, mandate deployment schedules for certain kinds of switching and signaling technologies, and even regulate the number of seconds it takes to process a call.

True deregulation in telecommunications will never be possible without a competitive, unregulated market for interconnection and access. This book has shown that unregulated access competition is not an unthinkable option. The applicability of America's historical episode of access competition to the present time increases as alternative infrastructures, such as cable television systems and wireless telephone companies, proliferate. The idea that no firm is capable of duplicating the local access network of the telephone company is looking increasingly dated. In addition, the computer industry now provides a model (although not, of course, a perfect one) of how compatibility, interconnection, and unbundling can be achieved without pervasive regulation of terms and conditions.

15

Why the First-Generation Universal Service Debate Is Relevant Today

As noted earlier, widespread acceptance of the second-generation universal service concept has literally buried the older concept. The first-generation debate, however, is still relevant to the policy challenges of the next two decades. A better understanding of the basic policy choice faced in Vail's era is essential if we are to understand the implications of current developments in telecommunications and information.

The new information infrastructure is characterized by competing, overlapping, and often incompatible or imperfectly integrated technologies. The typical business card today carries three or four different user addresses—one each for a telephone, a cellular phone, a fax, an electronic mail address, or a pager. There may be additional information about internal, enterprise networks. Compared with that, the advertisements of the dual service era, in which businesses had to list two different telephone numbers, seem simple. Far from showing any signs of abating, the proliferation of communication devices and addresses continues with the development of new wireless telephone services, portable personal computers, the World Wide Web, enhanced pagers, and personal digital assistants. Indeed, a large number of users now have two incompatible and unconnected "telephones" on their desk. One is the traditional voice telephone connected to the public switched network, the other is a computer equipped with Internet voice transmission software.

Aside from the efflorescence of devices and applications, the number of service providers is also growing. No less than four prospective categories of service provider are now contending for a role in developing the information infrastructure: telephone companies, cable television systems, terrestrial and satellite radio communications providers, and Internet/on-line service providers. How those diverse systems will exchange traffic and achieve technical compatibility is anybody's guess.

Within that increasingly heterogeneous environment, technologists, policymakers, and businesses continue to hold out the promise of total, seamless integration. For more than two decades, we have been told that sometime in the near future a single device and an integrated network will deliver interactive voice, video, and data capabilities everywhere. That vision is, of course, a modern version of the first-generation universal service concept. It assumes that the panoply of information technology will someday achieve the uniformity, compatibility, and ubiquity of the telephone system of the regulated monopoly era.

It is an appealing vision. It may even happen eventually. If we are envisioning a twenty-first-century version of universal service, however, there is much we can learn from the earlier debate between dual service and universal service.

INTEGRATION IS A POLICY CHOICE, NOT A LAW OF NATURE

To begin with, universal integration of the information infrastructure really is a choice we face, not an inevitable product of technology or economics. Even in the era of the telephone, there was an alternative to complete integration, namely dual service. The replacement of dual service by universal service did not come about "naturally," via routine market processes, but required the major institutional innovations discussed in this book. Resolving the first-generation universal service debate took the better part of two decades, and those were simpler times.

It is possible that technological and institutional differences between the past and the present have tilted the social optimum away from integration and toward more tolerance of heterogeneity, fragmentation, and competition. The expansion of telecommunications access can no longer be considered an unqualified good, as it may have been in the era of Vail. As fears about privacy and security grow, and technologies such as voicemail and caller ID gain popularity, one can only conclude that today's users are as interested in controlling and restricting access as they are in broadening it. To many people, the indiscriminate intrusion of a universal "information superhighway" into their home or business is about as welcome as the presence of an eight-lane interstate highway in their backyards. We should not assume that the new information infrastructure will or should follow the trajectory of the telephone system. At the very least, our policy dialogue needs voices capable of articulating and defending a twenty-first–century version of dual service.

INTEGRATION HAS COSTS AS WELL AS BENEFITS

A historical perspective can make us more aware of the difficult trade-offs that must be made. Integration involves costs as well as benefits. History suggests that unification is driven by demand-side economies of scope. Compatibility and integration can benefit users by eliminating the need for duplicate investments in terminal equipment and access facilities and by eliminating the confusion and uncertainty caused by heterogeneous products and services. But the realization of demand-side economies of scope also creates market inertia. As the communications infrastructure matures and users converge on a single system or standard, it becomes increasingly difficult for new technologies or networks to gain a foothold in the market. In other words, there is an inherent trade-off between integration and competition.

Thus, it is likely that when or if the much-ballyhooed seamless integration of the information infrastructure actually arrives, many of us will not like it. The dominance of Microsoft in the software marketplace has already given us some inkling of the problems to be faced. Just as AT&T was the perennial focus of antitrust activity from 1910 to 1980, so Microsoft, and more generally the interface between computers, users, and software applications, will become the focal point of competition policy controversies in the near future. In both cases, the economic forces contributing to market power are the same: demand-side economies of scope.

Microsoft's success has been achieved in what is really only a small subset of the overall market for telecommunications and information. One can scarcely imagine the amount of market power that could be achieved by a company that succeeded in winning mass acceptance of a standardized software application and terminal for accessing and navigating a fully integrated, global information infrastructure. If or when that occurs, the tension between demand-side efficiencies and supply-side diversity may reach some kind of breaking point, as occurred between 1912 and 1920, and impose a policy choice upon us.

Unfortunately, the prevailing thinking about competition policy does not offer much help in making such a choice. The theoretical roots of antitrust policy are derived from natural monopoly theory. The natural monopoly doctrine, as we have seen, is equipped only to identify and remedy anticompetitive behavior based on supply-side abuses such as predatory pricing. Current antitrust doctrine gives us little guidance as to how to handle monopolies that originate in demand-side economies of scope. That is why the relationship between communications monopoly and the antitrust laws has historically been so ambiguous.

History Never Repeats Itself

There are three important structural differences between the first-generation universal service debate and what might be called the "third-generation" confrontation with that issue in the future. Although the parallels are significant, the differences need to be kept in mind as well.

One important difference pertains to the globalization of information and telecommunications markets. The institution of telephone monopoly was a response to the problem of creating a comprehensive and uniform communications capability across political units known as nation-states. Historically, the response to that challenge in the telecommunications sector was surprisingly uniform across the globe. In practically every nation, post, telephone, and telegraph (PTT) monopolies were created to make the telecommunications infrastructure an extension of the national state.[1]

National PTT systems lasted for eighty years, but are currently being eroded almost everywhere in the world. As these systems break down, the trade-off between fragmentation and competition versus integration and monopoly presents itself again. But the developmental process that took place at the national level in the late nineteenth and early twentieth centuries is now taking place at

---

1. Peter Cowhey, *The International Telecommunications Regime: The Political Roots of Regimes for High Technology*, 44 International Organization 69 (Spring 1990).

the international level. As a response, telecommunications service providers and manufacturers are becoming horizontally integrated across nations, which gives the twenty-first-century equivalent of dual service competition an added level of complexity. At the global level, there is more room for competing systems and standards to take hold, and it is more difficult for user convergence to take place in a coordinated fashion. On the other hand, the stronger linkages between markets in different countries and the transnational integration of firms makes it impossible for one country to ignore the systems and standards established in another.

Wireless personal communications hold the promise of the ultimate in universal service: two-way telecommunications that are available at any time in any part of the world. But the promise of ubiquity is undermined by the development of competing, incompatible television and wireless telephone standards in Europe, the United States, and Japan. The desire for and benefits of global compatibility are strong, but business competition, technological diversity, and national industrial policies make unification elusive. As information technology matures and the international economy becomes more dependent upon its capabilities, is it not possible that some sort of universal service drama will be acted out again, this time on a global scale?

The nature of technology is another important difference between the past and the present. One of the key economic features of the first-generation dual service–universal service debate was the diseconomy of scope associated with the growth of networks. In that context, vertical integration and monopoly may have been the most efficient ways of bringing about the demand-side economies of scope that users wanted.

Electronic and digital switching systems have conquered the supply-side diseconomy of scope. The unit cost of switching a given number of access lines actually declines now with the new technologies. In addition, digital signal processing is more robust and more easily interconnected and standardized than analogue or manual systems. In the present environment, it is easier to achieve various levels or gradations of compatibility and interconnection. Thus, it is unlikely that users will be confronted with the stark, binary choice between interconnection and no interconnection they faced in the past.

The universality of communications access will always be a salient public policy issue. Debate over the nature of the telecommunications infrastructure—whether it should be fragmented or integrated, competitive or monopolistic, more or less subsidized—can only increase in importance as information technology occupies an ever-larger role in society. This book sheds light on the historical origins of that debate and in so doing attempts to illuminate the contemporary debate as well.

References

Adams, Henry Carter, "The Relation of the State to Industrial Action," 1 *Publications of the American Economic Association* 465 (1887).

Allen, David, "New Telecommunications Services: Network Externalities and Critical Mass," 13 *Telecommunications Policy* 257 (1988).

American Telephone and Telegraph Co., *Exchange Statistics: 1880–1907*.

American Telephone and Telegraph Co., *The Telephone and Telegraph Atlas of the United States* (circa 1914).

American Telephone and Telegraph Co., *Telephone Statistics of the World* (1912).

American Telephone and Telegraph Co., *The World's Telephones* (1961).

Andrews, E., "Communications Bill Signed, and the Battle Begins Anew," *New York Times* (February 9, 1996).

Arthur, W. Brian, "Competing Technologies, Increasing Returns, and Lock-in by Historical Events," 99 *Economics Journal* 116 (1989).

Arthur, W. Brian, "On Generalized Urn Schemes of the Polya Kind," *Cybernetics* 61 (1983).

Baumol, William, John Panzar, and Robert Willig, *Contestable*

194   References

Markets and the Theory of Industry Structure (Harcourt, Brace, Jovanovich 1982).

Baumol, William J., and J. Gregory Sidak, "The Pricing of Inputs Sold to Competitors," *Yale Journal on Regulation* 171 (Winter 1994).

Baumol, William J., and J. Gregory Sidak, *Toward Competition in Local Telephony* (MIT Press and AEI Press 1994).

Bonbright, James, *Principles of Public Utility Regulation* (Columbia University Press 1961).

Brock, Gerald, *The Telecommunications Industry: The Dynamics of Market Structure* (Harvard University Press 1981).

Brock, Gerald, *Telecommunications Policy for the Information Age* (Harvard University Press 1994).

Brock, Gerald, "Telephone Pricing to Promote Universal Service and Economic Freedom," Federal Communications Commission Office of Plans and Policies, Working Paper 18 (1985).

Browning, John, "Universal Service: An Idea Whose Time Has Passed," 3 *Wired* 102 (September 1994).

Bruce, Robert, *Bell: Alexander Graham Bell and the Conquest of Solitude* (Little, Brown 1973).

California Railroad Commission, *Barker Report* (1914).

Cave, Martin, "Interconnection, Separate Accounting, and the Development of Competition in UK Telecommunications," Institute of Economic Affairs Lectures on Regulation (1993).

Chappelka, A. R., "History of Independent Telephone Operating Companies in the United States," Memorandum on Affirmative Topic No. 10, Civil Action No. 17-49 (1956).

Chicago City Council, Committee on Gas, Oil and Electric Light, Communications (1906, 1907).

Cohen, Jeffrey E. "The Telephone Problem and the Road to Telephone Regulation in the United States, 1876–1917," 3 *Journal of Policy History* 42 (1991).

Cowhey, Peter, "The International Telecommunications Regime: The Political Roots of Regimes for High Technology," 44 *International Organization* 69 (Spring 1990).

Crandall, Robert W., *After the Breakup: U.S. Telecommunications in a More Competitive Era* (Brookings Institution 1991).

Crandall, Robert W., and J. Gregory Sidak, "Competition and Regulatory Policies for Interactive Broadband Networks," 68 *Southern California Law Review* 1203 (1995).

David, Paul A., "Clio and the Economics of QWERTY," 75 *American Economic Review* 332 (May 1985).

David, Paul A., "Narrow Windows, Blind Giants, and Angry Orphans: The Dynamics of Systems Rivalries and the Dilemmas of Technology Policy," in *Innovation Diffusion* (F. Arcangeli et al. eds., Oxford University Press 1990).

Dordick, Herbert, "Toward a Universal Definition of Universal Service," in *Universal Telephone Service: Ready for the 21st Century?* (Institute for Information Studies 1991).

Economides, Nicholas, and Lawrence J. White, "One-Way Networks, Two-Way Networks, Compatibility and Antitrust," EC-93-14 (New York University 1993).

Evans, David S., ed., *Breaking up Bell* (North-Holland 1983).

Evans, David S., and James Heckman, "A Test for Subadditivity of the Cost Function with an Application to the Bell System," 74 *American Economic Review* 615 (1984).

Fagen, M. D., ed., *History of Engineering and Science in the Bell System* (AT&T 1975).

Farrah, Barbara J., and Mike Maxwell, "Building the American Infostructure," *Telephony* 45 (April 20, 1992).

Farrell, Joseph, and Garth Saloner, "Competition, Compatibility, and Standards: The Economics of Horses, Penguins, and Lemmings," in *Product Standardization as a Tool of Competitive Strategy* (H. Landis Gabel ed., North-Holland 1986).

Farrell, Joseph, and Garth Saloner, "Standardization, Compatibility, and Innovation," *RAND Journal of Economics* (Spring 1985).

Faulhaber, Gerald, "Cross Subsidization: Pricing in Public Enterprise," 65 *American Economic Review* 966 (1975).

Faulhaber, Gerald, *Telecommunications in Turmoil: Technology and Public Policy* (Ballinger 1987).

Federal Communications Commission, *Investigation of the Telephone Industry* (1939 and 1974 eds.).

Federal Communications Commission, *Statistics of Communications Common Carriers* (annual).

Field Research Corporation, "Affordability of Telephone Service: A Survey of Customers and Noncustomers" (1993).

Fischer, Claude, *America Calling: A Social History of the Telephone to 1940* (University of California 1993).

Fischer, Claude, "The Revolution in Rural Telephony, 1900–1920," 21 *Journal of Social History* 5 (Fall 1987).

Fuss, Melvyn, and Leonard Waverman, *The Regulation of Telecommunications in Canada*, Technical Report 7, Economic Council of Canada (March 1981).

Gabel, David, "Competition in a Network Industry: The Telephone Industry, 1894–1910," *Journal of Economic History* 543 (September 1994).

Gabel, David, "The Evolution of a Market: The Emergence of Regulation in the Telephone Industry of Wisconsin, 1893–1917," Ph.D. dissertation, University of Wisconsin-Madison (1987).

Gabel, David, "Technological Change, Contracting and the First Divestiture of AT&T" (1989).

Gabel, Richard, *The Development of Separations Concepts in the Telephone Industry* (Michigan State University Public Utilities Studies 1967).

Garnet, Robert, *The Telephone Enterprise: The Evolution of the Bell System's Horizontal Structure* (Johns Hopkins University/ AT&T Series in Telephone History 1985).

Garnham, Nicholas, "Universal Service in Western European Telecommunications," in *European Telecommunications Policy Research: Proceedings of the Communications Policy Research Conference, June 22–24, 1988* (Garnham and Aksoy eds., IOS 1989).

Greenstein, Shane, "Invisible Hands vs. Invisible Advisors: Coordination Mechanisms in Economic Networks" (January 1993).

Hausman, T. Tardiff, and A. Belinfante, "The Effects of the Breakup of AT&T on Telephone Penetration in the U.S.," 83 *American Economic Review* 178 (1993).

Herring, James M., and Gerald C. Gross, *Telecommunications: Economics and Regulation* (McGraw-Hill 1936).

Horrigan, John, and Lodis Rhodes, "The Evolution of Universal Service in Texas," working paper, LBJ School of Public Affairs (1995).

Horwitz, Robert Britt, *The Irony of Regulatory Reform: The Deregulation of American Telecommunications* (Oxford University Press 1989).

Institute for Information Studies, *Universal Telephone Service: Ready for the 21st Century?* Annual Review of the Institute for Information Studies, a joint program of Northern Telecom Inc. and the Aspen Institute (1991).

Jones, Eliot, and T. C. Bigham, *Principles of Public Utilities* (Macmillan 1933).

Kahn, Alfred E., *The Economics of Regulation: Principles and Institutions* (Wiley 1971; MIT rev. ed. 1988).

Kahn, Alfred E., and William E. Taylor, "The Pricing of Inputs Sold to Competitors: A Comment," *Yale Journal on Regulation* (1994).

Katz, Michael L., and Carl Shapiro, "Network Externalities, Competition, and Compatibility," 75 *American Economic Review* (1985).

Katz, Michael L., and Carl Shapiro, "Technology Adoption in the Presence of Network Externalities," 94 *Journal of Political Economy* 257 (1986).

Langdale, John V., "The Growth of Long-Distance Telephony in the Bell System, 1875–1907," 4 *Journal of Historical Geography* 145 (1975).

Latzke, Paul A., *A Fight with an Octopus* (Telephony Press 1906).

Lavey, W. J., "Universal Telecommunication Infrastructure for Information Services," *Federal Communications Law Journal* 42 (1990).

Leighton, Wayne, *Telecommunications Subsidies: Reach Out and Touch Someone (Whether You Want to or Not)* (Citizens for a Sound Economy Issues and Answers Series 1995).

Lipartito, Kenneth, *The Bell System and Regional Business: The Telephone in the South* (Johns Hopkins University/AT&T Series in Telephone History 1989).

Littlechild, Stephen C., *Elements of Telecommunications Economics* (Institute of Electrical Engineers 1979).

Lowry, Edward D., "Justification for Regulation: The Case for Natural Monopoly," *Public Utilities Fortnightly* 18 (November 8, 1973).

MacMeal, Harry B., *The Story of Independent Telephony* (Independent Pioneer Telephone Association 1934).

Marvin, Lloyd Heck, "The Telephone Situation in Los Angeles," master's thesis, Department of Economics, University of Southern California (1916).

Mueller, Milton L., "New Zealand Telecommunications and the Problem of Interconnecting Competing Networks," Reason Foundation Policy Study No. 177 (May 1994).

Mueller, Milton L., "The Switchboard Problem: Scale, Signaling and Organization in the Era of Manual Telephone Switching, 1878–1898," *Technology and Culture* (July 1989).

Mueller, Milton L., "The Telephone War: Competition, Interconnection and Monopoly in the Making of Universal Service," Ph.D. dissertation, University of Pennsylvania (1989).

Mueller, Milton L., and Jorge R. Schement, "Universal Service from the Bottom Up: A Profile of Telecommunications Access in Camden, New Jersey," 12 *Information Society* (1996).

Neu, Werner, and Karl-Heinz Neumann, "Interconnection Agreements in Telecommunications," Wissenschaftliches Institut fur Kommunikationsdienste Working Paper No. 106 (April 1993).

New York City Bureau of Franchises, "Result of Investigation of the Operation of a Dual System of Telephones in Various Cities" (1906).

O'Neill, Patrick, "Franchising the New Telephone Company," paper delivered at the 1988 Midwest Journalism Association Conference.

Organization for Economic Cooperation and Development, "The Benefits of Telecommunications Infrastructure Competition," DSTI/ICCP/TISP (rev. 1 (1993)).

Paine, Albert Bigelow, *In One Man's Life* (Harper & Brothers 1921).

Perl, L. S., *Residential Demand for Telephone Service* (National Economic Research Associates 1983).

Pleasance, C. A., *The Spirit of Independent Telephony* (Independent Telephone Books 1989).

Posner, Richard, "Natural Monopoly and Its Regulation," 21 *Stanford Law Review* 548 (1969).

Prescott, George Bartlett, *The Electric Telephone* (Appleton 1890).

Preliminary Report on Communication Companies, submitted by Sam Rayburn pursuant to H.R. 59 and House Joint Resolution 572, 72d Cong., H. Rept. No. 1273, April 18, 1934.

Raj, Baldev, and H. D. Vinod. "Bell System Scale Economies from a Randomly Varying Parameter Model," *Journal of Economics and Business* 247 (February 1982).

Rohlfs, Jeffrey, "A Theory of Interdependent Demand for a Communications Service," *Bell Journal of Economics and Management Science* (Spring 1974).

Rostow, Eugene V., "The Case for Congressional Action to Safeguard the Telephone Network as a Universal and Optimized System," paper based on the memorandum prepared for AT&T for use in the November 1975 hearings before the Subcommittee on Communications of the U.S. House of Representatives Committee on Interstate and Foreign Commerce.

Sawhney, S., "Universal Service: Prosaic Motives and Great Ideals," in *Toward a Competitive Telecommunications Industry: Selected Papers of the 1994 Telecommunications Policy Research Conference* (Gerald Brock ed., Lawrence Erlbaum Associates 1995).

Sharkey, William, *The Theory of Natural Monopoly* (Cambridge University Press 1982).

Shin, Richard T., and John S. Ying, "Unnatural Monopolies in Local Telephone," 23 *RAND Journal of Economics* 171 (1992).

Sidak, J. Gregory, "Debunking Predatory Innovation," 83 *Columbia Law Review* (June 1983).

Smith, George, *The Anatomy of a Business Strategy* (Johns Hopkins University/AT&T Series in Telephone History 1985).

Smith, J. B., and V. Corbo, "Economies of Scale and Economies of Scope in Bell Canada," working paper, Department of Economics, Concordia University (March 1979).

Stehman, J. Warren, *The Financial History of the American Telephone and Telegraph Company* (Houghton Mifflin 1925).

Stone, Alan, *Public Service Liberalism: Telecommunications and Transitions in Public Policy* (Princeton University Press 1991).

Tarr, Joel, with Thomas Finholt and David Goodman, "The City and the Telegraph: Urban Telecommunications in the Pre-Telephone Era," 14 *Journal of Urban History* 38 (November 1987).

Taylor, Lester, *Telecommunications Demand: A Survey and Critique* (Ballinger 1980).

Temin, Peter, and Louis Galambos, *The Fall of the Bell System* (Cambridge University Press 1987).

Thompson, C. W., and Wendell R. Smith, *Public Utility Economics* (McGraw-Hill 1941).

Trachsel, Herman, *Public Utility Regulation* (Irwin 1947).

U.S. Department of Commerce and Labor, Bureau of the Census, *Census of Population* (Government Printing Office 1900, 1910, 1920).

U.S. Department of Commerce and Labor, Bureau of the Census, *Electrical Industries Census 1902* (Government Printing Office 1905).

U.S. Department of Commerce and Labor, Bureau of the Census, *Farm Census 1920* (Government Printing Office).

U.S. Department of Commerce and Labor, Bureau of the Census, *Telephones: 1907* (Government Printing Office 1910).

U.S. Department of Commerce and Labor, Bureau of the Census, *Telephones and Telegraphs and Municipal Electric Fire Alarm and Police Patrol Signaling Systems* (Government Printing Office 1915).

Von Auw, Alvin, *Heritage and Destiny: Reflections on the Bell System in Transition* (Praeger 1983).

Wasserman, Neil, *From Invention to Innovation: Long Distance Telephone Transmission at the Turn of the Century* (Johns Hopkins University/AT&T Series in Telephone History 1986).

Weiman, David F., and Richard C. Levin, "Preying for Monopoly? The Case of Southern Bell Telephone Company, 1894–1912," 102 *Journal of Political Economy* 103 (1994).

Wenders, John T., *The Economics of Telecommunications* (Ballinger 1987).

Wilcox, Delos F., *Municipal Franchises* (Gervaise Press 1910).

Wilson, G. Lloyd, James M. Herring, and Roland B. Eutscher, *Public Utility Industries* (McGraw-Hill 1936).

Weinhaus, Carol, and Anthony Oettinger, *Behind the Telephone Debates* (Ablex 1988).

Case and Regulatory Proceeding Index

Name Index

Subject Index

Access competition
  Bell System extension, 74–75
  effect of, 153
  elimination (mid-1920s), 146
  factors in development of, 43–44
  outcome of pre-1920s, 147
  role in universal service, 25
  in scope and price of product, 26
  sublicensing in context of, 79–80
Access networks
  with competition, 22–25
  duplicated by users, 28
  output, 20–22, 27–30
Access price
  discriminatory scheme, 26
American Bell. *See* Bell Telephone
  Company
American Bell Telephone Company.
  See AT&T; Bell Telephone
  Company
American Telephone and Telegraph
  Company. *See* AT&T
Antitrust policy, 189
  See also Monopoly; Natural mo-
    nopoly concept
Appropriability, 27, 31, 181–82
AT&T
  center checking method, 75
  early long-distance service,
    40–41, 43
  Kingsbury Commitment (1913),
    10, 129–35
  Western Union holdings, 129–30

Bandwagon effects, 23
Baxter Overland Telephone and Telegraph Company, 34

Bell System
  buyouts of competing ex-
    changes, 111–13
  competition with independents
    (1894–1912), 3–4
  connection exclusion policy
    (1894–1902), 76–77
  defined, 43
  expansion (1894–1913), 86
  geographical biases, 56–57
  idea of universal service under,
    98–103
  in jurisdictional separations de-
    bate, 154
  license contracts of, 77
  monopoly (1880–94), 33–35
  overlap with independents
    (1898–1907), 60–69
  patents of, 34–35, 43
  relations with local operating
    companies, 37–42
  response to independent compe-
    tition (post-1894), 69–80
  universal service idea, 8
  See also AT&T; Operating com-
    panies, local; Western Elec-
    tric; Western Union Telegraph
    Company
Bell Telephone Company
  control of telephone industry
    (1880–94), 33
  goal of unified system, 37–39
  interconnection cases, 46–50
  local operating companies, 38–39
  opposition to interconnection,
    51–53
  Western Electric subsidiary, 35
Bundling
  of access units, 28

207

DATE DUE

The Library Store   #47-0106